A Handbook for Evidence-Based Juvenile Justice Systems

A Handbook for Evidence-Based Juvenile Justice Systems

James C. Howell,
Mark W. Lipsey, and
John J. Wilson

LEXINGTON BOOKS
Lanham • Boulder • New York • London

Published by Lexington Books
A wholly owned subsidary of Rowman & Littlefield
4501 Forbes Boulevard, Suite 200, Lanham, Maryland 20706
www.rowman.com

16 Carlisle Street, London W1D 3 BT, United Kingdom

British Library Cataloguing in Publication Information Available

Library of Congress Cataloging-in-Publication Data

Howell, James C.
  A handbook for evidence-based juvenile justice systems / James C. Howell,
Mark W. Lipsey, and John J. Wilson.
      pages cm
  Includes bibliographical references and index.
  ISBN 978-0-7391-8708-1 (cloth) — ISBN 978-0-7391-8709-8 (electronic) 1.
Juvenile justice, Administration of—United States. 2. Juvenile delinquency--
United States. 3. Juvenile corrections—United States. I. Lipsey, Mark W. II.
Wilson, John J., 1944- III. Title.
  HV9104.H757 2014
  364.360973—dc23

                                                        2014009810

Printed in the United States of America

Contents

Acknowledgements

The authors acknowledge important contributions to the details of this book. Foremost, Gabrielle Chapman, Vanderbilt University, has collaborated with Mark Lipsey in the meta-analyses reported herein, and in system reform work in various states. Special recognition is given to Megan Qually Howell for her unique contributions to this book, both as a "comprehensive strategies thinker" and leading juvenile justice analyst.

For their steadfast leadership, we are indebted to key officials in states who have worked closely with us in implementing juvenile justice system reforms, including Billy Lassiter, June Ward, Jesse Riggs, Nancy Hodges, Pam Stokes, Rich Smith, Scott Stoker, Cindy Porterfield, Linda Graney, Ron Tillman, Massey Whiteside (North Carolina); Rob Lubitz, Stacia Nowinski-Castro, David Redpath, and Jeanne Brandner (Arizona); Wansley Walters, Laura Moneyham, Joan Wimmer, Adrienne Conwell, Michael Baglivio, and Mark Greenwald (Florida); Keith Snyder and Robert Williams (Pennsylvania); and Steve Grant, Julie Revaz, and Antonio Donis (Connecticut). Expert juvenile justice analysts in North Carolina (Megan Howell), Florida (Michael Baglivio), Pennsylvania (Justine Fowler), Connecticut (Peter Kochol), and Arizona (David Redpath), have collaborated closely with us in conducting analyses of serious, violent, and chronic offender careers and drawing policy and program implications. Marion Kelly contributed to system alignment and use of best practice tools. The unique expertise of Chris Baird and Kristen Johnson (National Council on Crime and Delinquency) has enhanced our application of advanced technology in risk and need assessment practice. All of these professionals have enriched this book.

To Dan Oates, Library Director, and Suzanne Sinclair, Librarian, Health Sciences Library, First Health of the Carolinas, in Pinehurst, North Carolina, we owe special recognition for greatly assisting the first author in securing resource publications.

1

Introduction

The *cycle of juvenile justice* is a unique feature of approaches for responding to juvenile offenders in the United States. Here's how it works (Bernard, 1992). Americans have long held strong and conflicting views about juvenile delinquency and appropriate public responses. One group in our society believes that the juvenile justice system is too lenient in emphasizing treatment for juvenile offenders. They contend that the leniency of the system encourages delinquency, thus they call for harsher approaches for juvenile offenders. Increased use of incarceration typically follows. After these policies are put into effect, another group begins to oppose harsh punishments, pointing out that they do not appear to reduce juvenile crime. These arguments lead to the return of more emphasis on rehabilitation of juvenile offenders, beginning the cycle again. In each of these eras, the current cohort of delinquents was described as "worse than ever before." This characterization of juvenile delinquents is not unusual. "From antiquity every generation has entertained the opinion that many if not most of its youth are the most vicious in the history of the race" (Hamparian, Schuster, Dinitz et al., 1978, p. 11). The latest punishment-rehabilitation cycle, covering the past 20 years, has had important ramifications for evidence-based practice with juvenile offenders.

After many years of little change, juvenile delinquency arrests for serious offenses began to increase in the late 1980s and continued to climb each year thereafter, until a peak was reached in 1994 (Snyder and Sickmund, 2006). From the mid-1980s through the early 1990s, the violent juvenile arrest rate increased sharply, most notably in the number of juveniles arrested for homicide. A few researchers claimed that an "unprecedented

1

epidemic" of youth violence occurred in that decade (Blumstein, 1995; Cook and Laub, 1998; Fox, 1996), but, once multiple data sources are examined carefully, the conclusion that a general epidemic of juvenile violence occurred lacks empirical support (Howell, 2003b; Zimring, 1998). Though more juveniles were charged with violent crimes, their actual rate of violent behaviors had not increased. At the height of the so-called juvenile violence epidemic "only about 6 percent of all juvenile arrests were for violent crimes and less than one-tenth of one percent of their arrests were for homicides" (McCord, Widom, and Crowell, 2001, p. 33).

Nevertheless, a few analysts from outside the juvenile justice field greatly exaggerated the so-called epidemic. DiIulio (1995) and Wilson (1995) predicted a new "wave" of juvenile violence to occur between about 1995 and 2010, which they based in part on a projected tsunami of so-called juvenile "super predators" who were presumed to be younger killers and perpetrators of more and more violent crimes. None of these assumptions proved to be valid. The super predators never arrived; instead, juvenile arrests for violence dropped sharply. Between 1994 and 2009, the juvenile arrest rate for violent crimes fell nearly 50 percent (Puzzanchera and Adams, 2011).

Although the dire prediction of a new "wave" of juvenile violence never materialized, fear of young people had grown in the public's mind and the more punitive philosophy of the adult criminal justice system filtered down to the juvenile justice system. Further momentum was given to that movement by a review of correctional programs that erroneously concluded that "nothing works" (Lipton, Martinson, and Wilks, 1975; Martinson, 1974). Together, these developments ushered in significant changes in the boundaries of the juvenile justice system and in policies and procedures for handling juvenile offenders. New laws designated more juveniles as serious offenders, brought more minor offenders into the system, and extended periods of confinement in juvenile correctional facilities. Many states abandoned rehabilitative programs in favor of boot camps, "Scared Straight" programs, and increased confinement of youths in detention centers and juvenile reformatories. Increasingly more juvenile offenders were transferred to the criminal justice system (Kurlychek and Johnson, 2004), and transferred juveniles convicted of felonies were often given longer prison sentences than adults for the same offenses (Brown and Langan, 1998).

In the mid-1990s, the climate for juvenile justice systems began to change in a more constructive direction, with strong emphasis on providing programs that reduce recidivism. Principles of effective adult and juvenile correctional practice were derived from a growing body of research (Andrews, Bonta, and Hoge, 1990), and many juvenile justice interventions were identified that addressed juvenile offenders' multiple needs and were effective in reducing their recidivism (Lipsey, 1992; Lipsey, Wilson, and Cothern, 2000; Lipsey and Wilson, 1998). In the late 1990s, model prevention and rehabilitation programs called "blueprints" were widely promoted (Elliott, 1998; Mihalic, Irwin, Elliott et al., 2001) amidst increasing interest in the use of evidence-based programs. In subsequent years, several states passed legislation limiting public funding to evidence-based programs, though definitions of "evidence-based" varied widely. Developments on these fronts restored optimism that juvenile delinquency can be prevented and reduced through effective practice in juvenile justice systems.

Over the past decade or more, several federal and state agencies and private entrepreneurs have promoted a more active process for moving science to practice with widespread dissemination of information on what works and encouragement and support for implementation of effective programs. Yet efforts to disseminate evidence-based programs with fidelity to program requirements often fail to produce the expected outcomes, for example, in the fields of education (Hallfors and Godette, 2002), mental health (Knitzer, 1982; Knitzer and Cooper, 2006), social services (Fixsen, Blasé, Naoom, and Wallace, 2009), and juvenile justice (Lipsey and Howell, 2012; Welsh, Sullivan, and Olds, 2010). It is our hope that the research and tools described in this handbook will support the progress of those juvenile justice systems that aspire to make better use of available evidence to improve their effectiveness in pursuing better outcomes for errant youth and the increased public safety that follows.

In a recent national needs assessment of state, local, and tribal entities, more than half of the respondents said their most pressing needs were understanding what qualifies as "evidence-based," difficulties associated with finding such programs that are applicable to their contexts, and guidance in sustaining them (National Juvenile Justice Evaluation Center, 2012). Presently, a rich body of research is available that can provide guidance to juvenile justice systems for implementing evidence-based programs and services with good potential for preventing delinquency, reducing recidivism rates, and increasing public safety in the process. Our main interest in creating this handbook is to provide an accessible summary of that research and its implications for practice.

JUVENILE JUSTICE SYSTEM CHALLENGES

Juvenile justice (JJ) systems presently face several impediments to becoming evidence-based operations. Important obstacles are discussed herein that must be addressed before marked progress on the evidence-based program front can be achieved. First, juvenile court caseloads are more diverse than in the past. A larger proportion of juveniles are now brought into court for minor offenses than in the recent past. Compared with 1995, law enforcement agencies now refer larger proportions of runaway, truancy, and ungovernable cases (Puzzanchera, Adams, and Hockenberry, 2012). In the recent past, the number of delinquency cases involving females increased 86 percent, while for males the increase was only 17 percent (Puzzanchera et al., 2012). More gang-involved offenders are now on juvenile court caseloads, with increasing representation with deeper JJ system penetration, and these offenders tend to have multiple treatment needs (M.Q. Howell and Lassiter, 2011). Court-referred youth with mental health problems add to the diversity of juvenile offenders' presenting problems. "Prevalence studies indicate that as few as 30 percent and as many as 70 percent of youths involved with the juvenile justice system may meet criteria for a mental health disorder (Wasserman, McReynolds, Lucas, Fisher, and Santos, 2002)" (McReynolds, Schwalbe, and Wasserman, 2010, p. 204). Moreover, as many as 45 percent of boys and 50 percent of girls brought into JJ systems have at least one diagnosable psychiatric disorder (Wasserman, McReynolds, Ko, Katz, and Carpenter, 2005). Repeat offenders are, on average, more than 1.5 times more likely to meet criteria for mental health disorders (Wasserman, McReynolds, Schwalbe et al., 2010). Girls are at significantly higher risk (80 percent) than boys (67 percent) for any type of mental health disorder, with girls demonstrating higher rates than boys of internalizing disorders (Shufelt and Cocozza, 2006).

Second, overuse of confinement remains a problem in many states (Hockenberry, 2013). The juvenile incarceration rate in the United States (225 per 100,000 youth) is 3 times greater than in any other country (Justice for Families, 2012). Although the population of juvenile offenders in custody has declined by one-third since 1997, reductions are needed in high confinement rates for minority youth. Nationwide, the custody rate for black youth is more than 4.5 times the rate for white youth, and the custody rate for Hispanic youth is 1.8 times the rate for white youth. Although several states have down-sized juvenile corrections (Campaign for Youth Justice, 2013; Hockenberry, 2013), crowding is still a problem in many detention and correctional facilities (Hockenberry, Sickmund, and Sladky, 2011).

Third, many JJ systems find themselves in a fiscal conundrum. Although their budgets have been drastically reduced as a result of the recent U.S. economic crisis, the proportion of all juvenile offender cases handled formally has not shrunk (Puzzanchera et al., 2012, p. 37). Thus, many state JJ systems presently are overloaded at the front end.

The JJ system can be viewed as a funnel, in which proportionately fewer very serious cases penetrate the system further and wind up in secure correctional facilities. Less serious cases receive milder sanctions, for example, parent-child consultation or "diversion" to one or another community program, whereas formal court actions include secure confinement and waiver to the adult criminal justice system. About 60 percent of delinquency cases are formally referred to the courts from law enforcement; of those referred, approximately two-thirds are adjudicated as delinquent, and about a quarter of those adjudicated are referred for secure placement (Snyder and Sickmund, 2006). Following system intake, some youth (21 percent nationwide; Puzzanchera et al., 2012) are detained pretrial, generally to prevent interim disappearance or reoffending. Since placement decisions reflect offense seriousness and recidivism risk, youth who penetrate the system further should differ substantially from those who do not on these dimensions.

The challenge is to reduce caseloads, meet the challenges of higher risk offenders, and reduce juvenile delinquency with fewer resources. Although funding limitations have stimulated a noticeable shift from committing juveniles to high-cost residential facilities to lower-cost options, such as probation, day treatment, or other community-based sanctions (Hockenberry, 2013), use of these options has not kept pace with decreasing juvenile crime. Ways of meeting this challenge are presented in this handbook.

STATE RECIDIVISM RATES

For statewide recidivism rates, one must rely on individual state reports, but high-quality data are scarce, largely because of the limited capacity of most states' data collection systems. Few states publish statewide juvenile court recidivism rates. The best available national benchmark is this: Nationwide, 41 percent of youth return among those first referred to juvenile court (Snyder and Sickmund, 2006). [1]

Some states show much better averages although there are wide variations.

- In Arizona, for court referrals, the rate was 24 percent for a subsequent adjudication within one year (Baird, Johnson, Healy et al., 2013).
- A three-year follow-up in North Carolina found that 34 percent of all court-referred youth had a subsequent delinquent complaint but just 23 percent were re-arrested (Flinchum and Hevener, 2011).
- In Pennsylvania, only 20 percent of all referrals returned to court within one year (Pennsylvania Commission on Crime and Delinquency, 2013).

- In Florida, the recidivism rate (a subsequent delinquent complaint) for one year from standard probation completion during 2009–2010 was just 19 percent (Florida Department of Juvenile Justice, 2012).
- In Missouri, 23 percent of youth recidivated with a new court referral for a delinquent offense within one year (Office of State Courts Administrator, 2013).
- In the State of Washington, only 23 percent of adjudicated juvenile offenders were subsequently adjudicated in two and one-half years (Barnoski, 2004a).

A few states show much higher recidivism rates. A three-year follow-up on adjudicated juvenile probationers in Texas found that 66 percent had been re-arrested (Legislative Budget Board, 2011).

Reasonably good data are available that provide a rough approximation of recidivism rates among offenders released from state juvenile correctional facilities (Virginia Department of Juvenile Justice, 2005). In this compilation, some states measured recidivism by rearrests (9 states), others used reconvictions (12 states), and the final group used reincarceration (12 states). A total of 33 states provided data, so there is overlap in the formats in which data were reported (but only 4 states reported recidivism data using all three measures). The average recidivism rates following confinement were as follows: rearrests (57 percent), re-adjudication (33 percent), and reincarceration (20 percent). However, a few states have very high recidivism rates. In California, of youth released from the Department of Juvenile Justice during FY 2004–2005, 81 percent were rearrested and 56 percent were returned to state-level incarceration within three years (California Department of Corrections and Rehabilitation, 2010). In Texas, 76 percent of juvenile offenders released from secure placement were re-arrested within the same time frame (Legislative Budget Board, 2011). Therefore, there is much room for improvement in many states' juvenile correctional programming.

NOTE

1. See Baird, et al. (2013) for comparative state recidivism rates by risk level.

2

+

Research with Important Implications for Juvenile Justice Practice

IN BRIEF

There is now a considerable body of research that can provide guidance to juvenile justice systems in implementing effective evidence-based practices, with the potential to prevent delinquency, reduce recidivism rates, improve the outcomes for juvenile offenders, and increase public safety in the process.

One important finding is that most youth who run afoul of the law are not on a pathway that leads to adult criminal careers. Most delinquency is self-correcting as youth age, and much delinquency is not serious, violent, or chronic. Juvenile justice systems thus should not treat every case as if a failure to vigorously intervene will lead to a lifetime of crime. It is the serious, violent, and chronic cases that need to be the focus in allocating scarce resources, and they represent a relatively small proportion of the population of juvenile offenders.

Moreover, predictive risk and protective factors have been identified that can be used to assess the likelihood that a youth will become a serious, violent, or chronic offender. This information allows juveniles on high-risk pathways to be identified relatively early so the juvenile justice system can give them special attention. The "pathways" part of the picture shows a developmental progression (rather than more or less random delinquents and incidents) with the implication that these pathways can be interrupted by effective intervention. Moreover, there are different points of intervention along that pathway, ranging from early prevention to more intensive intervention, easily graduated according to where a juvenile is positioned in the developmental progression. Young offenders who begin to engage in delinquent behavior at an early age are at especially high risk for serious, violent, or chronic delinquency and warrant particular attention when they appear in the juvenile justice system.

JUVENILE OFFENDER CAREERS

Research on juvenile offender careers relies on three sources of data: arrest records, self-reports taken in interviews, and juvenile court records. The earliest studies of serious and chronic juvenile offender careers used arrest histories. These studies conclusively showed that a very small proportion of juvenile offenders were responsible for the majority of delinquent acts and the vast majority of serious acts of delinquency. In a study of nearly 10,000 boys born in Philadelphia in 1945 and followed up in official records to the eighteenth birthday, Wolfgang, Figlio, and Sellin (1972) found that just 6 percent of the birth cohort, all of whom had committed at least five offenses, accounted for 69 percent of all aggravated assaults, 71 percent of homicides, 73 percent of forcible rapes, and 82 percent of robberies. The discovery of these 6 percent, termed "chronic offenders," led to calls for their early identification as prime targets for intervention.

Subsequent research using data on self-reported delinquency also shows that that a small number of offenders account for a substantial proportion if not a majority of the offenses (Loeber, Farrington, and Waschbush, 1998) and that the relatively few chronic serious and chronic violent offenders account for an overwhelming proportion of all serious and violent offenses committed by samples of delinquents. In the Rochester study, the chronic violent offenders constituted only 15 percent of the total sample, yet self-reported having committed 75 percent of all of the violent offenses reported in the entire sample (Thornberry, Huizinga, and Loeber, 1998). In Denver, this 14 percent of the study sample committed 82 percent of all self-reported violent offenses.

Although most of the delinquent acts that youngsters commit are never brought to the attention of police or juvenile courts, most serious, violent, and chronic offenders eventually are arrested. Thornberry and colleagues (1998) report on studies in Rochester, Denver, and Pittsburgh which found that by age fourteen, most chronic violent adolescents (81 percent in Rochester, 97 percent in Denver, and 74 percent in Pittsburgh) had begun committing violent offenses, but only small proportions of the youths in these groups had been arrested (slightly more than one-third of them in Rochester and Denver, and about half in Pittsburgh). However, most chronic violent offenders were arrested at some point (two-thirds eventually were arrested in Rochester and about three-fourths in Denver and Pittsburgh). Still, a gap exists between arrests and court referrals. In the Pittsburgh site, two-thirds of the delinquents were not brought to juvenile court until several years following onset, and 40 percent of the worst delinquents did not have a court petition by age eighteen (Stouthamer-Loeber and Loeber, 2002). The point is that, while much information on delinquent careers is missed in JJ system records, there is some correspondence and, therefore, these records give some indication of career patterns as shown in Figure 2.1.

THE AGE-CRIME CURVE

Over time, the relationship between offending and age is bell-shaped, called the age-crime curve (Farrington, Loeber, and Jolliffe, 2008). Figure 2.1 depicts the typical shape of the age-crime curve as reflected in self-reported delinquent behavior. It has a beginning and an ending with groups of offenders traversing varying slopes in between. As seen in Figure 2.1, the percentage of youth involved in delinquency increases from late childhood (ages seven to twelve) to middle adolescence (ages thirteen

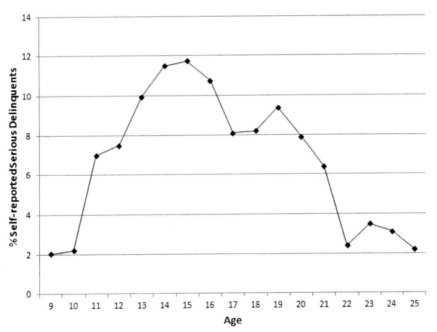

Figure 2.1.   The Age-Crime Curve of self-reported serious delinquents
Reprinted with permission from Springer

to sixteen) and the down-slope of the age-crime curve represents the decrease of criminal activities from late adolescence (ages seventeen to nineteen) into early adulthood (ages twenty to twenty-five) (Loeber, Farrington, Howell, and Hoeve, 2012). Studies clearly show that high-risk/high-rate (e.g., the most prolific) offenders dominate among juveniles and young adults (Macleod, Groves, and Farrington, 2012).

Some studies have revealed a small proportion of late bloomers whose frequency of offending is substantial, and whose careers peak slightly later, in their twenties (Thornberry, 2005; Van der Geest, Blokland, and Bijleveld, 2009). However, the frequency of offending usually peaks around ages seventeen to nineteen, and remains stable only among a small number of offenders over time. Most offenders desist naturally by their mid-twenties along with more mature brain functioning, including impulse control, planning ahead, reasoning, emotion regulation, gratification delays, abstract thinking, verbal memory, and resistance to peer influence (Farrington, Loeber, and Howell, 2012).

The percentage of juveniles who self-report continuous involvement in serious property and violent offenses across the adolescent period is very small. Across multiples studies, about 8–9 percent of young serious and violent offenders continue committing these types of offenses throughout adolescence (Lipsey and Derzon, 1998; Mulvey, Steinberg, Piquero et al., 2010; Thornberry et al., 1999). Although a similar life-course delinquency trajectory pattern is seen among girls as well as boys (Huizinga and Miller, 2013; Kempf-Leonard, Tracy, and Howell, 2001), a major difference is that a smaller portion of girls becomes persistent offenders. Prior studies also have suggested that violent offending peaks earlier among females than males, but the research is now mixed on this (Hipwell and Loeber, 2006).

In sum, delinquency is an age-related transitory stage for the large majority of offenders and thus most offenders will age out and not have serious or long careers. For the low risk/low rate non-serious offenders, then, the main objective of the juvenile justice system should be to do no harm. But there are persistent serious offenders and those who will not age out, and they need more attention. We next review research on serious, violent, and chronic offender careers.

SERIOUS, VIOLENT, AND CHRONIC OFFENDER CAREERS

"Juvenile" status, as codified in state laws (most often ages ten to seventeen), is an age-related transition stage between childhood and early adulthood, with the broader period generally referred to as "adolescence." During the teenage years, most offenders will age out of delinquency. For these minor offenders, often called experimenters, the goal of

JJ systems is minimal intervention. On the other hand, there are serious offenders who do not age out of juvenile delinquency. Offender career studies help sort the latter group (those who persist) from the larger group (those who desist). If the objectives of JJ systems are public safety and positive outcomes for the juveniles that come into the system, the most effective allocation of limited resources will be to focus them on the most dangerous and prolific offenders. These offenders represent a relatively small proportion of the juveniles who are adjudicated delinquent but account for an overwhelming majority of the total volume of offenses.

Five state-level studies have analyzed juvenile offender careers based on a typology developed specifically for the purpose of assisting JJ systems distinguish serious, violent, and chronic (SVC) offender careers from others (Wilson and Howell, 1993). In the first of these studies, Snyder's (1998) enormous sample included all children born from 1962 through 1977 (sixteen birth cohorts) in Maricopa County, Arizona, who later were referred to the juvenile court for a delinquency offense between their eighth and eighteenth birthdays.[1] Altogether, 151,209 youth in the sixteen birth cohorts had court careers.

Tracking the Wilson-Howell typology, the specific categorization of offenses that Snyder used in defining SVC offenders to distinguish them from ordinary delinquents follows (p. 429):

- Violent offenses included the offenses of murder and non-negligent manslaughter, kidnapping, violent sexual assault, robbery, and aggravated assault.
- Serious nonviolent offenses included burglary, serious larceny, motor vehicle theft, arson, weapons offenses, and drug trafficking.
- Non-serious delinquent offenses included such offenses as simple assault, possession of a controlled substance, disorderly conduct, vandalism, nonviolent sex offenses, minor larceny, liquor law offenses, and all other delinquent offenses.
- Chronic offenders were classified as those with four or more court complaints.

Snyder's analysis revealed that the group with ordinary delinquent careers (i.e., minor or non-serious offenders) is actually the largest group. This group of offenders represented almost two-thirds of all 151,209 juvenile court careers. In other words, nearly two-thirds (64 percent) of juvenile court careers were nonchronic and did not include any serious or violent offenses (Table 2.1). Just over one third (36 percent) of the delinquent careers involved serious, violent, or chronic offense histories. Nearly 18 percent of all careers contained a serious or violent referral but were nonchronic (fewer than four court referrals), 8 percent of all careers contained

Table 2.1.   Five States' Analyses of Serious, Violent, and Chronic Offender Careers

SVC Category	FL	PA	CT	NC	AZ
Non SVC	44%	79%	67%	66%	64%
Serious offenders	55%	6%	24%	29%	34%
Violent offenders	29%	6%	6%	3%	8%
Chronic offenders	16%	14%	14%	9%	15%
Serious, violent, and chronic (SVC)	9%	0.4%	2%	1%	3%

Note: FL: Juvenile court referrals in Fiscal Year 2008
PA: Juvenile offenders with a 2007 case closure
CT: Juvenile court referrals in 2005–2009
NC: Juvenile court referrals in Fiscal Year 2009–2010
AZ: Cohorts of juvenile court referrals turning 18 years of age during 1980–1995

Source: Material collection from collaborative work with state analysts.

a violent referral but were not chronic offenders, and only slightly more than 4 percent of all offender careers were chronic and included serious *and* violent offenses. In other words, only 4 percent of the careers contained serious property, violent, and chronic offense histories.

Four recent statewide analyses of SVC offender careers (in Florida, Pennsylvania, Connecticut, and North Carolina) were made to support evidence-based initiatives in each of the states that draw upon the framework and offender management tools for implementing the OJJDP Comprehensive Strategy for Serious, Violent, and Chronic Juvenile Offenders (Wilson and Howell, 1993). Each of the four comparative studies closely replicated Snyder's method of classifying juvenile offender careers. Statistical representations of offender career types are shown in Table 2.1. Readers should be aware that the figures in Table 2.1 will not add up to 100 percent per state because each offender type can overlap with others. For example, serious offender careers can contain serious offenses and be chronic, contain serious and violent offenses, or only have serious property offenses.

The first of these analyses, dissecting Florida juvenile court referrals in 2008–2012 (Baglivio, 2013a; Baglivio, et al., 2014), shows comparatively larger proportions of SVC offenders than Snyder reported in the Arizona study. As shown in Table 2.1, 55 percent of Florida offenders had at least one serious property or violent offense in their history, 29 percent had been referred for a violent offense, 16 percent were chronic offenders (4 or more court referrals), 9 percent were serious, violent, and chronic offenders (SVC); and 44 percent did not meet criteria for serious, violent, or chronic careers.

It can be seen that the Florida SVC offender subgroup is more than four times as large as that observed in North Carolina (Table 2.1). However, this difference can be explained, at least for the most part, by the younger juvenile offenders in North Carolina and the source of court referrals. Age fifteen presently is the upper limit of original juvenile court jurisdiction for delinquent offenses in North Carolina. Second, only those youth filed upon by prosecutors are referred to court in Florida, thus reducing the proportion of court-referred low risk offenders; whereas in North Carolina, 40 percent of court referrals come from schools, a large proportion of which are low risk offenders. Even so, the Venn diagram (Figure 2.2) graphically illustrates the overlap of serious, violent, and chronic offender careers in the younger North Carolina offender population (M.Q. Howell, 2013). Of the total cohort of youth referred to court in 2009–2010, with a three-year follow-up per juvenile, 29 percent had at least one serious property offense in their history, 9 percent were chronic offenders, 6 percent were serious and chronic, 3 percent were violent, just 1 percent were serious, violent, and chronic (SVC) offenders, and 66 percent did not meet criteria for serious, violent, or chronic careers (Figure 2.2).

Other than Florida—which can be expected to have a higher proportion of serious and violent offenders than the comparison states for reasons stated above—roughly two-thirds of all court-referred youth are

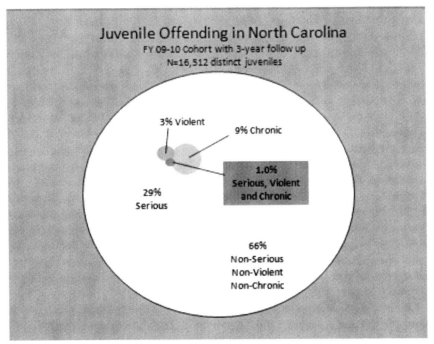

Figure 2.2.   Overlap of Serious, Violent, and Chronic Offender Careers in North Carolina
Reference: Howell, M. Q. (2013). Serious, violent and chronic (SVC) offenders in North Carolina. Paper presented at the Annual Meeting of the American Society of Criminology, November. Atlanta, Georgia.

non-serious, non-violent, and non-chronic in the four remaining states. Interestingly, excluding North Carolina's relatively younger offenders, the chronic offender group in the four remaining states is very similar in size, from 14 percent to 16 percent. The five states proportion of SVC offenders ranges from less than 1 percent in Pennsylvania to 9 percent in Florida. Importantly, in analyses not shown in Table 2.1, each of the states has a sizeable proportion of chronic serious property offenders.

Further analyses also revealed that the relatively small proportion of SVC offenders typically accounts for a large volume of total crimes in a state. For example, the North Carolina SVC offenders averaged fourteen court referrals each, and the total group of serious, violent, *or* chronic offenders—who represented 34 percent of all offenders—accounted for 62 percent of all delinquent offenses (M.Q. Howell, 2013). In Florida, among all court referrals in 2008–2013, the sizeable group of SVC offenders, a full 9 percent of all offenders, were responsible for 30 percent of all arrests, and 35 percent of the murder/manslaughters, 45 percent of the attempted murder/manslaughter arrests, 41 percent of the armed robberies, and 37 percent of all aggravated assault arrests over the five year period examined (Baglivio, 2013c).

In addition, though not surprising, SVC offenders have higher recidivism rates than other offender groups. But the magnitude of the difference is very important. Across the five states, analyses show that SVC offenders are far more likely to recidivate than non-SVC offenders (Baglivio, 2009; Fowler, 2013; M.Q. Howell, 2013; Kochol, 2013[2]; Snyder, 1998). In Pennsylvania, 48 percent of the SVC offenders recidivated, versus 31 percent of violent offenders and 34 percent of serious offenders, compared with an overall recidivism rate in the state of just 20 percent (Fowler, 2013). The proportion of SVC offenders in Florida that recidivated (within one year) was smaller, 35 percent, but SVC youth were almost 2.5 times more likely to be reconvicted than non- SVC youth, and over 3.5 times more likely than youth not meeting criteria for serious, violent, or chronic (Baglivio et al., 2014). In sum, Thornberry and colleagues (1998) observed that, "it is not possible to have much of an impact on the overall volume of adolescent violence without intervening successfully in the lives of chronic violent offenders. For example, even if we were 100 percent successful in preventing the nonchronic violent offenders from *ever* engaging in violence, we would reduce the level of violent behavior by only 25 percent" (p. 220).

In large cities with serious gang problems, gang members are often responsible for a large proportion of SVC offenders. Studies within high crime areas of several cities show that gang members account for more than seven in ten of self-reported violent offenses committed by all delinquents (Thornberry, 1998). There also is evidence that the smaller proportion of multi-year gang members commits an even larger proportion of the serious and violent offenses. In a Denver study, multi-year gang members represented just 8 percent of the total youth sample but they committed 71 percent of all the serious violent offenses (Huizinga, 2010). In the larger Rochester adolescent sample, two-thirds (66 percent) of the chronic violent offenders were gang members (Thornberry et al., 1998). Thus intervention strategies must take gang involvement into account, a matter that we address throughout this handbook.

Fortunately, SVC offenders have distinguishable risk factors and treatment needs that, if addressed early, can potentially reduce their recidivism. The North Carolina analysis (M.Q. Howell, 2013) examined risk factors and treatment needs of SVC versus non-SVC offenders. The proportion of SVC offenders classified as high risk of recidivism was 63 percent, whereas only 5 percent of the non-SVC offenders were high risk. Similarly, 67 percent of the SVC offenders displayed elevated treatment needs, in comparison with only 24 percent of the non-SVC offenders. The most prominent risk and need factors were mental health and substance abuse problems; school suspension, expulsion, and dropout; gang membership or associations; and family problems including conflict in the home, parents unwilling and/or unable to supervise their child/children, and a history of victimization by caregivers or others. Florida results show that SVC youth are exposed to substantial risk in school performance, relationships with peers, living arrangements and family history, antisocial attitudes, aggression, alcohol and substance use histories, and mental health problem histories (Baglivio et al., 2014). This Florida analysis also showed that SVC offenders are almost four times more likely to indicate gang association than youth not meeting criteria for SVC. In sum, the North Carolina and Florida analyses provide excellent guidance for formulation of comprehensive treatment plans for SVC offenders.

Several other Florida SVC analyses provide additional guidance for intervention strategies. The first of these supported other research in showing that higher risk youth more likely to re-offend (Baglivio, 2009; Baglivio and Jackowski, 2013). Another analysis supported the risk principle for low risk youth (Baglivio, 2013b). Diverted low risk youth who received services in less restrictive settings demonstrated significantly lower recidivism rates, indicating that diverting low risk youth is a very effective strategy in terms of reducing subsequent re-offending. Third, this analysis also identified a group of relatively low risk offenders who have considerably elevated treatment needs, that is, "low risk/high need" youth.

The predictive strength of risk and protective factors provides further guidance for intervention in SVC careers. Lipsey and Derzon (1998) reviewed violence predictors by using data drawn from an ongoing meta-analysis of prospective longitudinal studies of the development of antisocial behavior at Vanderbilt University. This meta-analysis—focused on serious property delinquency as well as violent outcomes—included sixty-six reports on thirty-four independent studies that measured risk factors at ages six to eleven and twelve to fourteen and serious and violent outcomes when the samples were ages fifteen to twenty-five—when such behavior tends to peak in adolescents and young adults.

Lipsey and Derzon's findings may be summarized as follows:

- At ages six to eleven, the best predictors of subsequent serious or violent offenses are involvement in delinquency (general offenses) at this early age and drug use. The second-strongest group of predictors are being a male, living in a poor family (low socioeconomic status), and having antisocial parents. A history of aggression and ethnicity are in the third-strongest group of predictors.
- For the twelve to fourteen age group, a lack of social ties and having antisocial peers are the strongest predictors of subsequent serious or violent offenses. Involvement in delinquency (general offenses) is the one predictor in the second ranking group. Several predictors are in the third-strongest group: a history of aggression, school attitude/performance, psychological condition (mental health), parent-adolescent relations, being a male, and a history of violence.
- Broken homes and abusive parents are among the weakest predictors of subsequent serious or violent offenses for both age groups.
- The significance of antisocial peers and substance abuse is reversed in the two age groups. Whereas having antisocial peers is the weakest predictor for the age six to eleven group, it is one of two very strong predictors for the twelve to fourteen age group. Conversely, in the six to eleven age group early onset of substance use is one of two very strong predictors; it is among the weakest predictors for the age twelve to fourteen group.

This meta-analysis is important for what it reveals about the relative strengths of predictors for the two different age groups, children (ages six to eleven) and adolescents (ages twelve to fourteen). The implications are important for prevention programming priorities. Early intervention efforts, with children, should target early delinquent behaviors, including drug use and displays of aggression, family poverty, and antisocial parents (Farrington and Welsh, 2007). In contrast, prevention efforts with adolescents should seek to reduce young people's associations with antisocial peers and involvement in delinquency, aggression, and physical violence while strengthening their social ties, improving their relationships with parents, and improving their mental health.

Malleable protective factors are discussed below. A comprehensive prevention approach that addresses predictors and protective factors in more than one risk factor domain (e.g., peer group and family) is likely to have the largest impact.

VERY YOUNG OFFENDERS

It has been well established that the court careers of early-onset offenders (children involved in delinquency before age thirteen) are more extensive and more likely to contain referrals for serious and violent offenses (Krohn, Thornberry, Rivera et al., 2001; Loeber and Farrington, 2001; Snyder, 2001). Research findings agree that the risk of later violence, serious offenses, and chronic offending is two to three times higher for early-onset offenders than for later-onset offenders, and this proportion applies to girls as well as boys (Loeber and Farrington, 2001). The early-onset offenders in a Pittsburgh study—who represented 10 percent of the total sample—had an average of 142 self-reported offenses through age seventeen (more than 50 percent of offenses committed by the entire sample) (Welsh, Loeber, Stevens et al., 2008).

Compared with offenders who start their career at a later age, child delinquents—particularly males—are at least twice as likely to become SVC offenders, to carry weapons, become gang members, and engage in substance use (Loeber, Farrington, Stouthamer-Loeber, White and Wei, 2008; Loeber, Slott, Van Der Laan et al., 2008), and their offending is more likely to persist into adulthood (Loeber and Farrington, 1998, 2001, 2012; Loeber, Hoeve, Slott, et al., 2012). In addition, many predictors of homicide are already in place during late childhood and early adolescence, particularly being suspended from school, disruptive behavior disorders, and having a positive attitude to delinquency (Loeber and Ahonen, 2013).

In Florida, the SVC group was almost three times more likely than non-SVC youth to have been first referred at twelve years old or younger (Baglivio et al., 2014). In Pennsylvania, 45 percent of child offenders were either a serious offender, a violent offender, or a chronic offender (Fowler, 2013). These analyses of younger SVCs provide assurance that states can distinguish this subgroup at a relatively early age and then attempt to intervene successfully with them.

IMPLICATIONS OF THE RESEARCH ON SERIOUS, VIOLENT, AND CHRONIC OFFENDER CAREERS

As seen in the research reviewed above, a large proportion of the offenses, especially more serious ones, are committed by a relatively small proportion of offenders, those we have referred to as serious, violent, and chronic offenders. To realize a significant reduction in delinquency, recidivism reductions must be seen in this group of offenders. It is important to take note of a critical finding in the initial SVC analysis: Snyder (1998) found that each time a youth returns to court on a new charge, there is a greater risk that it will be for a violent crime—that is, for advancing toward SVC status. Thus, Snyder insists, "to reduce juvenile violence, therefore, we must work to reduce the recidivism of juvenile offenders regardless of the act that has brought them to the attention of the juvenile justice system" (p. 444).

Cohen, Piquero, and Jennings (2010) estimate that a youth with six or more offenses over his or her lifetime costs $4.2–$7.2 million to society and victims. Researchers in a Pittsburgh study conservatively estimated that the entire cohort of 500 boys in a high crime area burden society in the form of victimization costs ranging from a low of $89 million to a high of $110 million (Welsh et al., 2008). Significant reductions in the number of offenses and shortening the length of SVC criminal careers would produce enormous savings in both dollars and harm to victims.

As noted earlier in examining SVC careers, we saw that most juvenile offenders are self-correcting; that is, they do not have lifetime careers and many never come to the attention of JJ systems. Diversion of these can reduce a large portion of the caseload. For many years, North Carolina has diverted almost a third of the youths referred to juvenile courts each year (M.Q. Howell and J. Bullock, 2013). Though this is a remarkable achievement, other states can follow suit by using risk and need assessment tools that facilitate matching juveniles with appropriate levels of supervision and services.

ADDRESS RISK AND PROTECTIVE FACTORS

As seen in the preceding section, a small proportion of offenders advance to become SVC offenders. However, for prevention and intervention purposes, a better understanding is needed of the risk factors that often propel them to that pinnacle. A social development model best explains the process by which delinquent careers begin, often persist to SVC levels, and gradually desist in most cases. Figure 2.3 illustrates the evolving influence of the major risk factor domains and their interaction with age. Researchers have noted the changes in "nested domains" of influences on children from middle-childhood onward, and in the course of social development, new risk factors are introduced over time, several of which persist with age, and thus are "stacked" over time (Loeber, Slott, and Stouthamer-Loeber, 2008). At a young age, the child is most affected by family influences, which in turn are affected by neighborhood conditions. "Very early onset offending is brought about by the *combination and inter-*

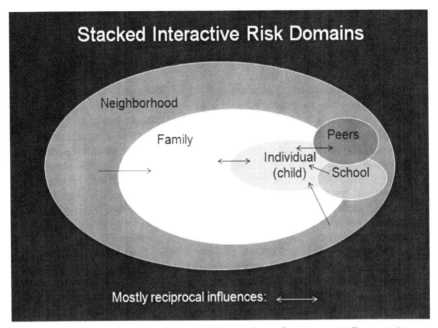

Figure 2.3. Developmental Domains and Interactive Influences on Delinquent Careers
Reprinted with permission from Ashgate

action of structural, individual, and parental influences" (Thornberry and Krohn, 2001, p. 295). During the preschool years, and especially in the elementary school period and onward, the array of risk factors expands, as some children are exposed to negative peer influences outside the home. Poor social skills, low academic achievement, and early alcohol/drug use are important individual risk factors. Peer rejection in the early school years may lead to greater susceptibility to the influence of deviant peers, including more aggressive and perhaps gang-involved peers. In time, as children become more mobile, they will be affected directly by neighborhood factors.

An important point about risk factors is that we will never see a well-validated comprehensive short list of, say, a half dozen risk factors for on-set and delinquency involvement. Delinquent behavior is not that easy to predict "because children's development from minor to serious, violent, and persistent offending entails intricate processes in which numerous factors have main effects on child deviancy and, sometimes, interaction effects over time as well" (Van Domburgh, Vermeiren, and Doreleijers, 2008, p. 170). Moreover, risk factors multiply with age and studies with large samples that follow youths throughout childhood and adolescence produce extensive lists.

BOX 2.1

TWO WAYS OF VIEWING PROTECTIVE FACTORS

Protective factors operate in two main ways (Lösel and Farrington, 2012). "Direct protective factors" insulate persons from risk factors and thus predict a low probability of violence. Operating in this way, protective factors are viewed as promoting prosocial behavior, sometimes called *promotive factors*. Generally speaking, professionals in some JJ systems think of protective factors as "strength factors." Indeed, a large body of research on protective factors is related to the topic of resilience, which refers to healthy development despite a high-risk status, and may involve biological mechanisms of protection, regeneration, and repair (Lösel and Bender, 2003). Because resilience shares many similarities with the concept of protective factors, this construct is not discussed separately here.

"Buffering protective factors" counter existing risk factors by helping youth overcome them, thus predicting a low probability of violence in the presence of risk. Given this dual role of protective factors, research typically does not specify the manner in which they are operating. Therefore, we do not at this time have the high level of research validation on protective factors that risk factors enjoy. Nevertheless, it is clear that in extremely high-risk conditions, youth need more than a simple majority of protective factors to overcome multiple risk factors (Stouthamer-Loeber, Loeber, Stallings et al., 2008). For example, Smith and colleagues (1995) found that adolescents living in high-crime areas who were exposed to at least eight protective factors were four times more likely to be resilient than those exposed to fewer than five protective factors. Therefore, the most effective approach is to reduce risk factors while increasing protective factors in an inverse dose-response relationship, meaning that the higher the number of protective factors an offender is exposed to, the lower the likelihood that the youth will continue delinquency involvement.

Tables 2.2a–2.2e show well-supported risk factors for juvenile delinquency and youth violence along with protective factors (that have less research validation). Numerous studies indicate a strong association between the number of risk factors and the probability of later violence. This well-documented dose-response relationship has been demonstrated for the full range of indicators of problem behaviors including violence and serious property crime.

Malleable risk factors follow that have the strongest research support for forestalling advancement in pathways to delinquent and criminal activity from childhood to later developmental stages (early adolescence, late adolescence, and early adulthood) (Tanner-Smith, Wilson, and Lipsey, 2013a, Table 5.3, p. 105).

Tables 2.2a–e. Risk Factors and Protective Factors for Delinquency (Including Violence)

Table 2.2a.   **Risk Factors within the Individual Domain**

Risk Factors	Protective Factors
Delinquency/violence	High academic achievement
Aggressive behavior	High perceived likelihood of getting caught
Impulsivity/hyperactivity	High self-esteem
Substance use	Lower perceived reward regarding offending
Externalizing problems	Substance abuse treatment
Low self-aspirations	Positive attitudes toward family and school
Drug exposure/attitudes	Low impulsivity and an easy temperament
Positive attitude toward delinquency	Low attention deficit hyperactive disorder
Anti-establishment attitudes	
High alcohol use	
Psychiatric disorders	
Violence victimization	
Gang membership/involvement	
Gun carrying	
Drug selling	

Table 2.2b.   **Risk and Protective Factors within the Family Domain**

Risk Factors	Protective Factors
Parenting skills	Close relationship to at least one parent
Low family cohesion/warmth	Intensive parental supervision
Harsh parenting	Parental disapproval of aggressive behavior
Family structure	Low physical punishment
Socioeconomic status	Intensive involvement in family activities
Family criminality	Family models of constructive coping
Child maltreatment	Positive parental attitudes toward child's education
	Low parental stress
	Parental support
	Parental involvement in conventional activities

Table 2.2c.   **Risk and Protective Factors within the School Domain**

Risk Factors	Protective Factors
Low achievement test performance	School achievement
Poor school performance (overall)	Bonding to school
Weak school motivation/attitudes	Strong work motivation
Negative school climate	Higher education
	Support and supervision by teachers
	Clear classroom rules
	Positive school climate

Table 2.2d. Risk and Protective Factors within the Peer Domain

Risk Factors	Protective Factors
Antisocial peers	Non-deviant good friends
Peer substance use	Peer groups who disapprove of aggression
Poor peer relations/popularity	Involvement in religious groups
Peer delinquency/criminality	Less association with antisocial peers
Peer attitudes toward deviance	Group conventional behavior

Table 2.2e. Risk and Protective Factors within the Community/Neighborhood Domain

Risk Factors	Protective Factors
Disadvantaged neighborhood	Non-deprived neighborhood
Residential instability	Non-violent neighborhood
Racial/ethnic transition	
Low resident cohesion/informal social control	
Exposure to firearm violence	
Availability of firearms	
Availability of drugs	
Low neighborhood attachment	
Feeling unsafe	
Youth often in trouble	

Note: Typical age at risk: six to fourteen; Typical age at outcome: twelve to seventeen; Typical ages at protection: six to seventeen. Only factors that are malleable in everyday practice are included.

Sources: Bushway, Krohn, Lizotte et al., 2013; Farrington et al., 2008; Howell, 2012; Krohn, Lizotte, Bushway et al., in press; Loeber, Farrington, Stouthamer-Loeber, White, and Wei, 2008; Loeber, Slott, and Stouthamer-Loeber, 2008; Lösel and Farrington, 2012; Loughran, Mulvey, Schubert et al., 2009; Loughran, Piquero, Fagan et al., 2012; Monahan and Piquero, 2009; Mulvey, 2011; Mulvey, Steinberg, Fagan et al., 2004; Mulvey, Schubert, and Chung 2007; Mulvey, Steinberg, Piquero et al., 2010; Stouthamer-Loeber et al., 2008; Tanner-Smith, 2012

Individual: Prior levels of delinquent and criminal behavior, including substance use, as well as general externalizing behavior. In particular, "violent or aggressive behavior, impulsivity/hyperactivity, and externalizing problem behaviors during childhood can all serve to identify the children who may benefit most from early intervention" (p. 108).

Family: Poor parental skills, supervision and monitoring, harsh parenting, and lack of family cohesion/warmth.

School: Mainly school performance, with weaker support for achievement test performance, school motivation/attitudes, and school climate

Peers: The delinquent and criminal behavior of peers, including substance use; peer attitudes toward deviance and conventionality; and general peer relations or popularity among peers.

Given that relatively few youth are referred to juvenile courts during childhood (before age twelve), it is important to know which of these risk factors measured during the early adolescent period have predictive strength to late adolescence and early adulthood. The longitudinal studies that Tanner-Smith and colleagues (2013a) synthesized in their meta-analysis revealed the following risk factors as having the strongest research support onward from age twelve.

> *Individual*: Prior levels of delinquent and criminal behavior, including substance use, externalizing problems, and anti-establishment attitudes.
>
> *Family*: Each of the family factors was most potent during childhood, but remained relevant into adulthood, with the exception of harsh parenting.
>
> *Peer*: Each of the peer factors remained relevant into adulthood, with the exception that peer substance use and relations lost strength in predicting recidivism from late adolescence to early adulthood.
>
> *School*: The strength of school factors waned into adulthood, with only school performance and school motivation/attitudes remaining important.

This array of relevant risk factors underscores the importance of crafting treatment plans that are multi-system—encompassing the individual, family, school, and peer domains—while concentrating in particular on age-appropriate risk factors. "There are important, and multiple risk factors in most domains at all developmental stages" (Tanner-Smith et al., 2013a, p. 108). Thus an intervention with a single focus will have only limited impact.

In addition, several of the risk factors that predict childhood onset and escalation of adolescent offending do not have a long reach into adulthood (Farrington, Loeber, Jolliffe, and Pardini, 2008; Ezell, 2007; Tanner-Smith et al., 2013a). The following are key findings from Tanner-Smith and colleagues' very comprehensive research synthesis:

- A number of risk factors clearly have value as potentially useful diagnostic indicators during childhood. School failure, violent or aggressive behavior, impulsivity or hyperactivity, and externalizing problem behaviors during childhood can all serve to identify the children who may benefit most from early intervention.
- Family risk factors measured during childhood are particularly salient risk factors for later criminal behavior. Prevention programs aimed at reducing criminal offending may benefit from including

parent training and parent education components that address family dynamics during the childhood years.

- Other important risk factors within the individual, family, peer, and school risk domains vary in strength across the developmental stages in adolescence and early adulthood, thus emphasizing the importance of future theory, research, and practice recognizing developmental specificity in risk for delinquent and criminal behavior.
- The strongest and most robust risk factors for crime during adolescence and early adulthood are those that represent prior delinquent or criminal behavior. Thus, prevention programs and JJ systems should first and foremost concern themselves with preventing the initiation and escalation of delinquency among children.

RISK AND PROTECTIVE FACTORS FOR GIRLS

It is clear that a small group of girls, just like boys, experience an early onset of disruptive behavior and their problem behavior shows a relatively stable pattern (Kroneman, Loeber, and Hipwell, 2004). It also is evident that there are more similarities in female and male delinquency careers than previously imagined (Borduin and Ronis, 2012; Wong, Slottboom, and Bijleveld, 2010). For example, in a Philadelphia study that examined continuity in offending among serious, violent, and chronic juvenile offender subgroups, Kempf-Leonard, Tracy, and Howell (2001) the male-to-female ratio was 3:1 among serious offenders (serious property and violent offenders), 4:1 among violent offenders, and 3:1 among chronic offenders. These researchers found larger gender differences when they examined repeated serious and violent offending.

Even though individual rates of serious delinquency remain considerably lower for girls compared with boys (Snyder and Sickmund, 2006; Steffensmeier, Zhong, Ackerman et al., 2006), girls commit the same types of offenses as boys, and self-report surveys of adolescents support the notion that the female-male ratio of delinquency involvement has increased substantially in recent years (Esbensen, Peterson, Taylor, and Freng, 2010; Hipwell and Loeber, 2006). Thus girls' involvement in delinquency should not be underestimated. Provided that JJ systems give special attention to reducing recidivism among girls as well as boys, larger overall system impacts can be seen.

There is considerable evidence of gender similarity in risk factor predictors of delinquency and violence (Hubbard and Pratt, 2002; Loeber, Farrington, Howell et al., 2012; Moffitt, Caspi, Rutter et al., 2001; Van der Put, Dekovic, Geert et al., 2011; Wong et al., 2010), but some important gender differences have been revealed. Indeed, recent research identifies areas in which females differ from males in rates of exposure to risk factors in several meta-analyses and other reviews of risk factors for adolescent and young adult female offenders (Hubbard and Pratt, 2002; see also Tanner-Smith et al., 2013a; Wong et al., 2010; Hawkins, Graham et al., 2009). A meta-analysis specifically of predictors of female delinquency (Hubbard and Pratt, 2002) found that antisocial personality and antisocial peers were the strongest predictors. In addition, school and family relationships and a history of physical and/or sexual assault, although less powerful predictors, also were robust predictors of female delinquency. Elevated individual factors are an antisocial personality, low intelligence, substance abuse, physical or sexual abuse, mental health problems, pubertal timing, and low levels of self-worth. Hipwell, White, Loeber and colleagues (2005) note that girls may be more vulnerable to persistent alcohol use, abuse, and dependence at an early age.

The largest discrepancy, however, is in sexual assault victimization. Although boys are more likely to report some assault victimization, females are ten times more likely to experience sexual assault than boys (McReynolds et al., 2010). Hubbard and Matthews (2008) isolate unique personality traits of girls that are believed to contribute to their antisocial behavior. Although girls possess four unique strengths (lower rates of hyperactivity and poor impulse control, stronger moral evaluations of behavior that enhance their ability to counteract negative peer influences, greater empathy, and more guilt proneness), they also have a greater tendency than boys to engage in self-debasing distortions (e.g., self-blame, negative thoughts about self) that can lead to internalizing behaviors and self-harm. Notably, girls also have a stronger desire than boys for affiliation and acceptance that can contribute to negative emotional (e.g., stress) and behavioral outcomes (e.g., risky sexual behavior).

In the family domain, important risk factors for girls are the quality of parent-child relationships, conflicts within the family, parental control, and family violence and having caregivers with a history of substance abuse or delinquency. In a comparison of brothers and sisters in a London study, Farrington and Painter (2004) found that socio-economic risk factors such as low social class, low family income, poor housing, and large family size predicted offending more strongly for sisters than for brothers. In addition, child-rearing risk factors such as low praise by the parents, harsh or erratic discipline, and poor parental supervision, and parental conflict, low parental interest in education, and low paternal interest in the children were also stronger predictors for sisters than for brothers.

In the peer domain, just as for boys, delinquent friends, gang membership, and the quality of peer relationships affect female delinquency (Petersen and Howell, 2013). The aggressive behavior of girls, even more so than boys, depends on their intimate relationships (Lösel and Farrington,

2012). Two features of peer relations have important implications for girls' involvement in delinquency (Hubbard and Matthews, 2008). First, girls who report having a mixed-sex friendship group are significantly more likely to engage in delinquency than girls with same-sex friendship groups (Peterson, 2012). Second, girls undermine the development of supportive friendships by engaging in what Brown (2003) dubbed "girlfighting," or the "emotional and discreet bullying of other girls (e.g., gossip, manipulation, teasing, and exclusion)" (p. 244).

Unique protective factors against delinquency and violence for girls have been investigated in just two major literature reviews. In the initial review, family connectedness, school connectedness, and religiosity provided significant protection for girls against violence perpetration (Hawkins, Graham, Williams, and Zahn, 2009). A subsequent literature examination also found that patterns of protective factors in women/girls seem to be "partially different" from those for boys (particularly in the greater relevance of relationship issues) (Lösel and Farrington, 2012, p. S19).[3] It also appears that the cumulative effects of risk factors may be worse for girls than for boys, requiring multimodal services (Hipwell and Loeber, 2006). These developmental differences have important implications for intervention with girls, which are discussed in the appendix to this book.

RISK AND PROTECTIVE FACTORS FOR GANG INVOLVEMENT

Youth gang membership is now recognized as a serious and persistent problem in the United States by both the Centers for Disease Control and Prevention and the U.S. Department of Justice (Simon, Ritter, and Mahendra, 2013). Nationwide, nearly one in twelve youth said that they belonged to a gang at some point during their teenage years (Snyder and Sickmund, 2006). Moreover, one in five students in grades six through twelve report that gangs are present in their school (Robers, Zhang, Truman et al., 2012) and almost half of high school students say that there are gangs or students who consider themselves to be part of a gang in their schools (National Center on Addiction and Substance Abuse, 2010).

Although the male-to-female gang ratio is approximately 2:1, that is 11 percent of males versus 6 percent females (Snyder and Sickmund, 2006), the proportion of females involved in gangs has increased the past few decades (Howell, 2012). More than one-third of all gang members are female (Peterson, 2012). Moreover, female gang members commit the same sorts of offenses. As seen in an eleven-city survey of eighth graders undertaken in the mid-1990s (Esbensen et al., 2010), more than 90 percent of both male and female gang members reported having engaged in one or more violent acts in the previous twelve months. The researchers also found that 75 percent of female gang members reported being involved in gang fights, and 37 percent reported having attacked someone with a weapon. Individual violent offending rates were similar except for hitting someone, general violence, and particularly serious violence (e.g., gun use), for which boys' rates were significantly higher.

Although research on the matter of whether or not risk factors for gang joining operate differently for males and females is sparse, a strong argument can be made that many risk factors affect boys and girls similarly. Studies in both Rochester (Thornberry, Krohn, Lizotte et al., 2003) and Seattle (Gilman, Hill, Hawkins, 2014) found no gender differences in risk factors across individual, family, school, neighborhood, and peer domains. Similarly, in an analysis of data gathered in the National Longitudinal Study of Adolescent Health, Bell (2009) found "little evidence that risk factors associated with gang involvement differ for males and females" (p. 379); gang membership for both genders was predicted by neighborhood disadvantage, negative parent-child relationship factors, school safety concerns, and exposure to violent peers—covering four of the five major risk factor sectors.

For boys and girls alike, conditions that contribute to one's decision to join a gang fall into two categories: gang attractions and risk factors. Moreover, similar constellations of risk factors elevate both boys' and girls' risk of gang joining, namely individual characteristics (early problem behaviors), family conditions, school experiences, peer group influences, and community contexts. We first discuss attractions to gangs.

Gang Attractions

Gang culture is intertwined with the general youth subculture via movies, music, and clothing styles. Most young people in urban areas recognize gang symbols and styles of dress. Gangs are often at the center of appealing social action, including parties, music, drugs, and opportunities to socialize with members of the opposite sex. In other words, the gang may be attractive because it meets a youth's social needs. Girls join gangs for similar reasons as boys. Both genders reported the following reasons for joining a gang, in the order of descending importance (Peterson, 2012):

- For fun.
- For protection.
- Because a friend was in the gang.
- To get respect.

Like boys, desired protection and social opportunities are the main reasons girls give for joining gangs. They want to feel safe and secure, and they want to be an integral part of the social scene. Many female adolescents are attracted to gangs because their friends or boyfriends have joined.

Risk Factors for Gang Joining

Factors that push youth toward gangs are more complex than gang attractions. While it is not possible to predict with acceptable accuracy whether a particular individual will join a gang, studies have shown that individuals who possess certain risk factors or who are surrounded by multiple risk factors have a greater chance of joining a gang. In short, youth who join gangs typically have multiple negative experiences in their lives—in their families, schools, neighborhoods, and peer groups, and likely have personal problems as well, such as early delinquency and drug and alcohol use. For boys and girls alike, a dose-response relationship is associated between an individual's multiple risk factors and an increased probability of adverse outcomes, including gang involvement. Thus, the more risk factors a youth experiences, the greater the likelihood of joining a gang.

This influence of risk factors on the decision to join a gang operates in two ways. First, the accumulation of a large number of risk factors leads to gang joining as opposed to general delinquency involvement. In a Seattle study, children under the age of twelve who experienced twenty-one of twenty-six measured risk factors were at an elevated risk of joining a gang (Hill, Howell, Hawkins et al., 1999), indicating that the predictors of gang membership are similar to predictors of delinquency, violence, and substance use. The following risk factors increased odds of joining a gang by more than three times: family structure (single parent family), low academic achievement in the fifth and sixth grades, early marijuana initiation, and availability of drugs in the neighborhood. Gang-specific protective factors have not been identified in credible research. It stands to reason, however, that protective factors that buffer youth from risk factors for delinquency would also apply because the two offender groups share the same constellation of risk factors.

Second, the presence of risk factors in multiple developmental domains further elevates risk of gang joining. In the Seattle study, children who evidenced seven risk factors that were present across domains were thirteen times more likely to join a gang than children with none or only one risk factor (Hill et al., 1999). In another study, Rochester, New York researchers (Thornberry et al., 2003) found that 61 percent of the boys and 40 percent of the girls with elevated scores in all measured risk factor domains later joined gangs.

Becoming a gang member typically commences in late childhood or early adolescence, peaks in mid-adolescence, and often substantially increases members' involvement in more serious criminal activities (Howell, 2012). To be sure, there is a high degree of overlap between gang membership and serious, violent, and chronic juvenile offending. The developmental pathways model (Figure 2.4) clearly illustrates how gang involvement is intertwined with delinquent behavior, including serious and violent offenses. Involvement in criminal activity on the part of gang members follows a parallel age-crime curve to that of ordinary delinquents. Becoming a gang member also commences in late childhood or early adolescence, and peaks in mid-adolescence. Most all youth who join gangs were already involved in delinquency, but while in gangs, their level of violence doubles or triples, and then declines once they desist from active gang participation (Krohn and Thornberry, 2008). Large proportions of gang members in the national Adolescent Health Survey admitted having committed the following offenses within the past year: had serious gang fights (62 percent), damaged property (40 percent), and shot or stabbed someone (21 percent) (Glesmann, Krisberg, and Marchionna, 2009). In late adolescence, gang involvement leads to drug trafficking and persistent gun carrying (Lizotte, Krohn, Howell et al., 2000).

IMPLICATIONS OF THE RESEARCH ON
RISK AND PROTECTIVE FACTORS

There are several important implications of knowing the particular risk factors that push a small proportion of disruptive and delinquent children to SVC offender status. The predictive value of the risk and protective factors is that they allow juveniles on high risk pathways to be identified relatively early so the JJ system can give them special attention. The prospects of successful early intervention are increased given that the "pathways" part of the picture shows a developmental progression—rather than more or less random delinquents and incidents—with the implication that it can be interrupted by effective intervention. This enterprise is complicated, though, by the reality that most offenders are intermittent offenders. Careful risk assessments are thus imperative. Moreover, there are various points of intervention along that pathway ranging from early prevention to more intensive intervention well into offenders' careers.

Early intervention is a prudent strategy for other reasons. This is the most opportune time because risk factors and co-occurring problems multiply with age, beginning in the individual, family, and school domains. Prevention and intervention programs are likely to be more effective if they do not restrict their focus to one risk domain or one risk factor within a domain. Owing to the changing influence of risk factors from one developmental period to another, individual assessments are imperative, and these must be graduated for more complex clients. Reducing risk while enhancing protection is the goal, although research is not as clear with respect to protective factors that should be targeted, that is, beyond the obvious ones such as good parental supervision and academic success.

The transitions from elementary to middle school and from middle school to high school are propitious intervention points because the influence of positive family influences diminishes with each of these transitions. Gang involvement is intertwined with advancements in delinquent pathways, progressively in more serious and violent offenses. Thus, targeting gang members' risk and protective factors in the community and on JJ system caseloads will help achieve more widespread delinquency reductions.

LEADING THEORIES OF PERSISTENT JUVENILE OFFENDING

Certain theories of delinquency are useful for their practical application in guiding strategic intervention in JJ systems. Three types of theories of persistent juvenile offending are most popular. "Static" theories suppose that the propensity to commit crimes is set early in life, and consequently is unaffected by events that occur over the life course. For example, self-control theorists hold the view that the propensity to engage in crime is a product of the person's level of self-control which is presumed to be established roughly by age eight (Gottfredson and Hirschi, 1990). The explanation for persistent offending in static theories such as this one is thus found mainly in low self-control, accompanied by family dysfunction and neuropsychological deficits that also are established during childhood.

Second, the most popular typological theory identifies two main groups of offenders (Moffitt, 1993): early onset life-course-persistent offenders and later onset adolescence-limited offenders. According to Moffitt (1993), the very small proportion of life-course-persistent offenders tend to engage in biting and hitting at age four, shoplifting and truancy at age ten, selling drugs and stealing cars at age sixteen, robbery and rape at age twenty-two, and fraud and child abuse at age thirty. In contrast, Moffitt's adolescence-limited offenders represent the larger proportion of adolescents in the mid-section of the age-crime curve. These offenders do not have childhood histories of antisocial behavior; rather, they engage in antisocial behavior only during adolescence.

Recent studies have challenged Moffitt's assumption of just two main groups of offenders. In the Rochester Youth Development Study, eight groups with diverging patterns of offending were observed, prompting Thornberry (2005, p. 160) to conclude that "offending can start earlier or later, but onset is not distinctly divided into neat patterns of *early starters* and *late starters* as hypothesized [by] Moffitt." However, Moffitt's theory is useful for identifying short-term offenders who commit delinquent acts only during the teenage years—the adolescence-limited offenders. Other career studies have dubbed these as intermittent or episodic offenders.

Most research has revealed four main adolescent offender career groups: those whose problem behavior remains low over time, those whose problem behavior increases, those whose problem behavior remains high over time, and those whose problem behavior decreases (Bushway, Thornberry, and Krohn, 2003; Loeber, Farrington, Stouthamer-Loeber, White and Wei, 2008; Farrington et al., 2008). Of course, those whose problem behavior increases and remains high are of greatest concern. It also is important to recognize that the group of late starters may be fairly substantial in some localities (Loeber, Farrington et al., 2008).

The third set of theories adopts a developmental, life course perspective on crime and offers a distinctively different explanation for patterns of offending during the adolescent years (Thornberry, Giordano, Uggen et al., 2012). While static and typological theories recognize that early characteristics retain some explanatory importance, according to developmental theorists the primary explanation for later offending is to be found in the changing social environment that individuals confront as they traverse the life course. Importantly, Thornberry and colleagues noted that "changing relationships with parents and peers, the timing and success of transitions along major life course trajectories such as family, school, and work, and the consequences of earlier involvement in delinquency and contact with the juvenile justice system are all expected to exert a strong influence on diverging patterns of offending such as persistence and desistance" (p. 57). Hence developmental theories have achieved widespread acceptance because these explain onset, escalation, de-escalation, and desistance in individuals' delinquent and criminal careers.

Two general developmental processes have been identified to account for persistence during the adolescent years (Thornberry et al., 2012). The first process stems from the stability of the causal factors that are associated with the onset of offending. Negative temperamental traits, ineffective parenting, poverty, school failure, and association with delinquent peers are all linked to the onset and maintenance of delinquent careers. The second process, an interactive one, has to do with the negative consequences of the earlier involvement in antisocial behavior, particularly involvement in delinquency, which disrupts later life course development, especially if it is prolonged and serious. In other words, early delinquents are likely to be alienated from parents and family, fail to graduate from high school, and become enmeshed in delinquent peer groups. The section that follows reviews offender career trajectories in more detail and provides a developmental theory that accounts for the main trajectories.

A pertinent question, then, is this: What are the stepping stones to the SVC level of delinquency involvement? Loeber and colleagues discovered three main developmental pathways, in the progression of delinquent careers from childhood to adolescence in the Pittsburgh Youth Study (Loeber, Slott, and Stouthamer-Loeber, 2008; Loeber, Wei, Stouthamer-Loeber et al., 1999; Loeber, Wung, Keenan et al., 1993; see also Kelley, Loeber, Keenan, and Zang, 1997). Shown in Figure 2.4, these are the authority conflict pathway, the covert pathway, and the overt pathway. The authority conflict pathway consists of predelinquent offenses, the covert pathway consists of concealing and serious property offenses, and the overt pathway consists of violent offenses. Loeber's pathways model has four important dimensions. First, the model shows an orderly progression over time from less serious to more serious offenses and delinquent behaviors. For many children, a pattern of stepping stones is observed over time, from less serious to more serious offenses and delinquent behaviors.

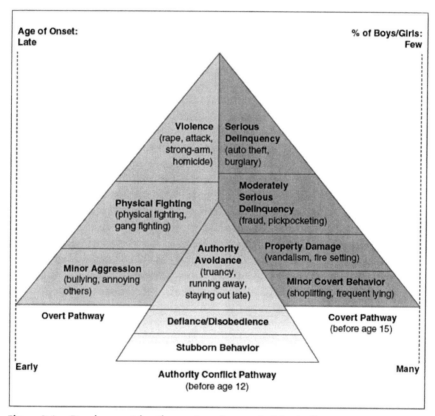

Figure 2.4. Developmental pathways to serious and violent offenses
Reprinted with permission from Ashgate

Second, the progressively narrowing width of the triangles illustrates the decreasing proportion of youth (from *many* to *few*) involved in particular problem behavior and delinquent offenses. Third, the model shows the general age of onset (from *early* to *late*). Fourth, the pathways are hierarchical in that those who have advanced to the most serious behavior in each of the pathways usually have displayed persistent problem behaviors characteristic of the earlier stages in each pathway. Problem behavior typically begins in the authority conflict pathway with stubborn behavior, followed by defiance or disobedience, then truancy, running away, or staying out late. Persistent offenders then typically move into either the overt pathway or the covert pathway. The first stage of the covert pathway is minor covert behavior (shoplifting, frequent lying); this is followed by property damage (vandalism, fire setting), and then moderately serious (fraud, pickpocketing) and serious delinquency (auto theft, burglary). The first stage of the overt pathway is minor aggression (bullying, annoying others); physical fighting follows (often including gang fighting), and then more serious violence (rape, physical attacks, and strong-arm robbery). In short, persistent offenders typically follow an orderly progression from less to more serious problem behaviors and delinquency from childhood to adolescence. The most prolific offenders, SVCs who represented 10 percent of the sample, had an average of 142 self-reported offenses through age seventeen (more than 50 percent of offenses committed by the entire sample) (Welsh et al., 2008).

The following proportions were observed in the original Pittsburgh sample (Loeber, Farrington, Stouthamer-Loeber, and White, 2008):

- About one-fourth of all children who engaged in pre-delinquent disruptive behavior escalated to minor delinquent acts.
- About one-third escalated to SVC delinquency.
- About two-thirds persisted in moderate to serious offending during adolescence.
- Nearly half of the persistent offender group (45 percent) offended at a high peak level of severity during adolescence, the serious persisters. The other half (55 percent) persisted offending at a minor to moderate peak level of severity.
- About a fifth of the sample (20 percent) of child delinquents desisted offending during adolescence.
- Altogether, the SVC offenders accounted for about half of all serious and violent offenses in adolescence and adulthood.

The three pathways have been verified in four large cities, and in a nationally representative U.S. sample of adolescents (Loeber, Slott, and Stouthamer-Loeber, 2008), and these pathways apply to girls as well as boys (Gorman-Smith and Loeber, 2005), and in a sample of African-Americans and Hispanic male adolescents in Chicago (Tolan, Gorman-Smith, and Loeber, 2000). In addition, higher percentages of youth follow the pathways in the most disadvantaged neighborhoods (Loeber and Wikstrom, 1993).

Loeber's explicit pathway model is particularly well suited for practical application in the juvenile justice system. As noted earlier, the covert and overt pathways correspond to the serious and violent offense categories, respectively. Taking into account multiple offense progression in the three pathways over time, Loeber's theoretical model also accounts for chronic offending. The next step in the practical application of Loeber's model is to link predictors (risk factors and protective factors) with offenders who advance in the covert (serious-chronic) and overt (violent-chronic) pathways. The risk factors in Tables 2.2a-e provide an excellent foundation along with Tanner-Smith and colleagues' (2013a) insightful analysis showing the changing influence of risk factors over time.

Other research on co-occurring problem behaviors among the relatively large group of "serious juvenile offenders" (with serious property and violent histories) is also instructive. A combination of persistent drug, school, and mental health problems greatly increase the likelihood of persistent serious delinquency. Researchers in Denver, Rochester, and Pittsburgh assessed the presence of these problems among "persistent serious delinquents," which they defined as self-reported offenders in serious assault or serious property offenses in at least two of the first three years of the respective samples of high-risk children and adolescents (Huizinga and Jakob-Chien, 1998; Huizinga, Loeber, Thornberry, and Cothern, 2000). This study found that the relationship between persistent serious delinquency and combinations of other persistent problem behaviors (drug, school, and mental health problems) was fairly consistent across the three study sites. For most male serious offenders, involvement in persistent serious delinquency and other problems go together. Among those who evidenced either two or three of these problems, as the number of problems increased, so did the chance of being a persistent serious delinquent. More than half (55–73 percent) of those with two or more problems were persistent serious delinquents. For females, the relationships between combinations of persistent problems were different and varied in the two sites that sampled females, so Huizinga and colleagues caution that generalizations are unwarranted for this gender.

Of the persistent males in the three sites, 25 percent were chronic serious delinquents, 15 percent were drug users, 7 percent had school problems, and 10 percent had mental health problems during adolescence. Of the persistent females in two sites, about 5 percent were chronic serious delinquents, 11–12 percent were drug users, 10–21 percent had school problems, and 6–11 percent had mental health problems. The most common pattern of occurrence of persistent serious delinquency, drug use, school problems, and mental health problems was an intermittent one across the three study sites. For all sites, the most common temporal pattern of each problem behavior was that it occurred for only one year, followed by two years, then three years. Therefore, the assessment of problem severity is critical.

When a young offender is first referred to juvenile court, juvenile justice system officials have a very limited view, only a snapshot, of that child or adolescent's early offending career, often based only on official records. Although most of the delinquent acts that youngsters commit are never brought to the attention of police or juvenile courts, most serious and violent offenders eventually are arrested, but not necessarily for their most serious offense. The narrow view of offense histories makes it very difficult to distinguish between potential SVC offenders and adolescence-limited offenders. However, early onset offenders are more likely to have official court records. Results from careful risk assessments that take into account prior JJ system involvement, and histories of family involvement in child welfare and social service interventions are key markers that help juvenile justice officials make informed decisions. The developmental theoretical perspective also helps in estimating progression in pathways toward SVC careers.

NOTES

1. Including Phoenix and its suburban areas in which more than half of all juvenile offenders in the state reside.

2. Personal communication, Peter Kochol, Program Manager, Court Support Services Division, Center for Research, Program Assessment, and Quality Improvement, May 20, 2013.

3. See Arthur, M. W., Hawkins, J. D., Pollard et al. (2002); Crosnoe, Erickson, and Dornbusch (2002); Fagan, Van Horn, Hawkins, and Arthur (2007); and Hart, O'Toole, Price-Sharps et al. (2007).

3

✦

A Comprehensive Strategy
for Evidence-based
Juvenile Justice Practice

IN BRIEF

This handbook promotes a comprehensive strategy for juvenile justice practice that is supported by the broad research base that is now available. This strategy recognizes, first, that a relatively small proportion of the juveniles who initially enter the juvenile justice system will prove to be serious, violent, or chronic offenders, but that group accounts for a large proportion of the overall amount of delinquency. Conversely, the majority of the juveniles who first make contact with the JJ system appear there for behaviors that are more symptomatic of adolescent development than potential for sustained criminal behavior. An important component of a comprehensive evidence-based JJ strategy, therefore, is distinguishing current or potential SVC offenders from the more adolescence-limited offenders, and focusing JJ attention and resources on that smaller SVC group. These groups can be distinguished by their risk factors, making systematic risk assessment, and differential JJ response on the basis of that risk assessment, a core element of effective JJ practice.

Second, a comprehensive strategy recognizes that serious, violent, or chronic delinquency emerges along developmental pathways that progress from less to more serious profiles of offending. The various stages of that progression are marked by increasingly serious and numerous risk factors, and diminishing protective or promotive factors, that will also be reflected in the results of systematic risk assessment. The main implication of this progression for a comprehensive strategy, however, is that effective intervention has the potential to disrupt the progression and reduce the numbers of juveniles whose SVC offending escalates along that pathway. The greatest effects can be achieved by intervening early in the progression, making early identification and treatment of juveniles on SVC pathways especially important, though effective intervention at any stage is also beneficial. As juveniles progress along SVC pathways, however, the JJ system must be increasingly concerned about public safety and calibrate the level of supervision and control of the juveniles' behavior to their level of risk.

The third major component of a comprehensive strategy, therefore, is effective intervention programs that are capable of reducing the recidivism of those juveniles at risk for further delinquency. More will be said about this component later in this volume, but the available evidence highlights several key features of effective intervention. First, there is no one-size-fits-all intervention for juveniles at risk for subsequent delinquency. Interventions must be well matched to the need and risk profiles of each juvenile. Assessment of needs as well as risk, therefore, is an important element of a sound intervention plan. The results will differentiate low need/low risk juveniles for whom little or no intervention is appropriate, high need/low risk juveniles best treated outside the JJ system, and high need/high risk juveniles for whom effective intervention by the JJ system is paramount. Second, not all programs, including some that are attractive to policymakers and the public, are actually effective for reducing recidivism and some can actually make it worse. Selecting programs proven in research to actually be capable of reducing recidivism is thus essential. Third, those programs must be implemented well enough to actually obtain the effects they are capable of producing.

The Comprehensive Strategy for Serious, Violent, and Chronic Juvenile Offenders is an administrative framework that supports a continuum of services that parallel offender careers across the age-crime curve. This framework emphasizes evidence-based programming specifically on recidivism reduction, and supports protocols for developing comprehensive treatment plans that match effective services with offender treatment needs along the life-course of delinquent careers, as they move from intake onward, to probation, community programs, confinement, and reentry. We turn next to a fuller description of the elements of this framework.

THE COMPREHENSIVE STRATEGY FOR SERIOUS, VIOLENT, AND CHRONIC JUVENILE OFFENDERS

A useful framework for incorporating evidence-based practice into JJ systems in everyday practice is the OJJDP Comprehensive Strategy (CS) for Serious, Violent, and Chronic Juvenile Offenders (Wilson and Howell, 1993, 1994, 1995; see also Howell, 2003a, 2003b, 2009). This forward-looking administrative framework is organized around risk management and promotes a statewide continuum of graduated sanctions and services that are aligned with offender careers (Figure 3.1). It incorporates best practice tools including validated risk and needs assessment instruments, a disposition matrix that guides placements in a manner that protects the public, and protocols for developing comprehensive treatment plans that improve the matching of effective services with offender treatment needs (Lipsey, Howell, Kelly et al., 2010).

The Comprehensive Strategy guides jurisdictions in developing a continuum of responses that parallel offender careers, beginning with prevention and followed by direct intervention and graduated sanctions. Rehabilitation programs in which SVC offenders are placed must be more structured and intensive, to address effectively the serious problems that more dangerous offenders present. The Comprehensive Strategy has been successfully implemented in a number of state juvenile justice systems (Howell, 2003b, pp. 292–300; Lipsey et al., 2012) and provides practitioners with a blueprint for making disposition decisions that take into account the developmental trajectories of system-involved youth.

The Comprehensive Strategy is based on the following core principles (Wilson and Howell, 1993):

- We must strengthen the family in its primary responsibility to instill moral values and provide guidance and support to children. Where there is no functional family unit, we must establish a family surrogate and help that entity to guide and nurture the child.
- We must support core social institutions such as schools, religious institutions, and community organizations in their roles of developing capable, mature, and responsible youth. A goal of each of these societal institutions should be to ensure that children have the opportunity and support to mature into productive, law-abiding citizens. In a nurturing community environment, core social institutions are actively involved in the lives of youth.
- We must promote delinquency prevention as the most cost-effective approach to reducing juvenile delinquency. Families, schools, religious institutions, and community organizations, including citizen volunteers and the private sector, must be enlisted in the nation's delinquency prevention efforts. These core socializing institutions must be strengthened and assisted in their efforts to ensure that children have the opportunity to become capable and responsible citizens. When children engage in acting-out behavior, such as status offenses, the family and community, in concert with child welfare agencies, must respond with appropriate treatment and support

services. Communities must take the lead in designing and building comprehensive prevention approaches that address known risk factors and target other youth at risk of delinquency.

- We must intervene immediately and effectively when delinquent behavior occurs to prevent delinquent offenders from becoming chronic offenders or committing progressively more serious and violent crimes. Initial intervention efforts, under an umbrella of system authorities (police, intake, and probation), should be centered in the family and other core societal institutions. Juvenile justice system authorities should ensure that an appropriate response occurs and act quickly and firmly if the need for formal system adjudication and sanctions is demonstrated.
- We must identify and control the small group of serious, violent, and chronic juvenile offenders who have committed felony offenses or have failed to respond to intervention and nonsecure community-based treatment and rehabilitation services offered by the juvenile justice system. Measures to address delinquent offenders who are a threat to community safety may include placement in secure community-based facilities, training schools, and other secure juvenile facilities. Even the most violent or intractable juveniles should not be moved into the criminal justice system before they graduate from the jurisdiction of the juvenile justice system.
- We must establish interagency teams that conduct in-depth assessments and craft comprehensive case plans for serious, violent, and chronic juvenile offenders that integrate treatment delivery and are implemented jointly. Members of these interagency teams should include juvenile justice, child welfare, social service, mental health, and educational system representatives.

Each of these principles is explicitly supported by research in longitudinal developmental studies of children and adolescents summarized in this handbook (see also Loeber, Farrington, Stouthamer-Loeber, and White, 2008, p. 329–334). Strong emphasis is placed on prevention and early intervention in the Comprehensive Strategy. These are linchpins in forestalling the development of SVC offender careers. By developing a continuum of integrated programs and sanctions, juvenile justice systems can match offenders' risk levels and treatment needs to appropriate services and supervision at any point in the development of offender careers. The following are potential benefits of using the Comprehensive Strategy:

- Fewer young people enter the juvenile justice system
- Enhanced responsiveness from the juvenile justice system
- Greater accountability on the part of youth

- Reduced confinement
- Decreased costs of juvenile corrections
- A more responsible juvenile justice system
- More effective juvenile justice programs
- Less delinquency
- Lower recidivism
- Fewer delinquents become SVC offenders
- Fewer delinquents become adult offenders

The CS is a two-tiered system for responding proactively to juvenile delinquency (Figure 3.1). In the first tier, delinquency prevention, youth development, and early intervention programs are relied on to prevent delinquency and reduce the likelihood that at-risk youth will appear in the juvenile justice system. If those efforts fail, then the juvenile justice system, the second tier, must make proactive responses by addressing the risk factors for recidivism and associated treatment needs of the offenders, particularly those with a high likelihood of becoming SVC offenders. In the CS framework, this latter supervision and control component is referred to as *graduated sanctions*, a term also used in this fashion in many juvenile justice systems.

More specifically, the CS framework is structured around seven levels of parallel program interventions and sanctions, moving from least to most restrictive, plus aftercare for youth released from secure facilities:

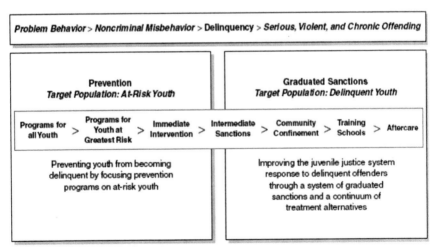

Figure 3.1. The Comprehensive Strategy for Serious, Violent, and Chronic Juvenile Offenders
Reference: Wilson, J. J., and Howell, J. C. (1993). A comprehensive strategy for serious, violent and chronic juvenile offenders. Washington, DC: Office of Juvenile Justice and Delinquency Prevention.

- Community primary prevention programs oriented toward reducing risk and enhancing strengths for all youth.
- Focused prevention programs for youth in the community at greatest risk but not involved with the JJ system, or perhaps diverted from it.
- Intervention programs tailored to identify risk and needs for first-time minor delinquent offenders provided under minimal sanctions, for example, diversion or administrative probation.
- Intervention programs tailored to identified risk and need factors for nonserious repeat offenders and moderately serious first-time offenders provided under intermediate sanctions, for example, regular probation.
- Intensive intervention programs tailored to identified risk and need factors for first-time serious or violent offenders provided with controls, for example, intensive probation supervision or residential facilities.
- Multi-component intensive intervention programs in secure correctional facilities for the most serious, violent, and chronic offenders which provide focus on both treatment and rehabilitation in the context of a restricted secure environment.
- Post-release supervision and reentry aftercare programs for offenders released from residential and correctional facilities.

As noted earlier, most minor juvenile offenders are self-correcting, that is, they do not have lifetime careers. In most cases this large group never comes to the attention of JJ systems. They either mature out of delinquency or desist on their own volition, perhaps in response to influence of parents, teachers, or prosocial peers. Hence not all youth who happen to be arrested or referred to juvenile courts need to be treated as if they are beginning a lifetime of crime. Well-designed and implemented risk assessment instruments are a valuable tool for distinguishing between those who will persist versus those who will desist, with the latter low risk cases being good candidates for diversion. Given that less than 10 percent of young serious and violent offenders continue committing these types of offenses throughout adolescence, JJ system attention needs to be especially focused on this relatively small chronic group.

When offenders persist in serious and violent delinquency, their position in a graduated sanctions system continuum should be advanced in the interest of public safety. To be most effective, program or facility placements must match the developmental history of the delinquent career and the risk of recidivism. Along the way "windows of opportunity" present themselves for engagement and intervention, particularly in early childhood, and the transition points following elementary school, middle school, and high school. A dispositional matrix should be used to guide the assignment of youth to levels of supervision and case management; including management of behavioral, non-criminal violations of probation and violations of parole conditions in accordance with severity and risk. As offenders progress in the graduated sanction system, linked rehabilitation programs must become more structured and intensive, to effectively deal with the stubborn problems that more dangerous offenders present while reserving secure confinement for the very small number of serious violent offenders.

Much of the Comprehensive Strategy's success hinges on the placement of offenders at graduated levels of intervention. Several considerations are important. For example, what criteria should be used to determine which non-court-involved youth would benefit from preventive services? Similarly, when confronted with a first-time violent offender, on what basis will the decision be made to place the youth under probation supervision as opposed to some more restrictive placement? What are the standards by which we judge fairly who will be securely confined as opposed to placed in a highly structured, community-based program? Any system predicated on graduated, differential intervention must have clearly specified criteria for the various programs and levels of intervention, adequate methods for assessing the degree to which individual youth meet those criteria, and a selection process that ensures that youth targeted for intervention at each level of the system are those who in fact are served at that level.

Some states are now reducing confinement in favor of community rehabilitative and other therapeutic contexts for treatment (Butts and Evans, 2011). Throughout the United States, more than one-fourth of all adjudicated juvenile offenders were placed out of home in 2009, largely for drug-related offenses (Puzzanchera et al., 2012). Prolonged confinement in the juvenile justice system often leads to higher rates of offending following release (Loughran et al., 2009). Alternatives to confinement should be used for most offenders while targeting serious, violent, and chronic offenders for intensive supervision and services. Treatment programs for juvenile offenders in nonsecure settings that were based on developmental knowledge and implemented with fidelity have been shown to be more effective in reducing juvenile recidivism and at a lower cost than incarceration (Drake, 2012; National Research Council, 2013; Zavlek, 2005).

PREVENTION TIER

The prevention component of the CS framework consists of the two initial program levels of the continuum: primary prevention and secondary prevention. In this framework, *primary prevention* refers to universal prevention programs, meaning that all youth are recipients in a community-wide program or a program provided to all youth in local school classrooms, community centers, and the like. *Secondary prevention* programs target children in the community with identified risk factors for delinquency and related adverse outcomes. These may be pre-delinquent youth who have not yet appeared in the juvenile justice system and who receive school or community-based programs. Or these may be youth referred to the juvenile justice system for minor offenses but judged to be sufficiently at risk to warrant services and be diverted to community or school-based prevention programs.

Use of a research-based risk and protection framework that is consistent with the public health model helps structure the delinquency prevention enterprise in communities. To be sure, this model is familiar to all practitioners, who know the importance of reducing risk factors and increasing protective factors from their own training and also to the public because of its widespread application in reducing cardiovascular and other diseases. Juvenile delinquency and other child and adolescent problem behaviors share many common risk and protective factors. Thus prevention programs oriented toward reducing risk and enhancing protective factors help ameliorate a range of adverse outcomes, including substance use and mental health problems.

Early on, programs may be needed that address family risk factors. In adolescence, peer influences are predominant and the most appropriate programs may be those that buffer the effects of exposure to delinquent peer influences and the spread of delinquency and violence in adolescence. Interventions that counter individual risk factors (e.g., substance abuse problems) and community risk factors (e.g., youth gangs) are needed all along the continuum, and developmentally appropriate across age groups. All such programs and services can be successfully developed by providing community stakeholders and JJ system managers with training and technical assistance in risk–protection assessment and strategic prevention planning.

Primary prevention is most advantageously managed at the county level. The best current model is found in North Carolina, because it promotes data-driven prevention programming along with local governance. The North Carolina Juvenile Justice Reform Act of 1998 (S.L. 1998–202) established Juvenile Crime Prevention Councils (JCPCs) in every county of the state to implement the prevention component of the CS. Each JCPC has a membership of not more than twenty-five people, including representatives of the full array of county government, social service, and education agencies, as well as youth representatives and representatives of the juvenile justice system, the faith community, and the business sector. The JCPCs are charged with developing comprehensive delinquency prevention plans; they also fund and monitor programs, ensuring that a wide variety of services and dispositional options are available. In sum, the JCPC programs in North Carolina may play a big role in the overall functioning of the state's juvenile justice system. The JCPC programs keep many youths out of the juvenile justice system by providing services to those who have elevated risk of delinquency involvement or minor delinquency (M.Q. Howell, Lassiter, and Anderson, 2012).

The Communities That Care (CTC) operating system has shown some success in targeting evidence-based programs to prevent minor forms of problem behavior (mainly alcohol, tobacco, and drug use) among low risk youth using a strategy that targets risk factors for delinquency (Hawkins, Oesterle, Brown et al., 2012). CTC was tested in a randomized controlled trial. Fifth graders were targeted with evidence-based programs. By the eighth grade, significantly fewer of the students in CTC communities had health and behavior problems than those from the control communities.[1]

The San Diego Breaking Cycles program is an excellent secondary prevention model (Burke and Pennell, 2001). The prevention component targets youth who have not yet entered the juvenile justice system but who clearly evidence problem behaviors such as chronic disobedience to parents, curfew violations, repeated truancy, multiple attempts to run away from home, and drug and alcohol use. These high risk youth are referred to community assessment centers. An evaluation of the Breaking Cycles program showed that the prevention strategy dramatically reduced the number of at-risk youths entering the juvenile justice system (Burke and Pennell, 2001). This model is recommended for secondary prevention because of the ease with which this approach can draw upon court referral data to target services geographically and intervene early with diversion programming using developmentally appropriate services for child delinquents.

INTERVENTION AND GRADUATED SANCTIONS TIER

The intervention and graduated sanctions component of the Comprehensive Strategy consists of the last five levels of the overall CS framework enumerated above in which treatment programs are combined with levels of supervision or control appropriate to the nature and severity of juveniles' offenses and their risk for reoffending.

What does the targeting of SVC offenders mean for state juvenile justice systems? Overall, the prospect of truncating their careers looks very promising. For one thing, the percentage of offenders brought into juvenile court whose careers consist of SVC offenses is relatively small. Successfully intervening with these offenders will require an understanding of how they got that way and use of this information to arrange systematic interventions with evidence-based services. In sum, the most effective allocation of limited resources will be to focus them on the relatively few offenders with potential for SVC careers. High-risk females and males alike should be targeted for intensive supervision and services. Further analysis should focus on recidivism reductions that accrue from service matching and program improvements in each state.

Low risk youth with low likelihood of becoming SVC offenders should be diverted out of the system immediately. Moderate and high risk offenders should receive increasingly progressive sanctions and intensive services. Well-implemented structured decision making tools will facilitate matching of evidence-based services to offenders' individualized treatment needs. Key management tools including validated risk and needs assessment instruments, a disposition matrix that guides placements in a manner that protects the public, and protocols for developing comprehensive treatment plans that improve the matching of effective services with offender treatment needs.

Early intervention in the community with first-time or low risk offenders is the first priority. For young offenders who become chronic offenders (six or more police contacts through age twenty-six), costs imposed in the early ages (through age ten) are relatively low—about $3,000 at age ten (Cohen et al., 2010). Over a lifetime, these costs aggregate to nearly $5.7 million. This demonstrates the cost-benefit argument for the value of diversion options and early interventions that target high-risk youth and child delinquents. Effective use of diversion options is vital. Findings from two meta-analyses of juvenile diversion programs show that diverted youth have lower recidivism rates than comparable youth not diverted, though the difference is not large (Schwalbe, Gearing, MacKenzie et al., 2012; Wilson and Hoge, 2013). Effective implementation of diversion strategies is the key to success. The North Carolina JJ system has diverted one-third of court-referred youth since implementing the Comprehensive Strategy framework, the majority of which (76 percent) do not receive another referral within two years (M.Q. Howell and J. Bullock, 2013).

Thus diversion with developmental services is an effective strategy. An evidence-based early diversion program, Coordination of Services (COS), provides a thirteen-hour educational class to groups of ten low risk juvenile offenders and their parents (Barnoski, 2009). The State of Washington uses this program in conjunction with a community outreach component to engage the various community juvenile justice and service providers. For aggressive children with SVC potential, the leading evidence-based program is the Stop Now and Plan (SNAP®) program (Augimeri, Walsh, and Slater, 2011) that is described later in this handbook.

Utmost confidence can be placed in Lipsey's (2009) meta-analysis which concluded that treatment programs are about equally effective for juveniles at any risk level whether delivered in conjunction with prevention, diversion, community supervision, or confinement settings. Other research shows that diversion programs and teen courts also are cost effective (Drake, Aos, and Miller, 2009). Moreover, some research strongly suggests that probation and confinement can have a detrimental impact on low risk youth, likely because even intermittent separation of youth from their everyday interactions may disrupt their prosocial community networks (Lowenkamp and Latessa, 2004) and healthy social development (Sweeten, 2006).

As a first option, the diversion of very low risk cases can be accomplished in two ways: reducing school referrals and providing alternatives to arrests. The first of these two approaches addresses excessive referrals of youth to court from school officials (largely for disruptive behaviors at school that should have been addressed as disciplinary matters)—which can amount to up to four out of ten court referrals each year. These high volume referrals are often made by school resource officers, associated with "zero tolerance" policies. This problem is addressed directly in the Georgia Clayton County initiative (Teske and Huff, 2011). In a collaborative initiative with the School Superintendent and Chief of Police, a Memorandum of Understanding (MOU) titled the "School Referral Reduction Protocol (SRRP)" was executed to: (1) reduce suspensions, expulsions, and arrests, and (2) develop alternatives to suspension and arrests, including assessment and treatment measures for chronically disruptive students. The SRRP identified misdemeanor offenses no longer eligible for referral to the juvenile court unless the student had exhausted a two-tier process that includes: (1) warning on the first offense to student and parent; (2) referral to a conflict skills workshop on the second offense; and (3) referral to the court on the third offense. A second MOU created a multidisciplinary panel to serve as a single point of entry for all child service agencies, including schools, when referring children, youth, and families at risk for petition to the court. The panel, called the Clayton County Collaborative Child Study Team, meets regularly to assess the needs of students at risk for court referral and recommends an integrated services action plan to address the student's disruptive behavior. Immediately following the SRRP, referrals to the court were reduced by 67 percent. By the end of the 2011–2012 school term, the number of students referred to the juvenile court for school offenses was reduced by 83 percent. The number of youth of color referred to the court for school offenses was reduced by 43 percent. According to Judge Teske, "when prohibited from making arrests, school police began to engage students and developed an understanding that discipline should be applied on a case-by-case basis. This resulted in greater reductions in referrals."[2]

Use of civil citations in lieu of arrest is also a promising option for community-level diversion with or without services, as appropriate. The Florida Civil Citation (Florida Statutes 985.12) has been in place since 2011, and its provisions give law enforcement the discretion of issuing a citation rather than filing a formal complaint. Only first-time misdemeanor offenders are eligible for the civil citation or similar diversion program. Law enforcement officers who issue a civil citation may follow one of the two procedures: (1) transport an eligible juvenile to the Juvenile Assessment Center for booking as an arrestee; or (2) issue a civil citation in the field and release the youth to a parent, relative, guardian, or other responsible adult. The four goals of Civil Citation are to divert the youth at the time of arrest, hold the youth accountable for delinquent behavior, involve the parents in sanctioning and correcting the youth, and prevent the youth's further involvement in the juvenile justice system. Civil Citation providers oversee youth who are required to receive an assessment of needs, perform community service hours, and complete various sanctions, which may include reparations and treatment services. Civil Citation is also much more cost-effective than formally processing a youth in the court and juvenile justice system, and offers the youth an opportunity to receive sanctions, treatment, and to make reparations without obtaining a delinquency record that may interfere with educational, work, and military service opportunities for many years into the future.

Juvenile Assessment Centers (JACs) are viewed as a key mechanism for early intervention. JACs can provide a single point of entry or intake and assessment, typically at the point of police apprehension or arrest (Oldenettel and Wordes, 2000). Pioneering JAC development in Florida (Dembo, Schmeidler, and Walters, 2004; Cocozza, Veysey, Chapin et al., 2005) provided a springboard for JACs elsewhere that also have proved useful for diverting low risk youth from JJ system handling. Two cautionary notes are in order, however. First, the opportunity should not be missed at JAC intake to identity youth's mental health service needs and attempt to establish protocols of referral for services from mental health providers located in the community (McReynolds, Wasserman, DeComo et al., 2008). Second, care must be exercised to guard against net-widening to the disadvantage of minority youth (Bechard, Ireland, Berg, and Vogel, 2011).

For SVC offenders, a continuum of programs aimed at different points along the life course has a much better chance of succeeding than a single intervention. This is illustrated in a RAND cost-benefit study of juvenile delinquency prevention and treatment programs (Greenwood, Model, Rydell, and Chiesa, 1996). The researchers calculated that, if implemented statewide, a combination of four delinquency prevention and treatment programs (graduation incentives, parent training, intensive supervision linked with graduated sanctions[3], and home visits with day care) could achieve more serious crime reduction than California's "three strikes" law, which mandated imprisonment for the third strike. The RAND researchers projected that the four juvenile delinquency prevention and treatment programs would cost less than $1 billion per year to implement throughout California, compared with about $5.5 billion per year for "three strikes." Thus, at less than one-fifth the cost, the four programs could potentially double the crime reduction that had been achieved with imprisonment alone.

Research showing that a combination of persistent drug, school, and mental health problems which greatly increase the likelihood of persistent serious delinquency has very important implications for intervention. First, not all persistent serious offenders need drug treatment, as often assumed. Second, individual assessments are extremely important for case plan development and service matching. Third, the prospect of reducing juvenile offending levels appears to be within reach, provided that progression of at-risk juveniles along the pathways to delinquency can be forestalled. About 40–60 percent of juvenile offenders desist from offending by early adulthood, but correspondingly, about 40–60 percent persist into early adulthood, though the percentage of persisters substantially decreases thereafter (Loeber et al., 2012). This is important because a high proportion of adult offenders begin their careers as juvenile offenders. For example, 73 percent of adult offenders in prison in Washington had previously been in Washington's juvenile justice system (Aos, Miller, and Drake, 2006). However, the rates of persistence are not immutable.

But most of the window of opportunity for early intervention will have passed before juvenile court intervention typically occurs. Stouthamer-Loeber and Loeber (2002) found that by the time a youngster got to court for an index offense in Pittsburgh, his or her parents likely had coped for several years with the child's problem behavior. Almost half of the boys who eventually became self-reported persistent serious delinquents had an onset of serious delinquency before age twelve. Hence there is a compelling need to effectively integrate mental health, child welfare, education, and juvenile justice system services (Howell, Kelly, Palmer, and Mangum, 2004). This is imperative because the extremely costly and largely ineffective residential facilities of the child caring systems are all overloaded, as both public and private agencies are over-reliant on residential care (Henggeler and Schoewald, 2011). Thus a major objective is to avoid confinement whenever possible and use less costly and more effective family- and child-centered treatment interventions. This is not as simple as it sounds, however. Most children and youths destined for the deep end of these systems have experienced cumulative problems and juvenile or social service system mishandling for several years (Burns, Landsverk, Kelleher et al., 2001; Stouthamer-Loeber and Loeber, 2002). In the absence of effective services, youths' problems tend to become stacked on one another with time, often requiring intensive serves to peel them off one another.

JUVENILE JUSTICE SYSTEM EFFECTIVENESS WITH GRADUATED SANCTIONS

The use of graduated sanctions raises an important issue: Can these be effective? It is well established that deterrence measures do not reduce recidivism and, in fact, can have the opposite effect of increasing recidivism (Lipsey, 2009). Labeling theory proponents argue that worsening behavior stems from the stigmatizing effect of being labeled "delinquent." However, the experience of being brought to court itself may have beneficial effects for many referred youth. The corrective actions of judges can be very influential, in the same manner as corrective actions that family elders, neighbors, parents, school authorities, and others exert. In fact, law-related education was found to have beneficial effects in a meta-analysis of academic programs (Maguin and Loeber, 1996). "Perhaps . . . in providing ceremonial condemnation, the courts clarify boundaries for acceptable behavior" (McCord, 1985, p. 81). At the individual level, for active serious and violent juvenile offenders in the Denver Youth Survey, a modest deterrent effect of perceived certainty of arrest was reported (Matsueda, Kreager, and Huizinga, 2006). Although Shannon (1991) found no evidence of deterrence based on severity of sanctions, his Racine, Wisconsin, study suggests that future offense seriousness may be reduced by frequent interventions. These two high-quality studies suggest that a rational choice process may well be at work in either reducing crimes or the seriousness of them among some active offenders (see also Loughran and colleagues, 2012). Other research suggests that offenders with the highest self-reported criminality (not lowest) tend to show the most responsiveness to the risk of sanctions (Schneider, 1990; Schneider and Ervin, 1990; Wright, Caspi, Moffitt et al., 2004). Schneider states, "This suggests that there may be a point in a juvenile career where some of the youths recognize the severity of future actions and intentionally reduce their criminal activity" (p. 109).

Individualizing sanctions in large state systems is challenging (Mears, Cochran, Greenman et al., 2011). Clearly, juvenile probation and parole supervision by themselves produce only small reductions in recidivism (Andrews et al., 1990; Aos, Lee, Drake, Pennucci et al., 2012; Lipsey, 2009; Lipsey and Wilson, 1998), only about a 6 percent reduction, on average (see Figure 4.1). Lipsey (1999b) found that some intensive supervision programs are effective, linked either with probation or with parole. Intensive supervision coupled with graduated sanctions has produced more impressive results. This practice is not new in the United States. The first structured decision making tools for JJ systems were created in the mid-1980s, in a "Model Case Management System" for juvenile corrections (Baird, Storrs, and Connelly, 1984). Soon services were successfully coupled with probation-based intensive supervision (Sametz and Hamparian, 1990; Wiebush and Hamparian, 1991), a practice that quickly spread to multiple sites in Ohio and elsewhere.[4]

The Comprehensive Strategy has been most widely implemented in courts of state juvenile justice systems (Howell, 2003b, 2009; Lipsey et al., 2010). In the initial implementation of the graduated sanctions component of the Comprehensive Strategy, Orange County, California, probation officials targeted potential chronic and serious offenders among first-time court referrals, using a risk assessment instrument generated from an analysis of recidivism predictors for an earlier cohort of probationers in the county. The 8% Early Intervention Program (also called "The 8% Solution," Schumacher and Kurz, 2000), consisting of very intensive services tailored for youth and their caretakers, was developed for the highest-risk offenders (the 8 percent group), whereas the medium-risk group (22 percent) was assigned to intensive probation linked with services, and the remainder (70 percent) was assigned to an immediate accountability program, supervised by volunteer probation officers. This three-part framework consisting of well-structured sanctions and matching program services proved cost-beneficial (Greenwood et al., 1996).

Patterned after The 8% Solution, the San Diego County Breaking Cycles program places offenders in the graduated sanctions component administered by Juvenile Field Services using the San Diego Risk and Resiliency Checkup (SDRRC) instrument that was validated in the county (Pearl, Ashcraft, and Geis, 2009). Based on the assessment of risk and protective factors, a Breaking Cycles case plan is then developed for each youth. Youth are assigned for variable lengths of program participation—90, 150, 240, or 365 days—depending on risk severity and treatment needs. The following continuum of placement options is used:

- Home placement (e.g., the Community Unit)
- Community-based placement (e.g., day treatment in the Reflections Program)
- Institutional placement (e.g., minimum-security custody)

Each of these intervention levels is linked with community programs and resources that are needed to carry out the comprehensive treatment plan. An evaluation of the program showed that the graduated sanction component was effective in deterring offenders from progressing to more serious delinquency (Burke and Pennell, 2001). Regardless of commitment length, youth in the Breaking Cycles program were less likely than control youth to have a court referral for a felony offense or to be adjudicated for a felony offense during the eighteen-month follow-up period. Breaking Cycles youth also were less likely to be committed to long-term state correctional facilities, less likely to be using alcohol or drugs, and more likely to be enrolled in school during the follow-up period.

A recent study shows that well-managed JJ systems can promote desistance among most serious and violent offenders. Among more than one thousand adolescents adjudicated for serious offenses in Philadelphia (Philadelphia County), Pennsylvania, and in Phoenix (Maricopa County), Arizona, researchers found that juvenile justice system services and supervision reduced levels of involvement in antisocial activities (Mulvey et al., 2010). Almost six out of ten offenders in this two-city sample of 1,338 adjudicated juveniles (87 percent of which were boys ages fourteen to seventeen years of age) evidenced very low levels of involvement in antisocial activities during the *entire* three-year follow-up period, and less than 9 percent of the sample continuously reported high levels of offending.

This important study also found that juvenile court-based programs are more effective than confinement in juvenile correctional facilities and that periods of confinement beyond three to six months did not reduce recidivism (Loughran et al., 2009; Mulvey, 2011). Following release, a combination of community services and intensive supervision produced a sharp decrease in recidivism, in both rearrests and self-reported offending over a six-month reentry period (Chung, Schubert, and Mulvey, 2007). Pennsylvania uses a local court control model in which the supervision of reentry offenders is overseen by juvenile court-based probation officers who work as agents of the court, thereby increasing close supervision following release. In addition, at the time of this follow-up study Philadelphia County was involved in a state-initiated multi-year effort to improve aftercare services (Griffin, 2004). The Maricopa County JJ system has employed a Juvenile Intensive Probation Supervision program for many years that incorporates reasonably well-defined graduated sanctions levels. This research suggests that local court supervision of reentry offenders by juvenile court-based probation officers—rather than a separate track—produces the best outcomes.

In the most stringent study of graduated sanctions for young offenders committed to residential and non-residential placement, researchers compared recidivism rates for equivalent groups of juveniles in Florida who were transferred to criminal court or retained in the JJ system (Johnson, Lanza-Kaduce, and Woolard, 2011). More intensive treatment was provided in conjunction with four graduated levels of supervision (from probation to maximum-risk residential). Only 36 percent of the juveniles who received graduated interventions reoffended, compared with 58 percent of those who were transferred to criminal court and did not receive graduated interventions. "After controlling for other variables, graduated interventions were related to less recidivism." Failure to use graduated treatment interventions, specifically by leapfrogging over graduated sanctions, increased recidivism among this sample of juvenile offenders" p. 771). Juveniles who experienced this form of "leapfrog" were 1.5 times more likely to reoffend after age eighteen than juveniles who were not leapfrogged. "The results suggest that graduated interventions may constitute sound crime control policy because it is linked to lower recidivism." In addition this research suggests that transfer should be used for SVC offenders only if it is the next step in graduated interventions.

In sum, the outcome research reviewed here strongly supports the effectiveness of graduated sanctions with serious and violent offenders, as seen in Phoenix and Philadelphia (Chung et al., 2007), and statewide in Florida (Johnson et al., 2011). But few JJ systems have well-structured graduated sanction schemes, without which less impact on recidivism can be expected. Any system predicated on graduated, differential intervention must have the components that follow:

- Clearly specified criteria for the various programs and levels of intervention,
- Adequate methods for assessing the degree to which individual youth meet those criteria, and
- A selection process that ensures that youth targeted for intervention at each level of the system are those who in fact are served at that level.

COMPREHENSIVE STRATEGY IMPLEMENTATION PROCESS

Implementation of the Comprehensive Strategy framework—whether statewide or in selected cities or counties—involves a four-step process: mobilization, problem assessment, planning, and implementation and evaluation. As with any other social problem, mobilizing community stakeholders to act in a concerted fashion is the critical first step.

To be successful in this endeavor, Comprehensive Strategy implementation must be a collaborative process. Ideally, an interagency leadership team should be established to lead and manage a system-wide strategic plan. States that have a service orientation, well-respected supervisors, embrace data-driven policy-making, and establish on-site work teams have much better prospects for overcoming organizational cynicism,

BOX 3.1

THE COMPREHENSIVE STRATEGY PLANNING PROCESS

Mobilization: Community leaders are enlisted and organized to participate in the CS planning process. A formal community planning team is created to receive training and technical assistance and to develop a long-term strategic plan. Representatives of all sectors of the community are engaged in the planning process, including youth development agencies, citizen volunteers, private organizations, schools, law enforcement agencies, prosecutors, courts, corrections agencies, social service agencies, civic organizations, religious groups, parents, and teens.

Problem Assessment: Quantitative data are gathered and analyzed for use in the development of a baseline profile of the community's risk and need factors and a comprehensive juvenile justice profile. The data can guide decision making about long-term program planning, coordination, and optimum resource allocation.

Planning: A five-year strategic plan is created for building a continuum of services to address the community's priority risk and need factors, based on best practices. The plan clearly articulates the community's vision, mission, goals, and objectives.

Implementation and evaluation: Systems and programs are developed according to the five-year strategic plan; these include a seamless continuum of prevention, intervention, and graduated sanctions and programs. Evaluation mechanisms and procedures are established.

Source: Howell, 2009, pp. 218–219.

properly using sanctions with evidence-based services, and right-sizing their systems (Farrell, Young, and Taxman, 2011). First, communities must conduct a comprehensive assessment of risk and protective factors for delinquency in their specific jurisdictions, instead of arbitrarily selecting prevention programs that may miss the mark. Second, juvenile justice system agencies must assess their delinquent populations for risk and treatment needs and strengths in order to classify and position offenders within a structured system of graduated sanctions to best protect the public, and to properly place offenders in program interventions that are appropriate for their treatment needs and strengths. Successful accomplishment of these two tasks not only engages communities in research-based practices, thus raising the comfort level, but also helps them see the potential value of using evidence-based program interventions. Third, community engagement and long-term strategic planning entail four sequential steps: *mobilization, assessment, planning,* and *implementation.*

This strategic planning process should lead to development of an integrated continuum of prevention and intervention programs and graduated sanctions options that parallel offender career trajectories. The key segments of such a continuum are described below.

CONTINUUM BUILDING WITH THE COMPREHENSIVE STRATEGY

The Comprehensive Strategy provides a framework and management tools that can be used across entire juvenile justice systems for promoting close matches between evidence-based programs and offender treatment needs on an ongoing basis. As noted earlier, the Comprehensive Strategy is a forward-looking administrative framework organized around a statewide continuum of prevention and intervention programs and graduated sanctions options that parallel offender career trajectories. It incorporates best practice tools including validated risk and needs assessment instruments, a disposition matrix to guide placements in a manner that protects the public, protocols for developing comprehensive treatment plans, and evidence-based treatment programs monitored for quality control.

Successfully lowering the juvenile crime rate will require consistent, extensive, and appropriate use of programs that are supported by evidence of effectiveness. But a challenge is in the forefront of this goal—matching services with the offenders that will most benefit them. Not every program addresses the conditions in a juvenile's life that propel their problem behavior. The effective programs found through research, such as those included in the meta-analyses described above, necessarily involve some matching of offender needs and circumstances to the nature of the program, though the basis for that matching is not always well documented. Programs that do not address the criminogenic factors that most contribute to a juvenile's delinquent behavior cannot be expected to significantly reduce that behavior no matter how potent they are on average.

Primary and Secondary Prevention

Universal prevention approaches are necessary to reach the entire youth population and reduce the number of youth who become involved in delinquency and other problem behaviors. For primary and secondary prevention, the ideal arrangement would be for each state to establish

Juvenile Crime Prevention Councils (JCPCs) in every county of the state (described earlier, as operating in North Carolina) to implement data-driven and research-based prevention programming. JCPC-funded agencies, schools, Juvenile Assessment Centers, and the like could serve as portals for connecting at-risk youth with effective services and model programs. A risk assessment tool must be administered on all referrals for prevention services to ensure that services match the risk level of clients and also are developmentally appropriate. Low- and moderate-risk youth can be served in various county- and city-supported child development programs.

At the school level, systems across the United States are implementing the federal Office of Special Education Program's Positive Behavioral Interventions and Supports (PBIS) framework (www.pbis.org). A three-tiered model for instruction and intervention, PBIS is based on the principle that academic and behavioral supports must be provided at a school-wide level to effectively address the needs of all students in a school (referred to as Tier 1, core, universal instruction and supports). Because not all students will respond to the same curricula and teaching strategies, some students with identified needs receive supplemental or targeted instruction and intervention in Tier 2 (targeted, supplemental interventions and supports). Lastly, in Tier 3, intensive, individualized interventions and supports are provided for the relatively few students with the most severe needs, requiring intensive and individualized behavioral treatment and academic support. As an example, the G.R.E.A.T. curriculum produced improvements in several risk factors—such as having less anger, more use of refusal skills, and less risk-seeking among elementary and middle-school students (Esbensen, Osgood, Peterson, Taylor, and Carson, 2013). This program has merit for adoption within Tier 1 of the PBIS framework as a universal prevention program that also has proved effective for reducing gang membership (Howell, 2013a). As an effective program for reducing gang membership, improvements in student attitudes toward law enforcement, and reductions in several risk factors for delinquency and joining gangs, the G.R.E.A.T. curriculum fits very well within Tier 1 of the PBIS framework. Individually targeted programs (in Tier 2) and intensive programs (in Tier 3) address students' specific intervention needs.

Early Intervention

This strategy is advised because of the large savings that can accrue before costly multiple problem behaviors develop (Cohen et al., 2010). Diversion is a mainstay strategy for early intervention in JJ systems, particularly for very young court referrals who are beginning to advance in delinquency pathways (Howell and Bullock, 2013). We drew attention earlier to noteworthy diversion strategies in North Carolina and Florida. At this time, more outcome data are available on North Carolina diversions, showing that two options (closed complaints or plans/contracts) have proved successful in helping juveniles avoid committing further delinquent or "undisciplined" acts. With both groups, there are many possibilities as to treatment and supervision actions taken by the parent/guardian/custodian or the school system. Court counselors also refer juveniles to local developmental and mental health programs across the state. These options have proved to be remarkably effective, in 76 percent of diverted cases (Howell and Bullock, 2013).

JUVENILE JUSTICE SYSTEM CONTINUUM

A forward-looking JJ system, that is, a preventive risk-management model of juvenile justice (Slobogin, 2013; Slobogin and Fondacaro, 2011), uses services in tandem with sanctions and service that effectively reduce risk of offending. Effective services are paramount, and these are discussed in the next chapter. Description of a practical tool for assessing the effectiveness of existing programs, together with guidelines for improving them, follows in chapter 5. Use of objective structured decision-making tools (chapter 7)—particularly a validated risk assessment instrument, treatment needs assessments, and a disposition matrix—can be relied upon to guide the placement of offenders and facilitate matching offender treatment needs with effective services in comprehensive case plans, while diverting low risk offenders. Use of these tools will assist JJ managers in undertaking system reforms that should make their systems more effective and just. The outcome should be a data-driven, age-graded, and developmentally-appropriate continuum of services and sanctions that demonstrably reduces recidivism.

NOTES

1. The online CTC web platform introduces the process and supports participating sites: http://www.communitiesthatcare.net/.
2. The Honorable Steven C. Teske, Chief Judge, Clayton County Juvenile Court, Georgia. Testimony before the Senate Subcommittee on The Constitution, Civil Rights, and Human Rights Subcommittee Hearing on "Ending the School to Prison Pipeline," December 12, 2012.
3. *The 8% Solution* (Schumacher and Kurz, 2000).
4. See Howell (2003b) for numerous other applications of graduated sanctions.

4

✛

Effective Evidence-based Prevention and Intervention Programs for Juvenile Offenders

IN BRIEF

There is now no doubt that credible research demonstrates the effectiveness of many prevention and intervention programs for reducing the subsequent offenses of juvenile offenders and juveniles at high risk of becoming offenders. What is not so clear is how juvenile justice systems should use research to ensure that the programs they administer are effective. For that challenge, there are three options of successively broader scope, each described below. None of these is the universal solution for establishing evidence-based programs. Each has advantages and disadvantages and they may be readily mixed in any juvenile justice system.[1]

THREE APPROACHES TO IDENTIFYING EVIDENCE-BASED PROGRAMS

The key component of a comprehensive strategy for reducing serious, violent, and chronic offending is a continuum of prevention and intervention programs that are truly effective for reducing the subsequent delinquency of the juveniles who enter the juvenile justice system. A myth that nothing works in adult or juvenile corrections was erroneously pronounced in the 1970s, based on a faulty review of the evidence. This myth persisted until it was gradually overturned by a group of scholars working over the past thirty years who examined the evidence more carefully and systematically (Cullen, 2005, dubs them the "twelve disciples of rehabilitation").

Among these "disciples of rehabilitation" were several early leaders who took a systematic approach to identifying what interventions actually work for reducing the recidivism of offenders. Program reviews made by Lipsey, using meta-analysis techniques, focused specifically on programs for juvenile offenders and demonstrated that the available research provided ample evidence that many programs were effective in reducing offense rates (e.g., Lipsey, 1992, 1998, 1999a, 1999b). At about the same time, a team of Canadian-American criminologists led by Andrews and colleagues also used meta-analysis techniques to identify effective programs for both juvenile and adult offenders. For the Canadians, this work led to what they called a "psychologically informed approach to correctional treatment" that was grounded in three principles they derived from the research, referred to as the risk-need-responsivity (RNR) model (Andrews and Bonta, 2010a; Andrews et al., 1990; Andrews, Zinger, Hodge et al., 1990).

Within the context of these scholars' revised interpretation of the evidence for effective rehabilitation programs, and other reviews that followed, certain specific programs could be identified that had sufficient supporting evidence of effectiveness to allow them to be promoted for use to prevent or reduce delinquent behavior. The Blueprints for Violence Prevention Project was an early authoritative source for identifying such programs (Mihalic et al., 2001) and soon produced a list of recommended research-supported programs that could be adopted by juvenile justice and social service systems. Other organizations also began sponsoring reviews of research aimed at identifying these "model" or "exemplary" programs. Examples of such other efforts that encompass programs for juvenile offenders include the National Registry of Evidence-based Programs and Practices (NREPP), the Office of Juvenile Justice and Delinquency Prevention (OJJDP) Model Programs Guide, and CrimeSolutions.gov.

Three main approaches can be used to translate research evidence on effective programs into practice for everyday use by practitioners and policymakers. The first approach is direct evaluation of each individual program used in practice to confirm its effectiveness and, if it is found ineffective, to use that evidence to improve or terminate it. A second is to implement with fidelity a program from a list of model programs certified by an authoritative source as having acceptable evidence of effectiveness. A third approach is to implement a type of program that has been shown to be effective on average by a meta-analysis of many studies of that program type, but to do so in the manner that the research indicates will yield that average effect or better.

DIRECT IMPACT EVALUATION OF PROGRAMS IN USE

A very direct way to use research to ensure that any prevention or intervention program is effective for reducing delinquency is to conduct an impact evaluation of that program as it is actually implemented in the local setting. This, after all, is the way all the available research evidence on program effectiveness originally was generated. To provide credible results about the impact of the program on offense rates, the evaluation must use a control group of comparable juveniles who do not receive the program, preferably assigned randomly to the program and control conditions. An evaluation of this quality on a specific program can provide credible evidence of effectiveness and, with positive results, that program can rightly claim to be evidence-based.

The advantage of direct evaluation is that the results apply specifically to the program in question, that is, the program as it is actually administered in the sponsoring juvenile justice system to the juveniles actually served by that program. The main disadvantage of this approach is the difficulty of conducting methodologically sound evaluations of this sort. They require creation of appropriate control groups, sufficiently large numbers of participating juveniles to yield statistically reliable results, and a relatively high level of research expertise.

A juvenile justice system would not likely undertake impact evaluations of this sort for all the programs it makes use of, but it might do so for a promising, innovative "home-grown" program as part of a commitment to evidence-based practice. It would also often be wise to conduct an independent evaluation on a model evidence-based program when it is first implemented in a particular jurisdiction to be sure that it is as effective in the local circumstances as it was where the original research on it was conducted (see Barnoski, 2002 and 2004a, for examples). Indeed, the best time to conduct an impact evaluation of a program is often when it is first implemented and it is relatively easy to randomly assign some juveniles to this new program while others are assigned to the prior practice as usual for such juveniles as a control condition.

ADOPTION OF EVIDENCE-BASED
BRAND NAME PROGRAM MODELS

Another option for using research to help ensure that the programs used by a juvenile justice system are effective is to adopt a program from one of the lists of model programs certified by an authoritative source as having acceptable evidence of effectiveness. The main repositories of effective programs for juvenile offenders are the Blueprints for Violence Prevention, the OJJDP Model Programs Guide, and CrimeSolutions.gov.

To assure that one of these model programs has a high probability of being effective when used locally, it must be implemented with fidelity to the program developer's specifications for how it is to be delivered, and it must be applied to juveniles substantially similar to those for whom the research evidence on that program was established. There are many familiar examples of these evidence-based model programs appropriate for use in juvenile justice systems, for example, Functional Family Therapy (FFT), Multisystemic Therapy (MST), Multidimensional Treatment Foster Care (MTFC), Aggression Replacement Training (ART), and the like.

The main advantage of this type of evidence-based program model is the plausible expectation that it will be effective if implemented with fidelity to the program specifications with an appropriate juvenile clientele. A substantial additional advantage is that such programs typically come with a detailed manual specifying how and for whom they are to be delivered. For those supported by well-developed vendor organizations, training and technical assistance resources are generally also available.

Adoption of evidence-based model programs is the most common approach to using research to ensure that effective programs are employed in juvenile justice systems. Indeed, it has become the conventional approach and the phrase, "evidence-based program," is widely taken to only mean a model program identified on one of the respected lists of such programs. However, there are some limitations associated with this approach to ensuring effective juvenile justice programming. For one, there are relatively few certified programs tested specifically for effects on juvenile offending on these lists and those may not match all the needs of the juveniles served in a juvenile justice system. Moreover, the local program infrastructure in most jurisdictions is generally dominated by more generic programs, often called "homegrown" programs that are established, politically active, and provide credible services that may well be perceived as effective. The providers of such programs have not generally been eager to convert to, or be replaced by, one of the evidence-based model programs.

For model programs that are implemented, there are challenges associated with moving them into routine practice in a way that closely replicates the relevant circumstances of the original research (Lipsey and Howell, 2012; Welsh, Sullivan, and Olds, 2010). For example, major shortcomings in achieving high fidelity with evidence-based substance abuse and violence prevention programs in community settings have been documented (Fagan, Hanson, Hawkins et al., 2008). Two national assessments found poor implementation for many delinquency and violence prevention programs that public schools had attempted to adopt (Gottfredson and Gottfredson, 2002).

Some slippage appears inevitable once even carefully implemented model programs are moved into everyday use (Rhoades, Bumbarger, and Moore, 2012). There are a number of reasons why such slippage might occur. The service infrastructure for delivering the program is likely to be weaker in routine practice than the infrastructure organized by the program developer when conducting the evaluation research. Sufficient resources, such as trained service providers and funds for personnel and capital expenditures, may not be available in everyday practice settings to fully meet the requirements of a model program when it is rolled out at scale. Also, it may not be possible to restrict the scaled-up program to the same population represented in the research. In real-world settings, for example, the program may serve a more heterogeneous population than was used in the research. As a result, the desirable program effects on delinquency and subsequent offending found in the supporting research studies often are attenuated when those programs are scaled up or rolled-out for general application (Rhoades et al., 2012; Welsh et al., 2010).

These limitations and challenges are perhaps why, despite considerable interest, evidence-based model programs constitute only a small proportion of all the programs used with juvenile offenders and a relatively small proportion of offenders receive services from those programs. Henggeler and Schoewald (2011), for instance, estimated that only 5 percent of eligible high-risk offenders are treated with evidence-based blueprint or model programs annually.

APPROPRIATE IMPLEMENTATION
OF EVIDENCE-BASED GENERIC PROGRAMS

In the third approach to evidence-based programming, effective generic types of programs are identified in meta-analyses of the results of numerous studies of programs of a particular type (see Box 4.1: What is Meta-Analysis?). What is meant by a generic program type in this context is a family of programs defined broadly as those that are substantially similar with regard to the nature and focus of the services provided. Familiar examples include cognitive-behavioral therapy, family counseling, mentoring, victim-offender mediation, and the like. Programs that provide services such as these are evidence-based if those services are (a) of a type for which multiple studies show positive average effects and (b) they are implemented in a way that matches what those studies show to be the most effective versions of that program type. The main advantage of this approach is that the scope of what can be identified as evidence-based programs may include many established local programs that already are of a type supported by research or that can be readily modified to match the research findings. Because of the broader scope of this approach to evidence-based programming, and its potential for statewide improvements in existing programs, a fuller description is provided here along with examples.

Meta-analysis of Research on the Effects of Intervention Programs for Juvenile Offenders[2]

Dozens of meta-analyses have been conducted on evaluations of the effects of programs on the recidivism of juvenile offenders (Lipsey and Cullen, 2007). Almost all of these, however, have had a somewhat limited scope. They have focused on one type of program or program area (e.g., boot camps, cognitive behavioral therapy, behavioral programs), or one type of offender (e.g., sex offenders), or a single named program (e.g., Multisystemic Therapy). The results of this work have been very informative for the respective topic areas and have generally confirmed the effectiveness of rehabilitative treatments for offenders. Nonetheless, it is difficult to piece such meta-analyses together into an overall picture of current knowledge about the nature of the most effective programs. A meta-analysis of, say, cognitive-behavioral programs may demonstrate that they have positive effects on recidivism while another meta-analysis shows that family counseling also has positive effects. But which programs are most effective and for whom and under what circumstances? Answers to those questions are especially critical for practitioners interested in using the most effective programs applicable to their situations.

Rather than focusing on a predefined kind of program or offender, an alternate approach is to collect and meta-analyze all the available research on the effects of intervention with juvenile offenders, sorting it according to the types of interventions found, whatever they may be. Examination of the full body of research on delinquency programs in a single meta-analysis allows for an integrated analysis of the comparative effectiveness of different program types and approaches. One of the authors of this volume, Mark Lipsey, began conducting meta-analyses of the findings of all the available research on the effects of interventions with juvenile offenders in the mid-1980s and has continued, with periodic updates, to the present day. The results of this large body of meta-analysis research on juvenile justice and delinquency prevention programs have been reported in numerous publications over the years (e.g., Lipsey, 1992; 1995; 1999a, 1999b, 2002, 2009; Lipsey et al., 2000; Lipsey and Cullen, 2007; Lipsey and Landenberger, 2006; Lipsey and Wilson, 1993, 1998). The most recent meta-analysis (Lipsey, 2009), however, is the most comprehensive both in terms of the number of studies included in the database and the detailed guidelines on effective evidence-based programs that are drawn from the analysis.

BOX 4.1

WHAT IS META-ANALYSIS?

Meta-analysis is a technique for extracting and analyzing information about intervention effects and the characteristics of the interventions producing those effects from a body of qualifying research studies (Lipsey and Wilson, 2001). This method of analysis allows researchers to analyze the characteristics of a large number of programs and synthesize the research findings about the effects of those programs in a systematic, replicable manner. Studies are eligible for inclusion in a meta-analysis based on explicit criteria and are collected through an extensive literature search. In the case of program evaluations, the key data elements are statistical estimates of the treatment effects, known as effect sizes. An effect size represents the magnitude of the difference on the outcome variable (e.g., recidivism) for the individuals receiving intervention and that for a comparable group not receiving the intervention; that is, the effect of the program on the treatment group versus the untreated control group. Effect sizes help researchers summarize results of many studies and generalize conclusions across a broad literature area such as juvenile delinquency programs. Meta-analysis techniques are well established and widely used to provide systematic syntheses of intervention research in education, social welfare, public health, and medicine as well as in juvenile and criminal justice.

EFFECTIVE PREVENTION AND INTERVENTION PROGRAMS

Lipsey's (2009) meta-analysis found first, that different generic program types had different average effects on reoffending rates—some types of programs are simply more effective than others, all else being equal. At the broadest level, there are differences related to the overarching philosophy of the program. "Philosophy" in this context means the global approach to altering juvenile behavior taken by the program. From this perspective, two broad program philosophies can be distinguished. The first emphasizes external control techniques for suppressing delinquency. The three most common types of programs found in the research literature that generally embody that philosophy, for example, are:

- Programs oriented toward instilling discipline (e.g., paramilitary regimens in boot camps).
- Programs aiming at deterrence through fear of the consequences of bad behavior (e.g., prison visitation programs such as Scared Straight).

- Programs emphasizing surveillance to detect and sanction bad behavior (e.g., intensive probation or parole supervision).

A contrasting program philosophy involves attempts to bring about behavior change by facilitating personal development through improved skills, relationships, insight, and the like. This "therapeutic" philosophy is embodied in various types of programs that can be sorted into the following broad categories:

- Restorative programs aimed at repairing or providing restitution for the harm done by delinquent behavior (e.g., community service restitution, victim-offender mediation).
- Skill-building programs that facilitate the development of positive abilities (e.g., building cognitive/thinking skills, social skills, academic, or vocational skills).
- Counseling programs based on relationships with a trained counselor (e.g., individual, group, and family counseling; mentoring).
- Multiple coordinated services (e.g., case management and service brokering arrangements).

When the mean effects on reoffending rates were compared for the programs associated with these two broad philosophies, the programs with a therapeutic orientation were notably more effective than those with a control orientation. Figure 4.1 shows the average effects on recidivism for

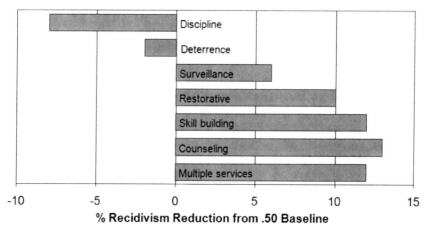

% Recidivism Reduction from .50 Baseline

Figure 4.1. Mean Recidivism Effects for the Program Categories Representing Control and Therapeutic Philosophies
Reprinted with permission from the Justice Research and Statistics Association from: Howell, J. C., and Lipsey, M. W. (2012). Research-based guidelines for juvenile justice programs. *Justice Research and Policy*, 14, 17–34.

the program categories within each of these philosophies. The zero (0) point in that chart indicates no program effect while positive values represent reductions in recidivism and negative values represent increases in recidivism. As can be seen, the programs in two of the control categories on average had negative effects.[3] The third category, programs relying mainly on surveillance, showed positive effects, but smaller ones than for any of the therapeutic program categories. The surveillance category includes mainly intensive probation programs, which often have significant counseling components by the probation officers. This combination thus most likely represents a mix of control and therapeutic strategies.

For purposes of guiding juvenile justice systems toward programs that are effective in reducing juvenile offending, the advice that follows from this portion of the meta-analysis is straightforward. To optimize the effects on recidivism and related outcomes, programs from the therapeutic categories should be favored and those from the control categories should be avoided as much as possible except when integrated in a graduated sanctions format coupled tightly with services tailored to offenders.

Within each of the program categories identified in Figure 4.1 that fall within the broad therapeutic grouping, the programs represented can be further classified into subcategories according to the primary type of service they provide. For example, in the subcategory of counseling programs, different kinds of counseling can be distinguished that vary in their effects on reoffending rates. Figure 4.2 shows the average effects

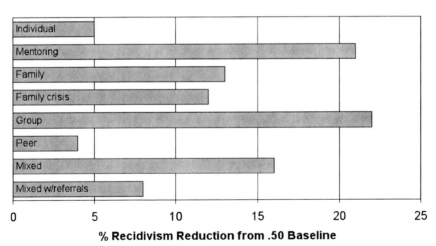

Figure 4.2.   Mean Recidivism Effects for the Generic Program Types within the Counseling Category
Reprinted with permission from the Justice Research and Statistics Association from: Howell, J. C., and Lipsey, M. W. (2012). Research-based guidelines for juvenile justice programs. *Justice Research and Policy*, 14, 17–34.

BOX 4.2

IS THERE AN IATROGENIC EFFECT OF MIXING LOW AND HIGH RISK JUVENILE OFFENDERS?

An *iatrogenic* effect refers to a situation in which the problem being addressed is inadvertently caused or made worse by the treatment procedure. Three studies are often cited as suggesting that programs which create intense group interactions among antisocial youths might actually increase the forms of behavior they are intended to prevent because of "peer contagion" (see Dishion, McCord, and Poulin, 1999; Dodge, Dishion, and Landsford, 2006; Gatti, Tremblay, and Vitaro, 2009). However, this claim is not supported by a meta-analysis of studies on group treatment of adolescent offenders (Lipsey, 2006). Lipsey's meta-analysis did not reveal *negative* effects associated with therapeutic programs that worked with offenders in groups, such as cognitive-behavioral therapy and group counseling. It did find slightly diminished, but still positive effects for mixed groups that included low and high risk youth, particularly for prevention programs, though not especially for adjudicated offenders. Skilled therapists appear to be capable of managing mixed risk groups in ways that minimize negative peer influences. To be sure, Lipsey advises that care should be taken in intermingling low and high risk offenders in prevention programs because favorable outcomes can be dampened as a result, and also cautions that very young offenders could be victimized by older males in secure residential facilities. In general, however, negative peer contagion seems to be more of a concern when antisocial youth interact in unsupervised settings than in professionally run treatment services.

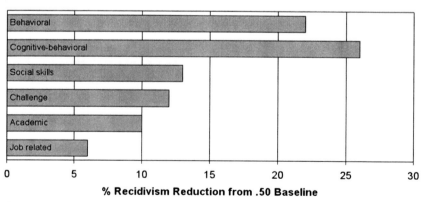

Figure 4.3.   Mean Recidivism Effects for the Generic Program Types Within the Skill-Building Category
Reprinted with permission from the Justice Research and Statistics Association from: Howell, J. C., and Lipsey, M. W. (2012). Research-based guidelines for juvenile justice programs. *Justice Research and Policy*, 14, 17–34.

for the major generic types of counseling. Though they all show positive effects, the largest effects are found for group counseling and mentoring programs. Group counseling is notable in this regard because of claims that have been made that treating offenders in groups may increase their recidivism as a result of the negative peer influences they have on each other, especially when low and high risk youth are mixed in the groups (see Box 4.2 for more on this topic).

Similar variation across generic program types is seen in the other therapeutic program categories. Behind counseling, the next largest category of programs with research evidence is skill building programs. Figure 4.3 shows that all the skill-building program types also produce positive effects, on average, with behavioral programs (e.g., behavior contracting) and cognitive behavioral programs showing the largest mean effects.

Embedded within many of these generic program types are specific brand name model programs that have been included in the evaluation research covered in the meta-analysis. These generally show positive effects on recidivism, as would be expected. However, they do not necessarily show notably better effects than the no-name programs of the same type. For example, Functional Family Therapy (FFT) and Multisystemic Therapy (MST) are both included in the generic program type labeled "family counseling" in Figure 4.2. As can be seen in Figure 4.2, the programs of the family counseling type, on average, had positive effects on recidivism. The effect estimates from the FFT and MST studies fall well within the range of those for the other family programs in this collection, but their effects were not notably larger than those of other more generic family counseling programs and, indeed, some of the no-name programs showed effects that were even larger than those found for the model programs.

In this example, we see that the model programs are indeed effective, and thus deserve their designation as evidence-based programs. At the same time, there is evidence for the effectiveness of family counseling programs as a generic type, so it is not unreasonable to say that family counseling programs are also evidence-based. However, some of the studies of family counseling programs showed near-zero or even negative effects, so a careful specification of the family programs that are evidence-based would also include identification of the characteristics those programs must have to be on the high end of the effect distribution.

There are several implications of this portion of the meta-analysis for juvenile justice practice. First, as long as the program type matches the needs of an offender, the largest effects on recidivism can be expected from the program types that showed the biggest average effects in the applicable research studies. For a specific program of any given type, selecting a model program if one is available and can be implemented with fidelity should generally be a good choice. Local programs of that same type might also be expected to be effective, but they too must be implemented in a way that is consistent with evidence-based guidelines. In those cases, it should be possible to achieve effective implementation by ensuring that the program has the distinguishing characteristics of those similar programs found in the research with above average effects and avoids the characteristics of those with negligible or negative effects.

Lipsey (2009) explored the evidence from 548 independent studies in an analysis aimed at identifying the general program characteristics that were most strongly associated with their effects on reoffending rates. He found that a relatively small set of rather straightforward program characteristics were capable of distinguishing the programs with larger effects from those with smaller, and even null and negative, effects. Those distinguishing characteristics include, first, the program type. As shown by the examples presented in Figures 4.2 and 4.3, the average effects on recidivism are larger for some types of programs than others. The quality of service delivery, that is, how well the specific service is implemented, matters a great deal. Even the most inherently effective program will not produce significant reductions in recidivism if it is not implemented well with a sufficient quality of service delivered. Beyond that, the amount of the service (contact hours and duration) provided is important. As might be expected, very small amounts of service, or programs that are poorly implemented, have smaller effects. Finally, the risk level of the juveniles served is an important factor. Higher risk juveniles have more room for improvement and, indeed, program effects on recidivism, all else being equal, are greater with higher risk offenders.

IMPORTANCE OF IMPLEMENTATION FIDELITY

For therapeutic programs, fidelity of implementation is as important as the treatment type. The evidence supporting this statement comes from Lipsey's (2007) analysis of 509 of the juvenile justice programs that provided sufficient detailed information about the quality of implementation. In this illustration, when implemented with high fidelity, programs in the group that generally were least effective reduced delinquency by about the same amount as the programs that were generally most effective but were implemented with low fidelity. That is, programs with less inherent effectiveness that are well implemented can show effects comparable to those of better programs that are poorly implemented. As Lipsey emphasized, therefore, it is a mistake to think of program effectiveness entirely in terms of the type of program used, as if there were a silver bullet type of program that, if found, would assure positive effects. How well a program is implemented is equally important. Although the largest effects are seen in the best program types when well implemented, a second important lesson comes from this analysis. It is that, when implemented with high quality, many homegrown programs can produce very worthwhile results—in many cases, comparable to model brand-name programs.

NOTES

1. Parts of this chapter are taken from the first and second authors' published articles: Howell, J. C., and Lipsey, M. W. (2012). Research-based guidelines for juvenile justice programs. *Justice Research and Policy*, 14, 17–34; and Lipsey, M. W., and Howell, J. C. (2012). A broader view of evidence-based programs reveals more options for state juvenile justice systems. *Criminology and Public Policy*, 11, 515–523.

2. Parts of this chapter are taken from Lipsey, M. W. (2009). The primary factors that characterize effective interventions with juvenile offenders: A meta-analytic overview. *Victims and Offenders*, 4, 124–147; and also from Howell, J. C., and Lipsey, M. W. (2012). Research-based guidelines for juvenile justice programs. *Justice Research and Policy*, 14, 17–34.

3. All estimates of the mean reoffense effect sizes have been adjusted for methodological differences between the studies.

5

The Standardized
Program Evaluation Protocol

IN BRIEF

The meta-analytic findings summarized above—drawn from more than 500 controlled studies—are informative for practitioners and policymakers in juvenile justice systems who wish to select effective programs for juvenile offenders. However, they fall short of providing specific guidance for how to ensure that the programs have the particular characteristics associated in the research with the most positive outcomes. For that purpose, more specific guidelines are needed that provide criteria by which local programs can be measured to assess the degree to which their characteristics match those of programs found in the research. Moreover, those guidelines need to be in a form that allows them to be easily used in a consistent and valid manner in routine practice by personnel who are not trained researchers. With such structured criteria, juvenile justice administrators can determine the extent to which their programs are supported by evidence of effectiveness and how to improve them if they fall short. It was with these considerations in mind that Lipsey developed a tool called the Standardized Program Evaluation Protocol (SPEP) to bridge between the large body of research included in the meta-analysis and practical application in juvenile justice settings.

The SPEP operationalizes research-based guidelines in the form of a program rating scheme that can be used by service providers and juvenile justice administrators to periodically assess their programs for juvenile offenders (Howell and Lipsey, 2012; Lipsey and Howell, 2012; Lipsey et al., 2010).

The characteristics of the programs with the largest effects on reoffending rates that were found in meta-analysis provide the basis for guidelines for effective programs that can be stated in general terms as follows (Lipsey, 2009):

- Use therapeutically oriented approaches, not control oriented ones.
- For the selected therapeutic approach, use one of the more effective intervention types within that category.
- For the selected intervention type:
  ○ Target high risk juveniles; low risk juveniles have little potential for recidivism.
  ○ Provide an amount of service that at least matches the average in the supporting research for that intervention type.
  ○ Implement the intervention with high quality; establish a treatment protocol and monitor service delivery for adherence to that protocol.

The general form of the SPEP rating scheme is shown in Figure 5.1. This scheme applies to any therapeutic program type for juvenile offenders for which there is sufficient supporting research in Lipsey's large meta-analytic database and assigns points to local programs of that type according to how closely their characteristics match those associated with the best recidivism outcomes for similar programs as identified in the meta-analysis. The maximum number of points available for each rated aspect of the program is proportionate to the strength of that factor for predicting recidivism effects in the meta-analysis. The program aspects rated are listed and described in more detail below.

Primary and Supplemental Service Types

All juvenile justice systems use a mixture of brand name and generic services. To rate programs with the SPEP instrument, the different services in the overall service array must be classified according to the primary type of service represented using descriptive information from the provider and a glossary of service descriptions derived from the associated research studies. When the program includes a therapeutic supplemental service that is also supported by favorable research in addition to the primary service, additional points are awarded.

Quality of Service Delivery

The quality of service delivery is the most difficult item to define empirically because research studies do not typically provide detailed information on this aspect. The quality indicators that are identified in the meta-analysis focus on monitoring implementation to ensure that the program is implemented as intended. This data element is operationalized by

Standardized Program Evaluation Protocol (SPEP) for Services to Juvenile Offenders© Recalibrated version, 2012		
	Points Possible	Points Received
Primary and Supplemental Service Types [Identified according to definitions derived from the research]		

Primary Service Type for Program Being Rated
  Group 1 services (5 points)   Group 4 services (25 points)
  Group 2 services(10 points)   Group 5 services (30 points)
  Group 3 services(15 points)
	30	

Supplemental Service Type Qualifying supplemental service used Yes(5 points) No (0 points)	5	
Quality of Service Delivery [Determined from a systematic assessment of the relevant features of the provider and provider organization]		

Rated quality of services delivered:
  Low (5 points)
  Medium (10 points)
  High (20 points)
	20	

Amount of Service [Determined from data for the qualifying group of service recipients]		

Duration [Target number of weeks specified for each service type]
  % of youth who received at least the target weeks of service
    0% (0 points)   60% (6 points)
    20% (2 points)   80% (8 points)
    40% (4 points)   99% (10 points)
	10	

Contact Hours [Target number of hours specified for each service type]
  % of youth who received at least the target hours of service:
    0% (0 points)   60% (6 points)
    20% (2 points)   80% (8 points)
    40% (4 points)   99% (10 points)
	10	

Risk Level of Youth Served [Determined from risk ratings on a valid instrument for the qualifying group of service recipients]		

% of youth with medium or high
risk scores(greater than low):
  0% (0 points)   75% (7 points)
  30% (2 points) 85% (10 points)
  50% (5 points) 95% (12 points)   % of youth with high risk
scores (greater than medium):
  0% (0 points)   25% (8 points)
  15% (3 points) 30% (10 points)
  20% (5 points) 35% (13 points)
	25	

Provider's Total SPEP Score	100	(Insert Score)

Figure 5.1.   The General Form of the Standardized Program Evaluation Protocol

combining information about the following program features into a single rating for each program service that is to receive a SPEP score:

- Whether the provider agency has an explicit written protocol for delivery of the service (e.g., a treatment manual with which staff providing the service are familiar).

- Whether the staff persons providing the service have received training in that specific service type; the amount and recency of such training.
- Whether the agency has procedures in place (a) to monitor adherence to the protocol and other aspects of quality by those providing service, and (b) to take corrective action when significant departures from the protocol or lapses in quality are identified.

These elements must be assessed for the provider of each program rated by the SPEP in an objective manner that is supported by evidence from site visits to the programs, review of organizational procedures, and the like.

Amount of Service

Target values for treatment duration and hours of contact are set at the respective medians from the research on the intervention type being rated and vary for different intervention types. For manualized programs supported by research specifically on those programs, the amount of service targets specified by the developer are used instead. Data for rating the amount of service provided must come from a management information system or similar client tracking procedure that provides information for a sufficient number of juveniles served by the program in a recent period.

Risk Level

The risk level of the juveniles treated by the program must be determined from a valid risk assessment instrument administered routinely to each juvenile prior to treatment. As with the amount of service, the data needed to make the SPEP rating on this factor come from records for the juveniles served by the program during a recent period, with a minimum number of cases required before a rating can be made.

Experience with the SPEP indicates that it can be used by many service providers and juvenile justice agencies with only modest adaptations to their data collection and management information systems, thus permitting evaluations of a wide range of programs with an associated assessment of the extent to which their profile of characteristics is consistent with evidence of effectiveness. Those evaluations will identify programs that are not optimal for reducing recidivism but, perhaps more important, they will provide guidance for improving those programs. Programs may be providing a type of service for which there is supporting research, but not doing so in a way that coincides with what the research indicates are the practices of the most effective programs of that type. The SPEP helps identify the areas with the greatest discrepancies between the program's practices and the research-based effective practice guidelines and thus gives a program a blueprint for improvement. The rating scheme is tailored for each specific program type within the general framework shown in Figure 5.1.

PILOT TESTING AND VALIDATION OF THE SPEP

Demonstration projects with the SPEP have been conducted in the state juvenile justice agencies of North Carolina (the original pilot state) and Arizona, and others are underway in Tennessee, Florida, Pennsylvania, Connecticut, Delaware, Iowa, and Milwaukee. North Carolina data showed that the SPEP scores for rated programs were related to their recidivism rates (Lipsey, Howell, and Tidd, 2007). A validation study in Arizona (Lipsey, 2008) compared the risk-adjusted recidivism rates for juveniles served by programs with low SPEP ratings with those for juveniles served by programs with high ratings. The six-month recidivism rate for juveniles served by the lower scoring programs was virtually the same as the rate predicted by their pretreatment risk factors. The recidivism rate for juveniles served by the higher rated programs, however, was 12 percentage points lower than expected on the basis of their risk level. The results were virtually the same for juveniles with twelve-month recidivism data. A replication of this analysis with more juveniles and SPEP-rated programs was conducted by the Arizona research staff after the SPEP had been rolled out statewide and showed similar results (Redpath and Brandner, 2010). These recidivism studies provide promising indications of the validity of the SPEP for identifying effective programs and guiding improvement for ineffective ones.

Most important, perhaps, this tool provides guidance for improving programs that do not measure up well. Programs may be providing a type of service for which there is supporting research, but not doing so in a way that coincides with what the research indicates are the practices of the most effective programs of that type. There typically is much room for improvement. Identifying the areas with the greatest discrepancies between the program's practices and the research-based best practice guidelines gives programs a blueprint for improvement.

BEST PRACTICES FOR REDUCING
RECIDIVISM WITH THE SPEP

The SPEP not only evaluates each service against an evidence-based effective practice profile, but provides guidance for improving programs that fall short in that evaluation. The overall SPEP score indicates how

closely the program service being scored matches the key characteristics of similar programs found in the available research to reduce
recidivism for juvenile offenders. The SPEP score indicates how much
room there is to improve the programs expected effects on recidivism.
It follows from the logic of the SPEP score that a program service that
finds constructive ways to increase its score should also increase its effectiveness for reducing the delinquency of the juveniles it serves. For
program improvement purposes, the scores for the individual SPEP
components have diagnostic value. The components with the lowest
scores relative to the maximum possible are those that, if addressed,
have the most potential to improve the overall effectiveness of the program service. For example, increasing the amount of service (duration
and/or contact hours), might be indicated as a particular area for potential improvement. As another example, it may be that the program
is working primarily with low risk youth who have little potential for
improvement and a shift in focus to higher risk youth might be considered. Working with service providers to properly interpret and respond to SPEP scores is an integral part of the SPEP process, generally
referred to as "program improvement planning."

USE OF THE SPEP PRIMARY SERVICE
TYPES IN SERVICE MATCHING

Matching elevated offender needs with primary (generic) services embodied in the SPEP is a straightforward process. Primary services—mentoring, individual counseling, group counseling, family counseling, and
the like—are specific, organized, planned, direct interactions with the
juvenile alone or with others (e.g., peers or family) intended to bring
about psychological or behavioral change. The service matching process
can begin with assignment of these primary service types in ways that
connect juveniles with services that have the capability of addressing the
domains of their greatest need. Standard treatment needs assessments for
juvenile justice system clients identify problems in family, school, peer,
individual, and community domains. For example, youth involved in
substance use (an individual-level problem) and also experiencing poor
family supervision could benefit from individual counseling for drug
dependence while his/her parents should receive family counseling. Of
course, multiple problems necessitate arrangement of a series of services,
while separating treatment events as much as practical so that the offender is capable of maintaining distinctions among the various treatment
ingredients to maximize learning opportunities.

When viewed system-wide, service matching necessarily involves making improvements in the array of programs. The first phase in this process is provider improvements. One example is increasing the frequency and/or duration of services, typically considered "low-hanging fruit" in the lexicon of provider improvements. The second phase involves matching offenders to services, as in the above example. In the third phase, systemic improvements may be needed so that all probationers who need a particular service have access to one that is evidence-based—that is, conforms to SPEP guidelines or is otherwise recognized as such. When a program is needed to fill a gap in the existing program repertoire, selecting an evidence-based model program may well be the best choice if an appropriate one is available (Lipsey and Howell, 2012). If service providers and juvenile justice managers can collaborate in making collective improvements, they should be able to achieve recidivism reductions across multiple program types and all along the service continuum (Howell and Lipsey, 2012).

OTHER BEST PRACTICE GUIDELINES FOR OFFENDER-SERVICE MATCHING

Guidelines for offender-service matching are now available in the form of a protocol for the development of service plans. An interdisciplinary team of service experts is needed to develop comprehensive case plans. If followed, several best practice principles will help greatly to achieve greater recidivism reductions with evidence-based programs. These are described below. A linchpin of the Comprehensive Strategy is its targeting of SVC offenders. Yet little progress has been made in systematizing the development of comprehensive case plans for this group. For this purpose, cross-system alignment in comprehensive case plans is the ideal (see Box 5.1).

Particularly for offenders at risk of residential placement, an interdisciplinary Community Planning Team (sometimes called a "service team") should manage the more in-depth clinical assessment, including a structured interview, and then use the results to develop comprehensive case plans that take into account each agency's experiences—including failures as well as successes—with the family at hand. At the screening stage, in most instances, court staff can complete both an actuarial risk assessment and an objective assessment of family strengths and needs. In some cases, clinical input will be needed in their completion (Shlonsky and Wagner, 2005). The Center for the Promotion of Mental Health in Juvenile Justice (2003) at Columbia University has developed a protocol for

BOX 5.1

CROSS-SYSTEM ALIGNMENT IN COMPREHENSIVE CASE PLANS

A Community Planning Team should be formed to align agency and community resources to execute comprehensive case plans. Headed by a coordinator, it would first assess youth and family treatment needs and then proceed to develop comprehensive case plans that are supported by pooled, blended, or "braided" funding in the wraparound tradition. The ideal components of the Community Planning Team are as follows (Howell, Kelly, and Mangum, 2004, p. 5).

Participants. The Team should include representatives of all sectors of the community that are engaged in the planning and service delivery processes, including juvenile justice, education, mental health, substance abuse, child welfare, child protection, other social service agencies, youth development agencies, citizen volunteers, private organizations, law enforcement agencies, prosecutors, courts, corrections agencies, civic organizations, faith organizations, parents, and teens.

Information exchange. Exchange of information is important for coordination, control, planning, and client assessment purposes. Confidentiality of client records often deters collaboration; however, barriers to information sharing can be reduced through identification of legal and policy barriers—and often removed, especially when youth and parents (or other caregivers) are actively involved in services planning. The Family Educational Rights and Privacy Act provides valuable guidance with respect to information sharing, particularly with regard to educational records (Medaris, 1998: Medaris, Campbell, and James, 1997).

Cross-agency client referrals. The key to successful cross-agency client referrals is each agency's need to see a return on interagency investments in the form of service resources for referred clients. The immediate targets for cross-agency referrals are youth presently in two or more systems. The primary clients, though, should be all youth currently in or at risk of residential placement because of the associated high cost and greater ineffectiveness of this option.

Networking Protocol. This refers to negotiated agreements between agencies that outline information exchange and cross-agency client referral conditions and procedures. Such agreements stimulate growth in communication and increased client sharing.

Integrated Services. Comprehensive and objective assessments of treatment needs provide the basis for development of client and family treatment plans involving multiple agencies and integrated services. The networking agreement should ensure that all youth and families receive the same assessment and case management protocols from the respective agencies at several locations. Information gathered by one service provider should be available for sharing with other service providers via an integrated management information system that links key agencies, including law enforcement, juvenile justice, education, mental health, substance abuse, and child welfare agencies.

the development of service plans for mental health problems, consisting of screening, assessment, referral, and treatment.

The assessment protocol is as important as the mental health assessments themselves. A standard protocol should be developed to include a checklist of information needed at the service team meetings, at which the results of the comprehensive mental health evaluation are presented. Pratt (2004), a leading expert on mental health assessments, also recommends that bachelor-level clinicians should be responsible for insuring that all the information is ready before the staff meeting and actually be responsible for the general presentation to the service team. This protocol helps insure that clinical mental health assessments are fully utilized in comprehensive case plan development and management. Pratt underscores the importance of using clinical interviews to support the standardized findings of mental health assessments, not the reverse. Wasserman, a leader in diagnosing and treating juvenile offenders' mental health problems, and her colleagues have for several years focused their efforts on identifying the specific forms of mental health problems and matching offenders in JJ systems with appropriate treatments (Wasserman, Ko, and McReynolds, 2004; Wasserman, McReynolds, Musabegovic et al., 2009).

Early Intervention with Very Young Offenders

There are three fundamental strategies for early intervention with delinquents (Welsh and Farrington, 2006). The first is to intervene at the individual level with at-risk children, particularly disruptive children. Tools and protocols are available now for conducting effective clinical risk assessments on child delinquents (Augimeri, Enebrink, Walsh, and Jiang, 2010) and numerous effective programs are available for children with mental health and disruptive behavior problems (Lee, Aos, Drake et al., 2012; Drake, 2012; Augimeri, Walsh, Liddon et al., 2011). The major risk assessment has been validated in two formats: the Early Assessment Risk Lists or EARL-20B V2 for boys (Augimeri, Koegl, Webster, and Levene, 2001), and the EARL-21G V1 for girls (Levene, Augimeri, Pepler et al., 2001; Augimeri et al., 2011). The EARL-PC is used when there is insufficient information to complete a full risk/needs assessment (EARL-20B or EARL-21G) such as those in educational and community organization settings. The EARL-PC guides users to exercise their best judgment in assessing areas of concern in order to determine appropriate community based services for these at risk children. It has been tested in multiple jurisdictions in Canada (Augimeri, Walsh, Jiang et al., 2010).

Augimeri and colleagues developed an evidence-based program designed specifically for aggressive, bullying, and delinquent behaviors in children (ages six to eleven), the Stop Now and Plan (SNAP®) for boys—and the corresponding Girls Connection (GC) (Augimeri et al.,

2011). Augimeri and Koegel (2012) also recommend community centers for referral and perhaps assessment settings as well. Services should be community-based and strengthen the child's context (e.g., family, peers, school, and neighborhood), and Augimeri and colleagues underscore several important features of service delivery:

- It should be individualized and comprehensive.
- It should be integrated into existing juvenile justice, social service, public health, and mental health systems.
- It should be sensitive to developmental level, gender, cultural/ religious context, and physical and mental health of the child.

Family prevention is the second recommended early intervention strategy. In this strategy, programs intervene with high-risk families that are most likely to produce child delinquents. A combination of home visiting and parent training is the most effective approach with these families. The single most popular program, and a very effective one, is the Nurse Family Partnership, which provides first-time, low-income mothers with home visitation services (Olds, Hill, Mihalic et al., 1998). This program has shown reductions in child abuse and neglect, reduced delinquency among the children, and has produced other favorable outcomes. School- and community-level prevention is the third recommended early intervention strategy. Certain school-based (Wilson, Lipsey, and Derzon, 2003) and afterschool (Gottfredson, Cross, and Soule, 2007) programs are evidence-based. In addition, mentoring is an evidence-based community-level prevention program that provides adult mentors who work one-on-one with troubled children and adolescents in a supportive, nonjudgmental manner while acting as role models.

Consider Special Offender Types

"Special needs" children demand utmost attention. Children with disabilities should never be placed in regular detention and correctional facilities. The same principle applies to children and adolescents with serious mental health problems. Other special offender types demand close attention. When secure care is appropriate, Wiebush (2002) constructed a secure care placement tree that helps govern placement of special needs cases separately from low, medium, and high risk offenders. For the most difficult cases (e.g., sex offenders, severe medical problems, chronic assault histories, severe mental health problems), facilities or units that provide programs or services for special needs should be available.

Active gang members require careful screening and often close supervision. It is important to immediately assess the level of gang involvement. Two considerations are important here: (1) whether the youth is only an associate of gang members, and not a bona fide member himself/herself; and (2) the centrality (degree) of gang participation (e.g., core member versus peripheral). Johnson (1987) developed a useful tool for assessing the individuals' levels of gang involvement. This is important for security reasons. Five levels are distinguished in this scheme (fantasy about gangs, at-risk of joining, an associate, a full-fledged member, and a hard-core gang member).

Matching services for juvenile sex offenders is not as challenging as previously thought. Public perception presumes sex offenders as specialists who require specific forms of treatment and control. To the contrary, most of these offenders display a pattern of versatility in offending; violent sex offenders, for instance, do not differ from other violent offenders on the large majority of risk factors (Rosenfeld, White, and Esbensen, 2012). Thus the juvenile sex offender "is characterized by a certain tendency to specialize in sexual crime over time against the backdrop of much versatility" (p. 138). In a recent study of sex offender types in a large sample of boys with a mean age of fifteen years (Van Der Put, Van Vugt, Stams et al., 2013), a comparison was made between the following groups: youth who have committed a nonsexual offense (NSOs), and three categories of youth who had committed a juvenile sex offense (JSO) of the following types: a misdemeanor sexual offense (MSOs) such as exhibitionism or voyeurism, a felony sexual offense (FSOs) such as indecent assault or rape, and a sexual offense against much younger children (CSOs). Regarding the impact of risk factors on general recidivism, the researchers found that the impact of most malleable risk factors was significantly greater among JSOs than among NSOs. "In other words, risk factors for general delinquency are less commonly found among JSOs than NSOs, but if they do occur, their impact on recidivism is much stronger" (p. 60). Two important implications for clinical practice were drawn from the study. First, "assessing the risk for general recidivism in JSOs can probably be performed in the same way as in NSOs, because the same risk factors predict recidivism in both groups [and] second, it appeared that dynamic risk factors for general delinquency have a relatively greater impact on general recidivism among JSOs compared to NSOs. The potential effect on recidivism from interventions that address these factors is therefore also relatively large among JSOs" (p. 63). In other words, it appears that treatments designed for general delinquency can also be effective with juvenile sex offenders "in reducing general recidivism and furthermore that the potential effect of these treatments is relatively high" for this category of offenders (p. 63).

Target Multiple Risk Factors in Multiple Developmental Domains

As shown earlier in this handbook, the first key consideration for effective intervention is the importance of targeting multiple risk factors in multiple developmental domains. Research has found "strong relations among the dynamic risk factors from all domains... suggesting that problems in the different domains frequently occur in combination with each other" (Van der Put, Dekovic, Stams et al., 2012, p. 313). Although not a new finding, this research underscores a very important principle of effective treatment of children and adolescents: "the high correlations among the different domains mean that there will often be problems in several domains in the higher risk groups" (p. 314). Most noteworthy is the relationship between chronic serious and violent delinquency and combinations of problems, including drug use and dealing, mental health problems, school problems, victimization histories, gang involvement, and gun carrying (Huizinga et al., 2000; see also Loeber, Farrington et al., 2008). This principle also applies generally to violence reduction (Bushway, Krohn, Lizotte et al., 2013) and also to truncating SVC offender career trajectories (Krohn et al., 2014).

Adjust Services to Constantly Changing Predictive Domains

The third service-matching principle, which also comes from many studies, is that the relative importance of the predictive domains changes as juveniles grow older. In a Washington study, the family domain showed the strongest association with recidivism at age twelve but, "at age thirteen, the relationships domain showed the strongest association, and from age fourteen, attitude was most strongly associated with recidivism" (Van der Put et al., 2012, p. 313). Other research also shows changes in the salience of risk factor domains from childhood to adulthood (Lipsey and Derzon, 1998; Loeber, Slott, and Stouthamer-Loeber, 2008; Tanner-Smith et al., 2013a; Van der Put et al., 2011).

Address both Risk and Protective Factors

"It is the mixture of risk and promotive [protective] effects that appears most crucial in determining the future risk of serious offending as well as the probability of full desistance or lower-level offending" (Loeber, Slott, and Stouthamer-Loeber, 2008, p. 159). These researchers also argue that "the next generation of risk assessment devices could potentially also benefit from an appraisal of juveniles' expected future exposure to risk *and* promotive factors based on knowledge gained from longitudinal survey studies" (p. 159). Indeed, this is the ultimate goal of risk assessment; that is, predicting youth's advancement in the multiple pathways to serious and violent offenders and to the SVC offender level.

Promote Desistance

Research has identified key hindering factors for desistance from serious and violent offenses (measured in middle adolescence): drug use, drug dealing, gun carrying, and gang membership (Loeber, Farrington et al., 2008; Loeber, Farrington et al., 2008). Among the particular hindering factors that have been identified in research are the following, arranged by domains (Loeber, Farrington et al., 2008; Loeber, Hoeve, Slott, and Van der Laan, 2012; Stouthamer-Loeber et al., 2008):

- Individual: High tobacco use
- Individual: High alcohol use
- Individual: High marijuana use
- Individual: High psychopathic features
- Individual: Depression
- Individual: High anxiety
- Individual: Drug dealing
- Individual: High violence victimization
- Individual: Gun carrying
- Peer: Continuing association with antisocial peers
- Peer: Gang membership/involvement
- System: Institutional confinement in lieu of probation supervision and services
- System: Longer stays in institutional placements

Several items in this listing are relatively new in desistance research. Juvenile offenders with a substance use disorder are at greater risk for escalations in offense seriousness over time (Hoeve, McReynolds, and Wasserman, 2013). A growing body of gang research shows that prolonged gang involvement ("embeddedness") delays desistance, as demonstrated in Phoenix (Pyrooz, Sweeten, and Piquero, 2013; Sweeten, Pyrooz, and Piquero, 2013). Although institutional confinement has long been recognized as detrimental for recidivism (though not for public safety from dangerous offenders), the most recent research underscores the importance of minimizing periods of secure confinement to less than three to six months (Chung et al., 2007; Loughran et al., 2009).

The Importance of Family Engagement

Successful implementation of comprehensive case plans for juvenile offenders necessarily involves family engagement. In their study of youths referred to the Newark Family Crisis Intervention Unit and community mental health centers, Lerman and Pottick (1995) found that most parents had relied on their own efforts in working with their children; they had tried behavior modification techniques, systems of rewards and punishments, and other forms of discipline, but to no avail. More than one-third had tried counseling or had contacted hospitals, doctors, or psychiatrists to get help—again, to no avail. Parents' talks with teachers were least likely to result in specific suggestions concerning agencies that likely could provide help. Contacts with police and court officials were most productive, followed by contacts with state youth workers and family workers. Remarkably, the parents in Lerman and Pottick's study sample said that none of the help sources they contacted appeared to understand the mental health problems experienced by their problem children, and professionals often made inappropriate suggestions for help. Each agency and program having contact with children and families involved in the justice system should hire or appoint a staff person, preferably a family member or former system-involved youth, to coordinate family engagement efforts and activities. State justice agencies and court systems should help develop a basic guide to the justice system for families that can be tailored or expanded for use by local jurisdictions. A *Family Guide to Pennsylvania's Juvenile Justice System* (Pennsylvania Commission on Crime and Delinquency, 2012a) is an excellent example. This guide was developed by the Family Involvement Committee of the Pennsylvania Council of Chief Juvenile Probation Officers—a committee of family advocates and juvenile justice practitioners—to help families understand Pennsylvania's juvenile justice system and be better prepared to work closely with juvenile justice staff to promote positive outcomes for justice involved youth.

Many abused and neglected children benefit greatly from Court Appointed Special Advocates (CASA) for Children, a national network of community-based programs that recruit, train, and support CASA advocates and guardian ad litem (GAL) volunteers who help abused and neglected children find safe, permanent homes. CASA volunteers are everyday citizens who have undergone screening and training with their local CASA/GAL program.[1]

COST-BENEFICIAL PROGRAMS

When evidence-based programs are used, it is important to take into account available information on their cost-benefits in making client-service matches. An excellent guide is the cost-benefit analyses conducted by the Washington State Institute for Public Policy (WSIPP[2]). This groundbreaking series of cost-benefit studies identified evidence-based public policy options for juvenile justice and demonstrated how investments in these options could decrease incarceration, save taxpayer dollars, and lower recidivism rates.

In the most recent WSIPP review, Drake (2012) identified a number of evidence-based options that can help policymakers achieve desired crime reductions while simultaneously offering taxpayers a good return on their investment with very low risk of failure—when implemented in the

State of Washington. A first-ever "measure of risk" of program failure is now calculated by Drake and colleagues. Probation-linked programs for which benefits greatly exceed costs include Functional Family Therapy (by $30,700 per participant), Aggression Replacement Training ($29,700), Multisystemic Therapy ($24,800), and less so for Drug Courts ($10,600) and victim offender mediation ($3,600). An alternative to confinement, community-based Multidimensional Treatment Foster Care ($31,300 savings per participant) is especially cost-beneficial (Drake et al., 2009).

For low risk offenders, diversion programs are particularly cost effective ($51,000), and teen courts are also cost-beneficial ($16,800) (Drake et al., 2009) in the State of Washington. Returns on investment are also summarized in a *Consumer Reports*-like list of what works and what does not, ranked by benefit-cost statistics and a metric of investment risk (Lee et al., 2012) for the program categories that follow: juvenile justice, adult criminal justice, child welfare, pre-K–12 education, children's mental health, general prevention programs for children and adolescents, substance abuse, adult mental health, and public health issues. The National Research Council (2013) suggests that the WSIPP cost-benefit findings are generalizable to other states.

The WSIPP studies highlighted three programs that proved cost-effective for institutionalized juvenile offenders (Lee et al., 2012), Functional Family Therapy ($67,100), Aggression Replacement Training ($61,400), and Family Integrated Transitions ($17,000). In sum, there are numerous effective programs that JJ systems can use without compromising public safety that are capable of reducing reoffense rates, especially for high risk offenders. Moreover, those programs can be effective while treating juveniles in the community and at lower cost than institutional care. When well-implemented and targeted on higher risk offenders, some programs can yield benefits that far exceed costs.

THE POTENTIAL OF EFFECTIVE JUVENILE JUSTICE PRACTICES TO LOWER THE AGE-CRIME CURVE

Before now, published evaluation studies have not shown the degree to which effective intervention could lower the age-crime curve across a given city or state. Such an exercise has been hampered for two reasons. First, there are few follow-ups of treated and untreated individuals throughout adolescence and into early adulthood. Second, program evaluations rarely encompass city-wide or state-wide samples. To demonstrate the feasibility of such an exercise, Loeber and colleagues (2012) used longitudinal data from the Pittsburgh Youth Study to simulate the impact of effective interventions on the long-term offending of at-risk youths.

These researchers selected the top third of high-risk offenders in three birth cohorts and simulated the effects of effective services that Lipsey and Wilson (1998) had identified in a review of programs serving serious and violent juvenile offenders that found an average effect of 30 percent reduction for the best programs. Figure 5.2 shows the comparison between the age-crime curve for serious delinquency without the "intervention" (the top line) and the curve with the "intervention," the lower line (simulated reductions are projected for Pittsburgh Youth Study offenders, as if the high risk offenders had actually received the effective program services).[3]

Figure 5.2 shows reduction in the percentage of serious delinquents amounting to approximately one-quarter from ages eleven to twenty-one. Other results (not shown in Figure 5.2) indicated that the simulated intervention also was associated with a decrease of 20 percent in the prevalence of arrest by the police, a 35 percent lower prevalence of homicide offenders and homicide victims, and a 29 percent reduction in the weeks of incarceration. Thus, the modeled interventions had a substantial benefit of lowering the age-crime curve by reducing the prevalence of self-reported serious offenders, officially recorded homicide offenders and homicide victims, and had benefits for the justice system by sharply reducing arrests

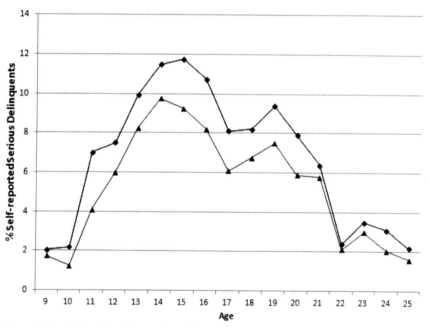

Figure 5.2.   A Simulated Reduction of the Age-Crime Curve
Reprinted with permission from Springer.

and convictions. This is a convincing illustration of the potential impact of effective services when matched to very high risk offenders.

Therefore, statewide reductions in recidivism appear to be within reach in a systematic approach that uses the Comprehensive Strategy framework and evidence-based programs to improve performance across the entire JJ system continuum. The SPEP provides juvenile justice systems with a tool for identifying such programs and improving those already in place to optimize their effects on recidivism, especially for the high risk juveniles with the most potential to reoffend. An effective service continuum might include a mix of brand name model programs and generic homegrown programs selected or developed on the basis of evidence of effectiveness from primary studies or meta-analysis. The prospects also are good that proper use of these tools to manage a spectrum of effective programs will improve the outcomes for juveniles who come into contact with the juvenile justice system and, with that, the cost effectiveness of the system itself.

The success of this effort hinges in large part on successful targeting of the most chronic, serious, and violent offenders. Recidivism rates for these juvenile offenders map onto the age-crime curve. Recidivism is lowest in early adolescence, peaks in middle adolescence, and diminishes in late adolescence (Van der Put et al., 2011). Yet, for the subgroup of SVC offenders, both basic research and statewide data show that recidivism rates remain high across these developmental periods. The implication is that a continuum of programs is needed to cover these three segments of offender careers, to reduce escalation of offense seriousness, lower recidivism rates, and truncate SVC offender careers in particular. If juvenile justice systems are successful in targeting offenders at high risk for serious, violent, or chronic offending before the point of confinement, the payoff can be enormous in terms of total crime reduction and reduced costs. Of course, providing evidence-based services is a critical linchpin. This entire enterprise can be evaluated statewide, using the design that follows.

A SYSTEM-WIDE EVALUATION FRAMEWORK

Figure 5.3 sketches the framework for evidence-based practice in juvenile justice that picks up at the point at which a juvenile is arrested. Prior to that point, of course, effective evidence-based prevention programs are important to minimize the number of arrests. Juveniles are first sorted into the appropriate level of supervision, an important consideration for public safety. This is the point where valid risk assessment plays a key role along with a disposition matrix that provides structured decision-making guidelines for aligning the level of supervision with the actual

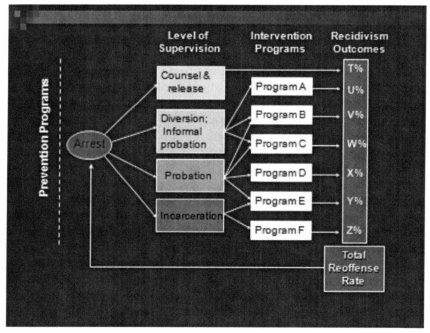

Figure 5.3.   A System-wide Evaluation Framework

risk level of a juvenile. Because higher levels of supervision by themselves have little or no long-term benefits for recidivism reduction, and strongly suggestive evidence indicates that it most likely increases recidivism, the objective here is to use the lowest level of supervision that will provide short-term control of the juvenile's behavior.

The part of the juvenile justice system that does have potential for producing sustained effects on reoffending rates is the repertoire of effective evidence-based therapeutic programs available to provide targeted services. At this juncture, systematic needs assessment and appropriate matching of services to offenders' needs and circumstances is pivotal. The growing body of research and availability of evidence-based needs assessment tools provides supports for this important function. Appropriate matching, however, will not produce the desired recidivism reductions unless the programs to which the juveniles are matched are actually effective for that purpose. This is where evidence-based treatment programs that provide a broad continuum of services play a central role.

The focal outcomes of this process are the recidivism rates of the juveniles managed at different levels of supervision and served by different programs. An appropriate management information system should track those recidivism rates and analyze them in relation to the characteristics of the juveniles and the procedures and programs applied to them. For instance, offenders could be grouped by risk levels and treatment need profiles to examine outcomes. Of primary importance, serious, violent, and chronic offenders can be examined to explore the influence of different combinations of supervision, sanctions, and services. The feedback from such analyses will help identify system functions needing improvement and support data-driven decision-making in accomplishing those improvements. The overall objective, of course, is to optimize the juvenile justice system's ability to reduce recidivism and thereby enhance public safety while also promoting other positive youth outcomes that support the prosocial development of the youth served and, moreover, to do so in the most cost-effective manner possible. The paths that youths take through juvenile justice systems are very important for determining whether these outcomes will be attained (Mears et al., 2011). Excessive use of sanctions such as detention and confinement can dampen the effects of evidence-based services.

NOTES

1. http://www.casaforchildren.org.
2. The Washington State Institute for Public Policy is an applied research group of the Washington State legislature.
3. The raw age-crime curve line was displayed in Figure 2.1 of this handbook. The simulation reported here was applied to the same delinquent sample.

6

Initiating and Sustaining Evidence-based Practice

IN BRIEF

There are many challenging issues associated with translating evidence-based programs into routine practice in a way that replicates the relevant circumstances of the research that produced that evidence. Common barriers include the following (Howell and Lipsey, 2012; Lipsey et al., 2010; Welsh et al., 2010):

- Uncertainty about whether the program will have the same effects in the local context as it had in the research sites;
- Difficulties in matching the explicit program requirements that were established in research settings to the real-life organizational constraints faced by practitioners, for example, large caseloads, and resource limits on the types, frequency, and duration of services;
- The costs associated with purchasing these programs and the required support;
- Staff buy-in, upper management support, inadequate resources, and inflexible payment systems;
- A more heterogeneous population than that for which the program was designed, and an insufficient service infrastructure;
- Resistance by established providers to changing to a new program;
- Sustaining the program over time in the face of management turnover that comes with gubernatorial elections and new political appointments; and
- The limited number of certified programs may not match all the needs of a juvenile justice system.

A growing number of reports with disappointing outcomes of initiatives that involve moving evidence-based programs into practice have been published over the past decade. For example, there have been major shortcomings in achieving high fidelity with evidence-based substance abuse and violence prevention programs in community settings (Fagan et al., 2008)."Delivering interventions in a manner congruent with the theory, content, and methods of delivery specified by program developers is important, yet communities often fail to achieve implementation fidelity outside of efficacy trials" (p. 257). In school systems, despite a major national evidence-based initiative, several widely used substance abuse programs/curricula do not qualify as such (including McGruff the Crime Dog) and two national assessments found poor implementation for many evidence-based delinquency and violence prevention programs that the schools attempted to adopt (Gottfredson and Gottfredson, 2002; Hallfors and Godette, 2002). In the 1990s, the mental health field, along with social services and child welfare, began to identify and disseminate summaries of particular programs, evidence-based treatments (EBTs) that evidenced strong empirical evidence of effectiveness. But, some fifteen years later, it was apparent that "the vast majority of EBTs are not in widespread use" (Suter and Bruns, 2009, p. 336).

The desirable program effects on delinquency and subsequent offending found in research studies are often attenuated when those programs are scaled up or "rolled-out" for general application (Welsh et al., 2010). Provider adaptations are common in this process (Fixen, Naoom, Blase et al., 2005). Researchers (Berkel, Mauricio, Schoenfelder et al., 2011) identify four dimensions of implementation that likely account for variation in program delivery: (1) fidelity, (2) quality of delivery (how well the program's activities and materials are conveyed to program clients), (3) participant responsiveness (the extent to which program clients are engaged with the program's activities and materials), and (4) program adaptation. Generally speaking, it appears that the positive effects of evidence-based programs are highest in experimental sites selected and managed by the program developers, lower in sites not chosen but managed by them, and lowest in sites neither chosen nor managed by the program developers. When high fidelity is not achieved, outcomes are attenuated.

PASSIVE VERSUS ACTIVE EVIDENCE-BASED PRACTICE

The business of using scientific knowledge to solve practical problems is not new. It has a long history, and many names are used to describe this process, including *technology transfer, information or research utilization, dissemination,* and *organizational change* (Backer, 1993). Three prominent

American examples are: agricultural innovations (1920–1960), applications of defense and space-related research (1960–1980), and recent improvements in personal health (Backer, 1993). Support for using research to develop effective practice in crime prevention and rehabilitation is growing, following the lead set in medicine (Welsh and Farrington, 2006), but progress has been slow. "For many years, science to service has been seen as a passive process that involves diffusion and dissemination of information that somehow makes its way into the hands of enlightened champions, leaders, and practitioners who then put the innovations into practice" (Fixsen et al., 2009, p. 532). In this passive approach, bifurcated roles are described for researchers (who do their part by publishing their findings); "then it is up to managers and practitioners to do their part by reading the literature and making use of the innovations in their work with consumers" (p. 532). As Fixsen and colleagues note, this *passive* process has long served as the foundation for most U.S. federal and state policies related to making use of evidence-based programs and other human service innovations. In the past decade, a more *active* process for moving science to service has been attempted; for example, mandatory model program replications as a condition of federal and state funding, or a demonstrated resolve on the part of key stakeholders in troubled states that find themselves the subject of a federal lawsuit or consent decree to improve services. On the whole, the consensus of many observers is that the *passive* approach to EBP has not produced noteworthy results. In contrast, two contrasting *active* approaches to statewide EBP are discussed below that stand out for their accomplishments.

Prompted by new evidence-based juvenile justice legislation, the State of Washington integrated three model programs and two otherwise evidence-based programs into thirty-three juvenile courts (Barnoski, 2009): mainly Functional Family Therapy (FFT) (fourteen courts), and Aggression Replacement Training (ART) (twenty-six courts). Because of problems implementing the evaluation design, no findings are associated with the third model program, Multi-Systemic Therapy (MST). The juvenile courts also adopted the new Washington State Juvenile Court Assessment (WSJCA) system into daily court operations to provide valid risk assessments and facilitate matching of youth with placements and services. This impressive complement of programs and structured decision making tools generated positive cost-benefits statewide (Barnoski, 2004b, 2009). This is a sound evidence-based practice approach, first introducing the program on a pilot basis and then evaluating its effectiveness in the local context before expanding.

Beginning in 1998, at their own volition, Pennsylvania leaders began investing millions of dollars in ten EBP model programs, accompanied by a highly structured support system to help insure high fidelity to the original program model (Bumbarger, 2012; Moore, Bumbarger, and Cooper,

2013). Although Pennsylvania' overall recidivism rate is relatively low across the state (Pennsylvania Commission on Crime and Delinquency, 2013), a statewide study reported considerable loss of program fidelity despite enormous efforts to ensure high-quality implementation and sustainability of evidence-based programs (Rhoades et al., 2012). In an implementation study of the State's full complement of model programs (Moore et al., 2013), researchers combined Berkel and colleagues' (2011) four dimensions of implementation under the rubric of program "adaptation." Almost half (44 percent) of the Pennsylvania program implementers reported that they had made program adaptations. Among those providers who did make adaptations, 43 percent changed the procedures (the location or timing of the program), 42 percent changed the dosage, 38 percent changed the content, 22 percent made cultural adaptations, and 12 percent made adaptations to the target populations (those for whom the program was designed). When asked why these changes were made, the main reasons given were: lack of time (80 percent); limited resources (72 percent); difficulty retaining participants (71 percent); resistance from implementers (64 percent); difficulty recruiting participants (62 percent); participant dissatisfaction (61 percent); difficulty finding adequate staff (59 percent); and lack of cultural appropriateness (43 percent). "The majority of adaptations were made because of the logistical barriers that implementers face when transporting EBPs into the real world [how well the mechanics of the program align with the current delivery; e.g., timing, setting, target audience]. Moreover, the present findings suggest that if a program does not fit the context in which it is implemented, implementers are more likely to make reactive adaptations to it, which may lead to poor implementation quality and ultimately less-than-optimal outcomes" (Moore et al., 2013, p. 158). The research team also noted that providers' legitimate self-interests should be respected: ". . . providers have the need to preserve their workforce and to maintain positive relationships with key stakeholders" (Rhoades et al., 2012, p. 398).

Other early adopter state juvenile justice systems have implemented a number of evidence-based model programs that were not previously part of their repertoire. Greenwood and colleagues (Greenwood and Welsh, 2012; Greenwood, Welsh, and Rocque, 2012), for example, highlight the efforts of Connecticut, California, Florida, Hawaii, Louisiana, Maine, Maryland, New Mexico, and New York along with Pennsylvania and Washington. These states have been impressively proactive and progressive in adopting evidence-based model programs, developments that represent an important step forward for evidence-based practice that may well improve outcomes for the youth served in those states. However, no evidence has yet been provided about whether these programs were implemented as intended or whether they produced better outcomes than the programs they replaced.

The findings from these EBP initiatives are instructive, pointing to both successes and difficulties associated with aligning juvenile justice systems with evidence-based program requirements. The Washington State (Barnoski, 2004b, 2009) and Pennsylvania (Moore et al., 2013; Rhoades et al., 2012) experiences demonstrated that effective use of "off-the-shelf" program models requires significant start-up costs, sustained ties to the original program developers, and an extraordinary quality assurance effort to ensure that these programs fulfill their promise in statewide initiatives. Even then, certain service provider adaptations are inevitable. These conditions may well dampen the impacts of EBP model programs relative to the potential they have shown in the research studies that support them. Achieving the benefits of evidence-based programming not only requires selection of effective programs, but sustained efforts to implement them well.

THE CHALLENGES OF EVIDENCE-BASED INITIATION AND SUSTAINABILITY

After having reviewed nearly 400 studies across the human services for the purpose of synthesizing research in the area of implementation as well as to determine what is known about relevant components and conditions of implementation, Fixsen and colleagues (2009) observed that in the enterprise of translating "science *to* service," the *to* service action represents a specific set of activities called "implementation." Moreover, these researchers identified six functional stages of implementation: *exploration, installation, initial implementation, full implementation, innovation,* and *sustainability*. Fixsen and colleagues are quick to point out that the stages are not linear as each can impact the others in complex ways. "For example, sustainability factors are very much a part of exploration and exploration directly impacts installation and initial implementation. Or, an organization may move from full implementation to initial implementation in the midst of unusually high levels of staff turnover. The stages of implementation can be thought of as components of a tight circle with two-headed arrows from each to every other component" (Fixsen et al., 2009, p. 533).

Based on our experience to date in working with evidence-based programming in state juvenile justice systems, we recognize the utility of the implementation stages that Fixsen and colleagues identify. However, their review of the literature (Fixsen, Naoom, Blasé et al., 2005) focused on implementation of individual name brand programs such as the evidence-based model programs discussed above. For our purposes here, we want to apply these implementation stages to the process of system-wide implementation of evidence-based practices. Further, we consider evidence-based programs for juvenile offenders as encompassing both model programs assessed for fidelity and local generic programs assessed through the SPEP process that was described earlier. In our view, these two complementary approaches are required to establish evidence-based programming throughout a juvenile justice system.

This entire implementation process should be led and managed by a system-wide interagency Leadership Team comprised of managers of juvenile justice, social service, child welfare, health, education, and other agency representatives that also receive substantial input from parents and youth themselves. The first task, *exploration*, should be an assessment of system readiness for implementation of a comprehensive strategy. An example of such an assessment is one that was conducted for the Delaware juvenile justice system (Wilson, Kelly, and Howell, 2012). This objective assessment also needs to examine the quality and utility of any risk and needs assessment instruments already in use. Our review of such tools in this handbook noted that many risk assessment instruments are not suitable for reliably classifying offenders into risk levels. The risk assessment instrument must be validated on the offender population to which it is applied (ideally, all court referrals). A validated instrument is one that consistently classifies offenders into distinctive risk levels (low, medium, and high). Once this procedure is followed, the process of matching offenders with services is enhanced. A well-designed disposition matrix facilitates this matching process. For example, in Florida, Level 3 offenders are placed in community supervision (e.g., probation), while Level 4 offenders are placed in non-secure residential treatment (low and moderate risk programs). Next, graduated need assessments determine the specific generic services that are to be prescribed in conjunction with compatible scheduled supervision (e.g., standard or intensive supervision).

It is imperative that high-risk offenders are targeted as a main priority. The Leadership Team must also determine the availability and quality of existing management information systems (or client tracking systems, as some are called) for providing necessary data and other information to support fidelity assessment, quality assurance, and the SPEP instrument.

Next, the Leadership Team selects a pilot city, county, or court circuit for *initial implementation* of the selected reforms and structured decision-making instruments. These innovations need to be institutionalized via policy and procedural directives or manuals and onsite training at the outset to ensure adequate preparation in the pilot jurisdiction.

Installation of the new elements of the comprehensive strategy first occurs in the pilot jurisdiction. After successful pilot *installation* is achieved, roll-out across the state occurs in *full implementation*. In preparation for full implementation, additional *innovation* may be needed. For example, it may be necessary to right-size the juvenile justice system to optimize program matches to take full advantage of the utility of the overall strategy. If probation is overloaded with low risk offenders, for instance, the recidivism-reduction potential of evidence-based services is undermined. The importance of a disposition matrix that guides placements in a manner that protects the public and improves the matching of effective services with offender treatment needs cannot be overstated.

The last stage, *sustainability*, comes from having integrated the SPEP and associated procedures in ongoing operations. Once in place, the data collection needed to support the use of these instruments should be automated and routinized to the extent possible so that extraordinary efforts are not required to sustain them. For example, some systems have portions of the risk assessment instrument filled in electronically from the juvenile's prior record. Similarly, guidance from the disposition matrix can be generated automatically from the risk and other relevant data, SPEP ratings can be periodically generated from program and client data, and so forth. In addition, tools are available to facilitate continuum building and identification of gaps in a state's repertoire of service programs given the risk and treatment need profiles of current offender caseloads. Sustainability naturally comes from shifting to a data-driven system in this manner, and from strengthening the JJ system infrastructure. The Florida Department of Juvenile Justice's progress in developing a data intensive system of this general sort provides an example of what can be accomplished.[1] The ideal is for JJ system managers and service providers to undertake this process in a constructive manner that builds on the common desire of all participants to provide the most effective services possible to juvenile offenders. Another example is "Pennsylvania's Juvenile Justice System Enhancement Strategy" (Pennsylvania Commission on Crime and Delinquency, 2012b).

NOTE

1. http://www.djj.state.fl.us/research/latest-initiatives/juvenile-justice-system-improvement-project-(jjsip).

7

✛

Eight Key Administrative Tools that Support Evidence-Based Programming

IN BRIEF

Structured decision-making tools used as part of standard operating procedures in JJ systems are vital for a sustained commitment to evidence-based practice in the face of the inevitable drift and variability of individual judgment, personnel turnover, and periodic changes in leadership and political context. Viewed broadly, these administrative tools undergird the Comprehensive Strategy framework by helping right-size JJ systems so that offenders are positioned at the proper risk level to protect the public and achieve good matches with existing services. State governments are statutorily mandated to protect the public, and JJ systems are required to accomplish this in dual roles, by constraining *and* rehabilitating juvenile offenders. To meet statutory mandates and succeed in rehabilitating juvenile offenders, three principles should be followed (Slobogin, 2013; Slobogin and Fondacaro, 2011). First, risk assessment should be continuous, not limited to intake or adjudication functions, so as to manage risk in all JJ system stages (including intake, detention, adjudication, probation, confinement, and reentry). Second, given the inexorably linked risk-treatment function, assessments must address both risk and rehabilitation of offenders, and *in concert*. Third, risk and need assessments should dovetail in a comprehensive but flexible risk management plan designed to ameliorate dynamic factors that exist outside offenders' static (unchangeable) offense histories. This general rehabilitative function is often characterized as increasing protective factors or reducing criminogenic factors—also called dynamic risk factors—that include negative peer associations, substance abuse, and antisocial attitudes, values, and beliefs supportive of criminal behavior. In this scheme, the philosophy of JJ systems is focused less on punishment than on prevention and risk management, and using graduated sanctions to stabilize offenders and give treatment a chance to work.

Many states are struggling with weak instruments for assessing risk of recidivism, and few of these have been validated on the population to which they are applied. The practice of combining assessments of risk and treatment needs in the same instrument has complicated matters. Tools proffered in many states for assessing treatment needs are ill-suited for this purpose, often measuring psychological problems and a large number of protective factors that cannot easily be addressed. As a result of these complications, many state juvenile justice systems are overwhelmed with unmanageable risk-need instruments that are misused, require excessive amounts of staff time to complete, and often produce a mound of data that program administrators and supervisors do not have the staff capacity to analyze nor put to good use in everyday practice.

Seven administrative tools empower JJ systems to meet their dual statutory mandates. First, valid risk assessment instruments (RAIs) can sort offenders into distinguishable risk categories for assignment to supervision levels to protect the public and themselves. Second, comprehensive assessments of treatment needs guide the selection of services most likely to reduce recidivism. These assessments should identify and prioritize services to address circumstances that contribute to delinquency in the developmentally relevant family, school, peer, individual, and/or community domains. Third, graduated assessments (increasingly in-depth) will be required for some offenders, particularly those with substance abuse and mental health problems, to obtain a more accurate assessment of presenting problems. Fourth, disposition matrices serve the dual goals of assigning offenders to appropriate supervision levels to protect the public and also facilitate matching offenders with developmentally appropriate services at the respective supervision levels. Fifth, comprehensive case plans integrate supervision strategies with treatment services. Sixth, quality assurance procedures must be established to ensure that case management plans are implemented with fidelity. Seventh, a management information system is needed to track clients and service delivery, and evaluate outcomes. Eighth, this entire process is best supported by formalized court standards.

BENEFITS OF STRUCTURED DECISION MAKING TOOLS

A broad strategy for optimizing the use of risk and needs assessment instruments focuses on statewide JJ systems with the aim of improving services across the entire system (Lipsey et al., 2010). Several administrative tools enable court and corrections officials to consistently and effectively carry out the mission of the juvenile justice system. The past decade has seen a virtual explosion of risk assessments instruments for a wide variety of child and adolescent problem behaviors, including delinquency, violence, substance abuse, mental health, abuse and neglect, and sex offending. The use of various "structured decision making" (SDM) tools, particularly risk and need assessment instruments (including rudimentary ones) grew from only one-third of all state JJ systems in 1990 (Towberman, 1992) to nearly nine out of ten states by 2011.[1] There are several key areas in which there is widespread agreement among researchers and practitioners on SDM instruments (Lipsey et al., 2010; Wiebush, 2002; Young, Moline, Farrell, and Bierie, 2006). Standardized instruments can:

- Lead to more effective treatment and placement decisions,
- Guide supervision plans,
- Reduce disparity in decisions,
- Improve the management of youth within juvenile justice system settings,
- Predict recidivism and institutional adjustment,
- Measure rehabilitative progress in treatment,
- Increase staff accountability and improve consistency in the treatment of youth, and
- Provide agencies with important information about the service use and gaps.

In short, SDM instruments can be of great utility in client risk assessment, problem diagnosis, service linkage, and case management. Unfortunately, the state-of-the-art of risk and treatment needs assessment and service matching in the United States presently is at a crossroad, having been complicated by misguided efforts. Key concerns internationally include the following (Baird et al., 2013; Miller and Maloney, 2013; Shook and Sarri, 2007; Van Domburg, Vermeiren, and Doreleijers, 2008):

- Lengthy instruments that are time-consuming for staff and may place an unnecessary burden on parents and youth.
- Assessment that is seldom based on multi-phase or longitudinal screening techniques.
- Inappropriate attempts to adapt instruments designed for older age groups for use with children.
- Differences that may appear in screening and assessment results and create confusion.

- Duplication of assessments that creates confusion in the parents and children, particularly in not knowing what can be expected from the various agencies.
- Lack of cooperation and sharing of results across agencies.
- Lengthy instruments that are not well-suited for everyday practice in JJ systems with a large volume of cases.

Two multi-state studies have compared everyday practice in risk/need assessment tool usage with expectations. In a study of twelve courts that implemented risk assessment procedures in four states in 1999–2000—Illinois, Indiana, Michigan, and Ohio—researchers found that use of risk and needs assessments can be challenging (Shook and Sarri, 2007). None of these states was following best-practice guidelines in risk and needs assessment procedures. Researchers surveyed probation officers, judges, defense attorneys, and prosecutors, asking them a variety of questions concerning current practices in their respective states and their opinion of SDM tools, as well as their perspectives on general and specific issues of juvenile justice system administration. Despite finding that most officials at both the court and state levels had positive views of SDM tools and felt that these had the potential to make case processing more fair and effective, only half of the court professionals (including probation officers) were consistently using the tools in their decision-making. Even when SDM tools were used, there were various constraints that affected their everyday use. The results also indicated that many court professionals did not place a high level of value on different SDM components and did not consider them to be particularly useful at various decision-making points. Of particular concern, the research revealed a lack of sensitivity to agency responsibilities at the moment a youth is referred to courts and social service agencies. As Shook and Sarri note (2007), "the broader evidence-based practice movement in social work and related fields advocates for practice to be informed by the best available evidence at the point of contact with the individual client" (p. 1350). Even so, practitioners sometimes attempt to alter or influence assessment results to fit their subjective judgments or personal goals for their clients (Gebo, Stracuzzi, and Hurst, 2006; Miller and Maloney, 2013).

A national survey of American Probation and Parole Association members (Miller and Maloney, 2013) explored the frequency of noncompliance in risk/need assessment tool usage among community corrections practitioners, whether groups of practitioners could be distinguished according to their patterns of compliance and noncompliance, and factors associated with these patterns. This study identified three distinct groups of practitioners, according to their patterns of compliance with respect to completing tools on clients and making decisions consistent with risk and need principles. Nearly half of the surveyed practitioners could be characterized as *substantive* compliers; that is, they largely completed tools carefully and honestly and made decisions in line with tool recommendations. Even so, this group was prone to seeking more restrictive options for offenders, or targeting needs not highlighted by the tool. The *bureaucratic* compliers—representing a substantial minority of the tool-using practitioners—by and large completed their tools as required but were generally less likely to make decisions based on the tool results. Last, a small group of *cynical* compliers was identified (comprising about one in eight of the tool-using practitioners). The members of this group subverted established procedures by manipulating results in accordance with their "clinical" judgment, and they often disregarded the final tool results in their decision-making.

RISK ASSESSMENT

The main purpose of risk assessment in the JJ system is to assess risk of committing another offense. Put simply, a risk factor means a variable associated with the probability of offending. Early and persistent delinquency involvement is the best predictor of future delinquency, thus actuarial risk instruments must prominently rely on *static factors* that can no longer be influenced (e.g., age of first arrest or conviction, number of previous arrests, convictions, or incarcerations, runaway episodes, etc.), but also include *dynamic factors* that are malleable (e.g., current peers, substance use, or family relationships) that can strengthen predictions. In constructing a risk assessment instrument, "each risk factor is given a specific weight depending on its presence or absence in the individual case examined and on its importance in the general pattern of risk" for a group of persons (Zara and Farrington, 2013, p. 235). In such instruments developed within the field of criminology, static predictive factors are integrated with dynamic factors. Some of the dynamic dimensions are of a psychological nature (e.g., criminal thinking errors), also called "criminogenic needs," those that are functionally related to criminal behavior. More broadly, "need is an indicator of the extent to which either daily functioning is altered or protective factors are reduced in warding off criminal engagement. If one way to enhance prediction is to focus on risk factors and to enhance protective factors, one way to serve prevention is to concentrate on a reliable process of risk assessment that looks at risks and needs in their temporal influential occurrence" (Zara and Farrington, 2013, p. 236).

Risk assessment and classification is one of the cornerstones of a systematic response to juvenile offenders that achieves twin goals of protecting the public and reducing their criminality. Achieving both of these goals

---

BOX 7.1

GENERATIONS OF RISK AND NEED ASSESSMENT INSTRUMENTS

The first generation of risk assessments was strictly clinical judgments, unstructured professional opinion. Risk levels were assigned by individual workers without the aid of actuarial instruments (defined below).

Second generation instruments were statistically derived, but relied heavily on static criminal history factors to assess risk. These tools typically were developed using local data for specific jurisdictions. Dynamic factors soon were included (changeable risk factors that can affect behavior) while restricting these instruments to fewer than a dozen factors.

Third generation tools utilize both clinical and actuarial methods to systematically measure static and "dynamic risk" or "criminogenic needs" factors, while including a broader sampling of dynamic risk items. These third generation tools tend to be more theoretically informed.

Fourth generation tools combined risk and need assessments and promote service planning and delivery. These tools also seek to identify key "responsivity characteristics" (amenability to treatment) to facilitate the matching of interventions to offenders.

> Definition: *Actuarial assessments* "are developed by observing the behavioral outcomes of interest to the predictive enterprise. Empirical research procedures are employed to identify a set of risk factors with a strong statistical relationship to the behavioral outcome. These are then weighted and combined to form an assessment tool that optimally classifies families or individuals according to the risk that they will exhibit the behavior" (Shlonsky and Wagner, 2005, p. 410).

Sources: Andrews, Bonta and Wormith, 2006; Baird et al., 2013; Shlonsky and Wagner, 2005

---

is more realistic when SVC offenders are selected for closer surveillance and more intensive treatment. "A valid, reliable, and equitable assessment of risk, when used in concert with sound clinical judgment and effective delivery of appropriate services, can be essential to treatment and rehabilitation" (Baird et al., 2013, p. 1). Some offenders require substantial service intervention and supervision (high risk), a broad group consists of moderately serious offenders (medium risk, for whom standard supervision is appropriate), and others who are unlikely to persist in delinquency (low risk, for whom diversion or only short-term supervision with only minimal services is needed). Research supporting the validity of RAIs has increased dramatically in recent years (Baird, 2009; Hoge and Andrews, 2010; Hoge, Vincent, and Guy, 2012; Olver, Stockdale, and Wormith, 2009;

Schwalbe, 2007) entirely, or largely, on literature reviews of prediction research; not on the population to which they are applied. In general, proper use of risk instruments is not particularly advanced at this time (Baird, 2009; Baird et al., 2013; Gottfredson and Moriarty, 2006). Two key issues presently confound the risk assessment enterprise: the issue of clinical judgment versus actuarial predictions, and the use of static versus dynamic predictors. Discussion of these issues follows, after which important risk assessment instrument performance criteria are presented.

The first issue concerns the utility of clinical judgment versus actuarial predictions. There are three basic approaches to risk assessment: staff judgments, clinical or psychological assessments, and assessments using actuarial (research-based) instruments (Gottfredson and Moriarty, 2006; Wiebush, 2002). A formal, structured approach to decision making is considered critical because subjective, informal methods result in inconsistent and frequently inappropriate decisions, often resulting in over-classification (i.e., too many false positives) (Wiebush, 2002). Inconsistencies in decision making can lead to handling youth with similar characteristics in very different ways, thereby violating a fundamental principle of justice. Dissatisfaction with the inconsistencies that came with use of unstructured clinical risk assessments prompted the development of actuarial risk instruments (Slobogin, 2013).

Clinical predictions have been shown to be significantly less accurate than assessments using empirically derived tools. In a comparison of clinical judgments with actuarial approaches, actuarial methods performed better than clinical procedures in 46 percent of the studies and equally well in 48 percent, whereas clinical judgments outperformed actuarial prediction in only 6 percent of the studies (Grove et al., 1990; for a summary of this study, see Grove and Meehl, 1996). In a more recent review of sixty-seven studies, the overall effect of clinical versus statistical prediction showed a somewhat greater accuracy for statistical methods in predicting a variety of outcomes (Ægisdóttir, White, Spengler et al., 2006). One area in which the statistical method proved clearly superior to clinical judgment is the prediction of violence. Out of 1,000 predictions of client violence, the statistical method can be expected to correctly identify 90 more violent clients than the clinical method. "The victims of violence would not consider this effect small" (p. 368).

The second confounding issue concerns the uses of static versus dynamic risk factors in risk assessment tools. Because earlier delinquency involvement is the best predictor of future delinquency, actuarial risk instruments must include *static factors* (e.g., age of first arrest or conviction, number of previous arrests, convictions, or incarcerations, runaway episodes, etc.) along with *dynamic factors*. In juvenile court files, the latter items are "social history" factors that increase risk of persistent delinquency, particularly substance use, poor school performance, parental abuse or neglect, family conflict, and association with delinquent peers. A combination of both sets of factors will yield the most reliable and current prediction. In fourteen actuarial risk assessment instrument validations, a combination of "static" factors and social history produced the most accurate overall predictions of recidivism and good separation of offenders into risk levels (Wiebush, 2002).

It is important to incorporate static factors in prediction instruments for another reason. The influence of most dynamic risk factors *decreases* as the age of the juveniles increases (Loeber, Slott, and Stouthamer-Loeber, 2008; Tanner-Smith et al., 2013a), indicating that the chances of reducing recidivism according to the needs principle is in large part limited to the childhood and early adolescent periods. In a state-wide Washington study using the Washington State Juvenile Court Assessment (WSJCA) instrument to identify recidivism predictors, researchers found that "the impact of almost all dynamic risk factors from almost every domain on recidivism was found to become weaker with increasing age" with an average decrease of 40 percent in the importance of the dynamic factors over the entire period of adolescence, and a 25 percent decrease between the ages of 12 and 13 (Van der Put, Dekovic, Stams et al., 2012, pp. 312, 314).

Much stock is wrongly placed in the overall predictive accuracy of an instrument, which is of little practical value for JJ system purposes. The key feature for JJ use is the degree to which instruments are capable of "discriminating between groups of youth with higher and lower rates of recidivism and the distribution of cases across the risk continuum" (Baird et al., 2013, p. 21). Studies show that risk assessment instruments have much higher validity when they are generated from actual recidivism data on the population to which they are to be applied in everyday practice (Austin, 2006; Baird, 2009; Baird et al., 2013; Weibush, 2002). Risk assessment tools should help JJ systems more effectively target limited resources to achieve desired outcomes.

A multi-state comparative study of risk assessment instruments was carried out in 2010–2012 to assess how widely used risk assessment tools perform in practice in JJ systems and to provide advice regarding the selection of the most appropriate instruments (Baird et al., 2013). This study examined the validity, reliability, equity, and cost of the following nine juvenile risk assessment instruments currently in use in JJ systems in several states:

- Juvenile Sanctions Center (JSC) Risk Assessment Instrument,
- Girls Link risk assessment instrument,
- Positive Achievement Change Tool (PACT),
- Youth Assessment and Screening Instrument (YASI),

BOX 7.2

A PRIMER ON RISK ASSESSMENT
INSTRUMENT PERFORMANCE CRITERIA

Juvenile justice system officials should consider four performance criteria when evaluating a risk assessment tool: validity, equity, reliability, and cost. In general, *validity* is the extent to which an instrument measures what it is intended to measure. For JJ system purposes, this outcome is recidivism. Although there are several statistical indicators of validity (Baird et al., 2013) the most important one for JJ system operations is "the level of separation in recidivism results attained between groups at various risk classifications and whether offenders are grouped into risk classifications of meaningful size" (p. 19). Thus, any RAI that demonstrates reasonably good separation (percentage groupings) between low, medium, and high risk groups that also predict co-varying recidivism rates has validity. "The combination of separation (or discrimination between recidivism rates for each classification) and the distribution of cases across the risk continuum is a meaningful measure of the risk assessment instrument's performance in practice" (p. 19). In sum, an actuarial risk assessment can a) identify the most relevant risk factors, b) assign appropriate weights to each factor, and c) determine effective thresholds for classifying placements into groups with distinctly different likelihoods of subsequent delinquency.

The importance of regular, comprehensive evaluation of an actuarial risk tool's performance under field conditions, including the policy context, cannot be overstated. Clearly, research supports risk assessment instruments that empower authorities to identify groups of juveniles with a relatively high probability of future offenses early in their careers so that more intensive intervention can be directed to them. Because different intervention programs address various risk factors, this research provides some basis for matching programs with offenders in ways that should improve outcomes. Without exception, it is essential to validate risk assessment instruments on the population to which they are applied. The validation process is straightforward (Baird et al., 2013; Dedel-Johnson and Hardyman, 2004). It also is important that these instruments accurately estimate recidivism likelihood across racial/ethnic, gender, and age groups. This is evidence that a risk assessment tool is *equitable*.

Reliability measures the consistency of assessments between officers and caseworkers, which is crucial for equity; ideally staff should assess risk in the same way when provided the same case information. A reliable risk assessment tool can help increase the consistency of workers' assessments by providing clear decision thresholds against which to measure evidence (also called inter-rater reliability). The key test of inter-rater reliability is whether

(continued)

BOX 7.2 *(Continued)*

staff consistently classifies offenders in the same subgroups or classes. If this requirement is not met at an acceptable level, the instruments cannot then attain high validity. Low reliability often occurs because the staff lacks adequate training and quality control monitoring, or instruments are used that are too lengthy and/or require high levels of subjective judgment or information that is not typically available. High inter-rater reliability is a basic requirement for consistent and equitable decision making about the juveniles being assessed. Low inter-rater reliability degrades instrument validity and reduces its everyday practical utility. Staff performing assessments must receive training, monitoring, and certification to bring practice into compliance with expected standards. Last, the risk assessment must not be costly with regard to either allocation of staff resources or expenditures. Some assessment procedures can require two or more hours to complete, greatly reducing their utility and possibly their reliability as well (Baird et al., 2013).

Unfortunately, the risk assessment instruments currently used in many states do not adequately group offenders by level of recidivism risk and thus are of limited utility in carrying out basic JJ system functions. To achieve the largest and most cost-effective benefits from evidence-based programs and services, it is essential that risk assessment instruments accurately classify low-, medium-, and high-risk youth, so as to allow predominantly high-risk offenders to be targeted for appropriate supervision and programming. In sum, the key principles for best practice are:

- Keep it simple. Short instruments are most easily implemented and have better inter-rater reliability.
- Use actuarial instruments that accurately, reliably, and equitably group offenders into risk levels.
- Include static and dynamic factors. This combination yields the best recidivism predictions.
- Re-administer risk instruments when new offenses occur to keep risk assessment current.
- Provide extensive staff training and monitoring on the assessment process and tools.
- Revalidate instruments periodically (every few years).

Perhaps most important, the inclusion of non-validated factors for recidivism introduces substantial "noise" and dilutes the relationship between legitimate risk factors and recidivism. In most cases, analysts can identify a parsimonious set of factors in lengthy instruments that can be relied upon to increase the validity of unwieldy and unreliable instruments.

- Youth Level of Service/Case Management Inventory (YLS/CMI),
- Comprehensive Risk and Needs Assessment (CRN, a derivative of COMPAS Youth),
- Arizona Administrative Office of the Courts risk assessment instrument,
- Arizona Department of Juvenile Correction Dynamic Risk Instrument (DRI), and the
- Oregon Juvenile Crime Prevention (JCP) Assessment.

In this landmark study—the only comparative juvenile offender risk assessment validation study to date in any country—comparable data from the state or county in which tested instruments had been deployed were used to test their validity and reliability.[2] The JSC Risk Assessment Instrument used in Solano County, California (in the populous San Francisco bay area), proved to be the most valid of the nine juvenile justice risk assessment instruments currently in use. "This assessment produced the highest absolute level of discrimination attained between high-, moderate-, and low-risk youth" (p. 86).

The JSC Risk Assessment Instrument is a composite tool generated from a total of fourteen validation studies in all regions of the United States (Wiebush, 2002).[3] It consists of just ten items:

1. Age at first referral to juvenile court intake
2. Number of referrals to intake
3. Number of referrals for violent offenses
4. Number of prior out-of-home placements
5. School discipline/attendance issues
6. Substance abuse
7. Peer relationships
8. Prior abuse or neglect
9. Parental supervision
10. Parent/sibling criminality

The first four items in this model instrument are static factors that reliably predict recidivism. The last six items are dynamic risk factors spanning the school (discipline/attendance), individual (substance abuse), peer (delinquent relationships), and family (child abuse or neglect, supervision, and parent/sibling criminality) domains.

There are two research-supported explanations for the superior performance of the JSC tool. First, it contains key risk factors in important developmental domains in studies that predict juvenile delinquency. "Data from prediction studies indicate that risk factors from each of the domains (individual, family, peers, schools and neighborhoods) contribute to the explanation of why some individuals and not others progress from minor problem behaviors such as bullying, to physical fighting and to violence" (Loeber, Slott, and Stouthamer-Loeber, 2008, p. 140). Second, the JSC instrument is a composite of fourteen previously validated actuarial instruments for predicting juvenile recidivism elsewhere. Each of those fourteen jurisdictions used similar instruments that were validated on cases therein. Items included on the JSC Risk Assessment Instrument were those that (1) appeared on all or nearly all instruments or (2) were found on the majority of instruments and exhibited particularly strong relationships to recidivism. A virtually identical combination of static and dynamic (social history) items was used in each of these well-validated instruments. The consistently best performing items comprise the model Juvenile Sanctions Center (JSC) Risk Assessment Instrument promulgated by the National Council of Juvenile and Family Court Judges' (NCJFCJ), an OJJDP-supported initiative (Wiebush, 2002).

To examine its broader utility, the NCCD research team simulated the use of the JSC instrument in two of the largest sites, Florida and Georgia, finding that it performed more effectively in those states than the risk tools currently in place (Baird et al., 2013). The Girls Link instrument did not produce results comparable to those produced for the boys' instrument. The degree of separation attained for outcomes, while substantial, was lower than that attained for boys. Minor revisions to the Girls Link instrument improved both the level of discrimination attained and the distribution across risk levels.

Across the multiple study sites, the instruments that performed poorly did not employ standard actuarial methods of development. Instead, those sub-standard instruments usually contained risk factors identified through literature reviews of research studies elsewhere and in some cases were based on theories of criminal behavior.

Two readily recognized instruments currently used by multiple states were not included in the NCCD study. A suitable database for a comparable study was not available at the time the study was launched to include the Ohio Youth Assessment System (OYAS) and the Washington State Juvenile Court Assessment Instrument (WSJCA), a risk assessment instrument developed in the state of Washington in the 1990s at the Washington State Institute of Public Policy that had been validated in 2004. The twenty-seven-item pre-screen risk assessment had moderate predictive ability in estimating the likelihood of recidivism (Barnoski, 2004a).

Another actuarial risk assessment instrument not included in the NCCD study has demonstrated excellent predictive validity. Modeled closely after the NCJFCJ JSC Risk Assessment Instrument, the *North Carolina Assessment of Risk* (NCAR) is comprised of both static risk factors and dynamic risk items. The NCAR is one of the fourteen validated tools upon which the model JSC RAI was constructed. The NCAR consists of just nine items that together comprise a total risk score in the same methodology as the JSC Risk Assessment Instrument. Overall, the NCAR has strong validation from tests of its predictive validity in four independent validations and also good evidence of high inter-rater reliability (Fraser, Day, and Schwalbe, 2002; Schwalbe, Fraser, and Day, 2007; Schwalbe, Fraser, Day, and Arnold, 2004; Schwalbe, Fraser, Day, and Cooley, 2006). Like the GSC Risk Assessment Instrument, the brevity of this tool gives it the advantage of being completed easily by juvenile justice personnel with very little staff training.

Several of the lengthy instruments commonly used also attempt to assess the presence of a broad range of protective factors that presumably help with risk reduction, but this approach can confound risk prediction. The inclusion of non-validated factors for recidivism introduces substantial "noise" and dilutes the relationship between legitimate risk factors and recidivism (Baird, 2009; Baird et al., 2013). Other recommendations that can improve instrument use include these (Miller and Maloney, 2013, p. 732):

- Agencies should select risk/needs assessment tools that assure confidence of both the agency managers and the frontline staff who are required to use it on a daily basis;

BOX 7.3

AN EXAMPLE OF AN EMPIRICALLY
GENERATED RISK ASSESSMENT INSTRUMENT

The Orange County, CA, 8% Early Intervention Program was based on an analysis of more than 6,000 prior court referrals that led to the creation of an actuarial risk assessment to screen referrals to the program. This analysis distinguished three groups of court referrals, a high risk SVC group (8 percent), a moderate risk group (22 percent) and a low risk group (70 percent) (Schumaker and Kurz, 2000). The criteria in offense and social histories that best predicted recidivism were: chronic family dysfunction (abuse/neglect, criminal family members, lack of parental supervision and control), significant school problems (truancy, failing multiple courses, and/or recent suspension or expulsion), a pattern of individual problems (drug and/or alcohol use), and predelinquent behavior patterns (youth gang involvement, chronic running away, and/or stealing). Youngsters with first-time court referrals who scored high in three of these four risk domains were very likely to become SVC offenders (i.e., appear later in the 8 percent group).

- Training curricula should be detailed, going beyond the technical aspects of tool use to encompass rationales for their use, and the local tool's correspondence with these principles; and
- Monitoring should focus on completed use, the quality of tool completion, and the fidelity of decision-making and case planning based on tool results.

NEEDS ASSESSMENT INSTRUMENTS

Use of treatment needs assessments instruments (NAIs) has a shorter history than RAIs. Needs assessments first came into vogue as a result of dissatisfaction with exclusive reliance on clinical assessments. Thus best practice standards for the use of needs assessments are less well formulated. Many of the items in lengthy widely promoted instruments that attempt to identify treatment needs do not map onto the main sectors of offenders' lives that can contribute to recidivism: particularly troubled families, school problems, deviant peer groups, and individual problems (e.g., substance use). If these problems are not properly assessed, then juvenile courts and correctional agencies are ill equipped to match offenders' treatment needs to services that reduce recidivism.

This process commences with pre-screens that are administered by court intake workers or court counselors/probation officers following a brief interview with the child and parents. Information also comes from collateral sources such as child welfare records, parent and mental health service reports, and school records. The most highly recommended instrument for this purpose is the "Model Youth and Family Assessment of Needs and Strengths" adopted by the NCJFCJ (Wiebush 2002). This tool is a "structured needs assessment" that provides a simple, easy-to-use overview of an offender's problems along with family treatment needs (and social strengths of both) for the case manager, program staff, and service providers. This model NAI tool also groups offenders into low, medium, and high need, which is useful in setting service priorities and for service matching purposes. Periodic reassessments of treatment needs also help case managers monitor client progress and can indicate when adjustments might be needed in individual treatment regimens. Finally, aggregated information derived from needs assessments provides a database for agency planning and evaluation, especially for determining whether there are sufficient treatment resources in the community to meet current client treatment needs.

The following are main purposes of treatment need assessments (Wiebush 2002).

- Provide a simple, easy-to-use overview of an individual's problems for the case manager, program staff, and service providers.

- Provide a brief profile of each offender's priority treatment needs.
- Ensure that all staff examine treatment issues consistently for all youth.
- Generate summaries of needs assessments that encapsulate information in a cumulative format so that it can be used in setting priorities (gaps in needed services).
- Devote more time to cases with elevated treatment needs.
- Periodic reassessments help case managers monitor client progress (at least monthly for probation clients; more often for confined youth).
- Pinpoint key treatment needs of juvenile offenders that are found in the following social development domains:
  - Family (poor parental supervision and family conflict)
  - School (attendance, performance, suspension, expulsion, drop-out)
  - Peers (peer delinquency and gang involvement)
  - Individual (substance abuse, mental health)

To facilitate matching of services to offender needs, it is important that NAIs target research-based developmental needs of adjudicated juvenile offenders. Two statewide treatment needs studies have compiled illustrative summaries. In the North Carolina analysis of nearly 9,000 youth adjudicated in 2008, the following priority and overlapping treatment needs were identified: serious school problems (drop-out, expulsion, long-term suspension), substance abuse; negative peer associations; and parents unwilling or unable to supervise their children (Lassiter, Clarkson, and Howell, 2009).The State of North Carolina uses the Model Youth and Family Assessment of Needs and Strengths instrument endorsed by the NCJFCJ Juvenile Sanctions Center (Wiebush, 2002). One of the important features of this tool is inclusion of indicators of gang involvement. Figure 7.1 illustrates how the predominant treatment needs can overlap, requiring the matching of multiple treatment services and supports.[4]

A similar Texas study (Kelly, Macy, and Mears, 2005) examined the need characteristics of more than 100,000 juveniles referred to seven county probation departments in the state. Combining both high and medium assessed needs, the most commonly identified needs were problems with parental supervision (47 percent), school attendance/enrollment (43 percent), family relationships (32 percent), and substance abuse (31 percent). Taken together, these two large-scale studies show the most common treatment needs and suggest the importance of prioritizing them in a continuum of services.

Surprisingly, research has not yet advanced to the point of demonstrating the prospect of lower recidivism when multiple treatment needs are addressed, though there is some evidence to this effect (Vieira, Skilling, and Peterson-Badali, 2009). "The present research suggests the need for

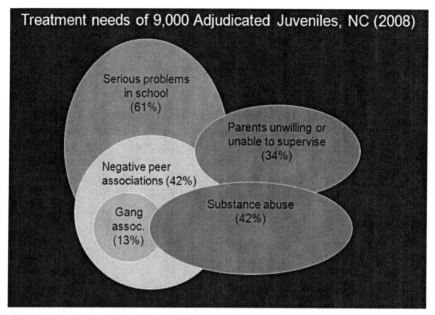

Figure 7.1.   Overlapping Treatment Needs
Reference: Lassiter, W., Clarkson, S., and Howell, M. Q. (2009). *North Carolina Department of Juvenile Justice and Delinquency Prevention Annual Report, 2008.* Raleigh, NC: North Carolina Department of Juvenile Justice and Delinquency Prevention.

efforts to ensure better and more consistent matching of services with youths' clinically identified needs, as doing so appears to lead to reduced recidivism and improvements in youths' functioning" (p. 396). Yet this is a challenging exercise, for youths' most pressing treatment needs often are not met (Kelly, Macy, and Mears, 2005; Singh, Desmarais, Sellers et al., 2013). Offender-service matching is discussed below, following some lead-in discussion of ways of achieving evidence-based practice and presentation of a general framework for managing offenders system-wide.

Every effort should be made to resist the temptation to ask court staff to do anything more than preliminary treatment need assessments. This effort will not prove useful because intake workers or probation officers are not trained to make diagnostic assessments (e.g., of mental health problems). Court intake workers are trained only to assemble available information—typically from police, school, and court records—along with interviews of parents, teachers, and the youths themselves in compiling what generally are called "social histories." Schwalbe and colleagues (2008), for example, implemented an instrument in a sample of courts that included questions about clinical behavioral problems. As a result of placing unwarranted expectations on court staff, distorted findings were produced. Most noticeably, this procedure failed to identify family-related problems among the top needs of juvenile offenders although these clearly are central to delinquency involvement as shown in the North Carolina and Texas studies noted above, and also in needs assessments in many other states (Wiebush, 2002).

Two blended risk-need assessment tools are widely used. Troubled by the findings of American researchers that "nothing works" in correctional treatment (Martinson, 1974), disbelieving Canadian criminologists (and an American, Francis Cullen, University of Cincinnati) set out to ascertain if this conclusion was justified in adult corrections. Discovering that some things do in fact work to reduce crime in adult criminals (Gendreau, 1981; Andrews, Bonta, and Hoge 1990; Andrews et al., 1990), these scholars sought to formulate principles of effective correctional intervention based on favorably evaluated programs and research on criminal orientations. This initiative led to the development of the risk-need-responsivity (RNR) model, a popular psychologically informed approach to adult correctional treatment that is grounded in three principles found in that research literature (Andrews and Bonta, 2006, 2010a, 2010b):

Risk principle: Match the level of service to the offender's risk to re-offend.
Need principle: Assess criminogenic needs and target them in treatment.
Responsivity principle: Maximize the offender's ability to learn from a rehabilitative intervention.

More recently, Andrews (2006, pp. 596–600) details the principles of effective correctional intervention as follows:

- Use structured and validated risk or needs assessment instruments.
- Never assign low risk cases to intensive service.
- Reserve intensive services for moderate and higher-risk cases.
- Always target a preponderance of relevant criminogenic needs.
- Always use cognitive-behavioral and social learning interpersonal influence strategies.
- Managers and supervisors must attend to the relationship and structural skills of service delivery staff.
- Clinical supervision entails regular ongoing high-level modeling and reinforcement of relationship and structuring skills.
- Make monitoring, feedback, and corrective action routine, as a matter of policy.

Despite Andrews' and colleagues' pioneering and salutary work, for many years the United States' criminal justice system did not make advancements in evidence-based practices such as those that have been adopted in many JJ systems. During most of the twentieth century, state sentencing policies were primarily offender-oriented, buttressed by a new "just deserts" philosophy in the latter decades (Tonry, 2009). Warren (2007), a former president of the National Center for State Courts, issued a clarion call to the United States criminal justice system to embrace evidence-based practices. Six years later, Taxman (2013a, 2013b) developed the Risk, Need, and Responsivity (RNR) Simulation Tool to help jurisdictions apply the RNR framework when working with adult offenders. The theoretical framework builds upon Andrews and Bonta's (2010a, 2010b) Risk-Need-Responsivity principles.

- *Risk Principle*: Offenders can vary by probability of recidivism, and the calculation of risk includes static factors that cannot decrease over time including age of first arrest, number of prior arrests, etc.
- *Need Principle*: "Criminogenic needs are dynamic factors that drive participation in criminal offending and are amenable to change. Supervision, correctional, and/or treatment staff can assess these factors and target them for reduction through treatment and controls. Targeting needs (i.e., drug dependence and criminal lifestyle) is one way to reduce individuals' overall risk of recidivism" (p. 2).
- *Responsivity Principle*: refers to matching individuals to appropriate treatment programming interventions geared toward the offender's abilities and motivation (generally cognitive behavioral or social learning interventions).

Modeled after the original RNR framework, a juvenile offender application has been developed, the Ohio Youth Assessment System (OYAS). It was designed to assist juvenile justice professionals in case management across the system in providing the most effective interventions for youth based on their likelihood to reoffend, their criminogenic needs, and their barriers to services, while using the least restrictive alternative (Latessa, Lovins, and Ostrowski, 2009; Lovins and Latessa, 2013; Lowenkamp, Makarios, and Latessa, 2010). Latessa and colleagues designed five instruments to assess youth at each stage of the JJS. The first two, OYAS-Diversion and OYAS-Detention, are used pre-adjudication and help juvenile justice professionals determine what type of interventions, if any, are appropriate to address the youth's level of risk and need. The next three, OYAS-Disposition, OYAS-Residential, and OYAS-Reentry, were created to manage youth following adjudication. Each tool is used at the appropriate stage to assess the criminogenic needs of the youth at that stage and to help guide decisions for appropriate interventions. A strong feature of the Ohio Youth Assessment System-Disposition (OYAS-DIS) tool is its actuarial base. It consists of 32 items across seven domains that were generated from statistical predictors of recidivism in Ohio (Lovins and Latessa, 2013).

A main limitation of other RNR tools is that they are not comprised of items generated directly from analyses of recidivism predictors. Hence, many of the factors in these tools may not be reliable predictors. This explains why Austin's (2006) validation of the LSI-R in Vermont found that only 11 of the 54 items in this scale predicted recidivism of adult inmates. This finding also underscores a very important point: every risk assessment instrument must be validated with data from the offender population to which it will be applied. The reason for this is that comparisons of outcomes across multiple states that used essentially the same risk assessment instrument found some differences in the relative strength of individual items, suggesting some state-specific variance (Wiebush, 2002; Wiebush, Baird, Krisberg, and Onek, 1995).

The *Washington State Juvenile Court Assessment* (WSJCA) (Barnoski, 2004a, 2004b) is an exception. This excellent two-component instrument combines actuarial risk items and needs assessment in a single tool. The risk assessment is implemented in a two-stage process. The first stage is a blended actuarial/criminogenic need pre-screen assessment completed for all youth placed on probation. The twenty-seven item pre-screen, an actuarial tool developed from recidivism predictors in the State of Washington (Barnoski, 2004a), is a shortened version of the full assessment that classifies youth at low-, moderate-, or high-risk to re-offend. The second stage, a full assessment, is required only for youth assessed as moderate or high risk on the pre-screen. The full assessment identifies a youth's risk and protective factor profile to guide development of treatment plans. The WSJCA has been adopted by more than a dozen states including New York, Illinois, Florida, Utah, and North Dakota, and service providers find it user-friendly (Barnoski, 2005).

A slightly modified version of the WSJCA, the *Positive Achievement Change Tool* (PACT), is utilized in the Probation and Community Intervention program of the Florida Department of Juvenile Justice (Baglivio, 2009; Olson, 2007). The PACT was designed to assess juvenile offenders' risks, needs, and protective factors and like the WSJCA, has an actuarial/criminogenic need pre-screen. The forty-six items on the pre-screen are used to assess risk level and the full assessment (126 items) is used for service matching. The overall risk to re-offend level as determined by the PACT has proven to be a significant predictor of recidivism for youth who were assessed and remain in the community, with higher risk youth more likely to re-offend (Baglivio, 2009; Baglivio and Jackowski, 2013; Winokur-Early, Hand, and Blankenship, 2012). In the comparative NCCD study, the pre-screening PACT component produced some separation of outcomes by risk level, though it did not perform as well in this regard as some other instruments tested in that study (Baird et al., 2013). However, the PACT works very well in distinguishing SVCs from non-SVCs and it also demonstrates practical utility in the formulation of comprehensive treatment plans for SVC offenders (Baglivio et al., 2014).

A GRADUATED ASSESSMENT PROCESS

Treatment need assessments should be structured in a two-step process: an immediate pre-screen, followed by graduated assessments (increasingly in-depth) for the purpose of developing comprehensive treatment plans. It is important to draw a clear distinction between preliminary screening and in-depth clinical needs assessment as practiced in the JJ systems and related youth service systems. For example, the focus of mental health screening is on a youth's *current* or *immediate* emotional, psychological, and behavioral functioning. In the first level, a general or global assessment—often called a pre-screen—should be made after collecting information that is readily available from agency records and a short structured interview with the offender. Purely actuarial instruments are ideal in this step; so are pre-screens, that is, shortened versions of some lengthy assessment instruments. Such information "is predictive enough to draw first conclusions and decisions" (Spanjaard, Van der Knaap, Van der Put, and and Stams, 2012, p. 129). A highly recommended instrument to screen for multiple forms of mental health disorders that has been widely used with youth in JJ systems, the Voice Diagnostic Interview Schedule for Children (DISC-IV), identifies mental health treatment needs of girls and boys alike, up to age seventeen (McReynolds et al., 2010; Wasserman and McReynolds, 2011).[5] This is a widely tested psychiatric screening instrument. Another screening tool designed specifically for children below the age of twelve, to assess risk of becoming persistent adolescent offenders and to help facilitate referrals to appropriate services, is the Early Assessment Risk List (EARL) (Augimeri et al., 2010). It was discussed earlier in the context of intervention with very young offenders. The Massachusetts Youth Screening Instrument Second Version (MAYSI-2) is a brief self-report inventory designed for use in juvenile justice settings to identify mental health problems among youth and to inform decisions about further evaluation and/or intervention. It has been found to be reliable for use in juvenile justice settings among youth entering the system, to identify quickly and efficiently those youths most likely to require psychological services (Vincent, Guy, and Grisso, 2012). It is widely used in juvenile probation, detention, or corrections settings in most U.S. states (for other screening tools, see Grisso and Underwood, 2004).

The second level of assessment is for the purpose of treatment plan development. This requires a comprehensive examination of individualized data, including arrest and court history (if any) and these assessments generally include the use of risk and needs assessment instruments. But this in-depth assessment requires more time than a screening instrument, often necessitating more specialized training, and can lead to more definitive conclusions about a youth's presenting behavior. Misuse occurs when in-depth psychological diagnostic methods are used in the first assessment level, that is, the pre-screen stage. It is vitally important that risk and need assessment tools are in sync with the developmental stages of offender careers. First, they must cover each of the developmental domains (family, school, peers, individual problems). Second, chosen instruments must support identification of priority treatment needs in each of these developmental domains, and as these change with age and criminal involvement. Used in tandem, RAIs help determine placements and levels of supervision, and NAIs facilitate matching services to treatment needs at each level of advancement in criminal careers and JJ system involvement.

Only brief risk assessments should be administered at intake and when a new offense occurs. Needs assessments come into play after intake in the course of more extensive diagnosis and development of treatment plans. While RAIs should be re-administered at the point of each JJ system penetration, a needs assessment should be repeated at regular intervals—within thirty days—or as needed to monitor client progress in accordance with treatment plans. In other words, risk and needs assessment serve distinctively different purposes.

DISPOSITION MATRICES

A disposition decision matrix is a central component of a well-managed JJ system. Such a matrix serves to guide dispositional decisions about the most appropriate level of supervision or custody for adjudicated offenders at the time of case disposition (Wiebush, 2002). Disposition matrices typically are designed with two dimensions: the presenting offense and risk level. The following are key points in a disposition matrix:

- Low risk offenders remain in the community with minimal supervision and low intensity services.
- Moderate risk offenders are typically placed in more structured community programs, with intensive probation supervision for higher risk youth and relatively intensive services.
- Residential placement is reserved for the highest risk offenders after community-based alternatives have been exhausted and continuous services are provided.

Next, a continuum of service options should be inserted at the intersections in the disposition matrix. To be most effective, program or facility placements must match the developmental status of offenders, their offense history, and recidivism risk. When offenders persist in serious and violent delinquency, their position in a graduated sanctions system should be advanced to protect the public. As offenders progress in the graduated sanction system, linked rehabilitation programs must become more structured and intensive, to effectively deal with the intractable problems that more dangerous offenders present while reserving secure confinement for the very small proportion of serious violent offenders. Offenders can be stepped up through the levels of sanctions as they progress in more serious and violent delinquent careers and stepped down as they decelerate or desist from delinquent activity. Aftercare/reentry is a critical component of a comprehensive system, because it constitutes step-down interventions and continuous treatment.

A disposition matrix is developed through a consensus-building process that typically involves a representative group of JJ system officials. Since they affect a pivotal decision in the system (placement in programs and facilities), most agencies are careful to involve judges, prosecutors, probation chiefs, and defense attorneys in the design stage. In other words, the design of a matrix reflects the developers' best thinking about what factors should be taken into account when making placement recommendations/decisions, and the appropriate level of custody/control for each possible combination of the selected criteria. After the design stage, it is ideal to have a matrix placed in statute so all juveniles receive level status in a standard manner. The matrix can still allow for flexibility within each grid box as to supervision length and required participation in programs.

The Florida Department of Juvenile Justice system uses a disposition recommendation matrix that designates specific service categories at each of the intersecting points, an excellent schematic for building a statewide service continuum (Figure 7.2). This disposition matrix and the alignment of services were developed in close collaboration with judges, prosecutors, court supervisors, and service providers. A well-designed disposition matrix empowers JJ systems to operate more efficiently, effectively, and economically by matching youth with appropriate services and supervision levels.

The explicit disposition recommendation matrix, recently put in play in Florida, links four risk-level groups (low-, moderate-, moderate-high-, and high-risk) with the most serious presenting offense categories (first-time misdemeanor, minor, serious, and violent) in a four-by-four matrix. Key points of the dispositional matrix include: (1) low-risk offenders remain in the community with minimal supervision; (2) moderate-risk

Florida Department of Juvenile Justice Disposition Recommendation Matrix
(Staff must always begin with the least restrictive setting within a particular disposition category. See SDM guidelines)

Most Serious Presenting Offense	PACT Risk Level to Re-Offend			
	Low-Risk to Re-offend	Moderate-Risk to Re-offend	Moderate/High-Risk to Re-offend	High-Risk to Re-offend
1st TIME MISDEMEANOR[1]	Level 1	Level 1	N/A	N/A
Minor[2]	Level 2 or 3a	Level 2 or 3a	Level 2 or 3a–c	Level 3a–c or 4
Serious[3]	Level 2 or 3a	Level 2 or 3a–b	Level 3a–c or 4	Level 3a–c or 4
Violent[4]	Level 2 or 3a–b	Level 2, 3a–c or 4	Level 3a–c, 4 or 5	Level 3a–c, 4 or 5

[1] – First time misdemeanor offenders with no history of arrest or participation in alternatives to arrest. Under Section 985.12, Florida Statutes, all first time misdemeanants eligible for civil citation. Youth deemed ineligible for civil citation (based on community standards) should be reviewed under the "Misdemeanor" category based on their P Risk Level to Reoffend.
[2] – All misdemeanor offenses.
[3] – Felony offenses that do not include violence.
[4] – Violent felony offenses (does not include misdemeanor assault/battery, which is captured under "minor").

Level 1 –Alternatives to Arrest	Level 2 –Diversion & Non-DJJ Probation
Level 3 –Community Supervision	Level 4 –Non Secure Residential Commitment (Low & Moderate Risk Programs)
(3a) –Probation supervision	Level 5 –Secure Residential Commitment (High & Maximum Risk Programs)
(3b) –Probation enhancement services (ART, LifeSkills, etc.)	
(3c) –Day Treatment, MST, FFT	

Figure 7.2. Florida Department of Juvenile Justice Disposition Recommendation Matrix
Reprinted with the permission of the Florida Department of Juvenile Justice

offenders typically placed in more structured community programs, with intensive probation supervision for higher risk youth; and (3) residential placement reserved for the highest risk offenders after community-based alternatives have been exhausted.

The recommended risk classifications are determined by the PACT risk-needs assessment tool (the forty-six item pre-screen). Specific service contexts and certain programs (Level 3, community supervision) are designated at each of the intersecting points. Level 4 (non-secure residential commitment) consists of low and moderate risk programs, and Level 5 (secure residential commitment) consists of high and maximum risk programs. Importantly, the dispositional matrix is to be implemented according to specific Florida DJJ guidelines: *Structured Decision-Making and the Dispositional Matrix.* This is an excellent schematic for building a service matrix, and a statewide continuum. A well-designed disposition matrix empowers JJ systems to operate more efficiently, effectively, and economically by matching youth with appropriate services and supervision levels in comprehensive case plans. Florida DJJ researchers presently are examining recidivism rates for offenders classified at the respective levels in the disposition matrix. This research will not only test the validity of the matrix for classifying offenders by risk level, but also reveal possible elevated recidivism rates when offenders' dispositions are at variance with the disposition guidelines.

COMPREHENSIVE CASE PLANS

Introduced earlier, some specific requirements of comprehensive case plans for adjudicated juvenile offenders are highlighted here. These plans should identify and schedule services that match treatment needs, set timetables for services, identify providers to deliver them, and specify treatment goals and objectives for the youth, families, schools, service agencies, and other particulars. Approaches to family involvement, and strategies for youth engagement must also be part of case plan execution. A cornerstone of JJ systems is family involvement. Motivational Interviewing (MI) is an excellent youth engagement approach, but MI should not be expected to accomplish more than this, because MI is not an evidence-based program for juvenile offenders, only an engagement strategy.

A recent study finds that providing juvenile justice-involved youths with systematic mental health assessment and linking those youths diagnosed with substance use disorder to mental health and substance use services likely reduces recidivism risk (Wasserman, McReynolds, Musabegovic et al., 2009). However, it is unreasonable to expect that solely providing treatment for mental health problems will reduce recidivism of serious offenders; other criminogenic factors must be addressed as well (Schubert, Mulvey, and Glasheen, 2011). Establishing a graduated assessment protocol is the first priority (Skowyra and Cocozza, 2006; Wasserman and Ko, 2003; Wasserman, Ko, and McReynolds, 2004). Evidence-based treatments for specific mental health and substance use disorders have been available for some time (Wasserman and Ko, 2003).

In juvenile justice practice, however, close attention to making appropriate matches often does not occur. Low stakeholder buy-in to effective programming (Henggeler and Schoenwald, 2011), difficulties associated with replication of whole-cloth evidence-based programs (Lipsey and Howell, 2012), a limited repertoire of service types, and, concomitantly, poor management information systems and insufficient data sharing among agencies who work with at-risk youth, are key factors contributing to the low percentage of matching high-risk youth with evidence-based programs.

North Carolina designs "Standardized Case Plans" that are standardized in the sense of following an established assessment protocol and consistent use of programs and generic services that specifically target priority treatment needs initiatlly identified in the statewide Model Youth and Family Assessment of Needs and Strengths. For case planning purposes, this tool requires identification of the three most serious problems to be addressed in the child and family case plan. This tool also requires specification of the youth's major strengths that can be used in case planning. In addition, as part of the assessment, court staffs identify problem areas in which there may be a need for additional, specialized assessments to determine the full extent or nature of a problem that requires more in-depth assessment. Services that match offenders' elevated treatment needs and developmental strengths along with family supports are selected from the Juvenile Justice Disposition Chart and Dispositional Alternatives matrix.

QUALITY ASSURANCE

The critical guide for agency Quality Assurance (QA) monitoring is the supervision plan (Wagner, 2009). This monitoring must ensure that planned service interventions are delivered as scheduled. A successful QA program should help the agency reduce recidivism and should be evaluated by that measure. Since recidivism is not likely to be reduced if case plans do not address a client's risk and needs or identified service interventions are not delivered, case plan fidelity is a logical focal point for QA. A Bureau of Quality Improvement in the Florida Department of Juvenile Justice sets the bar high for state QA management (http://www.djj.state.fl.us/partners/QI).

In Pennsylvania, a Juvenile Justice System Enhancement Strategy (JJSES) has been developed that provides a statewide organizing framework for promoting and monitoring evidence-based programs and services. A key component of the JJSES, a Resource Center for Evidence-Based Prevention and Intervention Programs and Practices (EPIS Center), has the QA benefits that follow:

- Supports the quality implementation of established evidence-based program models,
- Incorporates research-based principles and practices into existing local juvenile justice programs,
- Manages a continuous quality improvement and quality assurance process that includes building a continuum of effective programs that reduce recidivism, matching offenders to services based upon risk/needs, and
- Supports the development of graduated responses for SVC offenders.

A MANAGEMENT INFORMATION SYSTEM

Commonly called a MIS, a "management information system" is needed to track clients and service delivery, and evaluate services. An ideal MIS has the following features:

- manage statewide data on all juveniles served
- link data on juveniles from one component of the JJS to another
- support placement of offenders in the disposition matrix
- maintain risk and need assessment information on all youth
- maintain comprehensive case plans on all offenders
- provide data on the length and number of program or service events/contacts
- track youth outcomes, especially recidivism
- generate management reports regularly/as needed.

In other words, all JJ system functions should be data-driven. The Florida DJJ has integrated its web-based PACT (risk/needs assessment) with the State's Juvenile Justice Information System (JJIS) data base (Baglivio, 2009). The JJIS is an ideal MIS. Data Integrity Officers ensure that data and information entered into the JJIS is accurate throughout the Department of Juvenile Justice (http://www.djj.state.fl.us/research/delinquency-data/delinquency-profile).

The JJIS and PACT interface allows for automated scoring of the delinquency history domain (official prior criminal history). This feature is important, to pre-fill information that is already contained in the MIS. In addition, the PACT automates the assessment findings into the Youth Empowered Success (YES) plan that structures priority criminogenic needs to be addressed in the individualized case plan (Baglivio, 2009). Treatment teams then assign priority to those risk and protective factors that can be addressed while the youth is under supervision. Next, performance plan goals are established that address the rehabilitative needs of the youth in the Balanced and Restorative Justice areas of accountability, skill competency development, and community safety.

North Carolina practitioners and program development experts have developed a Juvenile Justice Planning Tool (JJPT) that is used to map the flow of juveniles across each county's juvenile justice system on an ongoing basis, and also support county-wide continuum building. Connected to the State MIS, the JJPT is structured in sections that correspond to the JJ system components (e.g., intake, diversion plans, approved for court, adjudicated, correctional commitments, and post-release supervision). Electronic client tracking data display the number of offenders that penetrate sequential system levels—the overall system flow of offenders—on an annual basis. The JJPT also enables program managers to determine the number of youths who need services in each level of the system and the risk-level of current clients, using the NCAR RAI tool (described earlier) for at-risk and court-referred youth. For the purposes of determining service availability and matching client needs, the JJPT serves as a repository for available developmental and rehabilitative services for JJ system clients.

For county-level planning purposes (service gap analysis), the JJPT displays a summary of the eligible risk level of youth served by existing programs, and in accord with their appropriate position in the county-wide continuum. Treatment needs are determined by compilations (for each county) of family strengths and individual needs assessments as indicated by the North Carolina NAI tool (described earlier). The system flow/program services feature is meant to be reviewed annually for the prior fiscal year in order to determine the array of juveniles served, and multiple years can be reviewed to determine trends. In providing a comparison between risk levels and treatment needs of existing clients at each JJ system component, the JJPT identifies gaps in existing services. In short, the JJPT is an important tool for maintaining a data-driven JJ system in North Carolina.

COURT STANDARDS

Performance standards are also an important component of a viable Case Management System. Missouri's Performance Standards for the Administration of Juvenile Justice are exemplary for helping balance individual rights and treatment needs with public protection (Office of State Courts Administrator, 2004; Waint, 2002). The performance standards help greatly to achieve a balanced system. As Waint explains, this does not come easily because JJ system roles include:

- protecting the community,
- promoting accountability so offenders decrease risk to re-offend,
- promoting competency to increase chances the youth will lead a productive life,
- sanctioning delinquent behavior, and,
- providing due process to those who appear before the court.

The model Missouri standards establish a common framework within which juvenile justice personnel can understand and assess the work of juvenile and family courts, enhance the courts' performance, and set forth expectations surrounding the administration and use of risk and needs assessment instruments and the development of case plans. As a result of implementing Missouri's Performance Standards, juvenile officers across the state have come to value them for "providing a framework for what they do, and setting the stage for juvenile office evaluation, assessment and improvement" (Waint, 2002, p. 61). An added benefit is that the performance standards bring consistency to multi-county circuits across the state in providing individual justice to individual juveniles and families in supporting the Missouri structured decision making tools (see the Missouri Structured Decision Making Tools sidebar). "The standards provide

BOX 7.4

MISSOURI STRUCTURED DECISION MAKING TOOLS

Missouri's history of treatment-oriented responses to juvenile offenders sets a very high standard for other states to follow (Abrams, 2003). Guided by the Comprehensive Strategy, in the mid-1990s Missouri created a structured decision-making model that uses risk and needs assessments and a classification matrix: the Missouri Juvenile Offender Risk and Needs Assessment and Classification System (Office of State Courts Administrator, 2002). A major goal of the state in establishing this classification system was to promote statewide consistency in the classification and supervision of juvenile offenders. The three SDM tools of the Missouri system are as follows:

- An actuarial risk assessment tool, completed before court adjudication, classifies youth into three categories: high, moderate, or low probability of reoffending. The risk assessment instrument has been revalidated twice (Johnson, Wagner, and Matthews, 2002; Yan, 2009).
- A classification matrix that recommends sanctions and service interventions appropriate to the youth's risk level and most serious adjudicated offense.
- A needs assessment instrument that recommends services that will reduce the likelihood of a youth's reoffending by reducing risk factors linked to recidivism—that help balance individual rights and treatment needs with public protection (described earlier).

A Missouri juvenile offender recidivism study revealed that most recidivists had three or four new charges; however, 11% of the sample had 4-6 new charges, and the most serious, violent, chronic recidivists, just 3% of the sample, had ten or more new charges (Yan, 2009). This research suggested that the benefits of juvenile offender risk assessment could be increased by adding community variables, which is a point well taken. Research along this line could help guide community prevention initiatives.

The state of Missouri has long had a treatment-oriented system (Abrams, 2003). Large congregate care training schools were dismantled in the early 1980s, replaced by a widely praised network of small, treatment-oriented youth facilities, and the re-confinement rate is just 16% (Mendel, 2011). The State's Division of Youth Services operates five regional networks of youth services that form a continuum, including secure juvenile corrections facilities (maximum capacity, fifty youths), non-secure group homes, day treatment programs, and post-release supervision by "trackers" (mentors). The Individual Treatment Plan (the master plan that outlines and defines the course of treatment for the youth) is a comprehensive and holistic plan that delineates the goals, objectives, resources and main "players" of the correctional treatment process. In treatment plans, the focus is on (1) individualized and group treatments with a clear treatment model, (2) supervision, not correctional coercion, (3) skill-building, (4) family partnership and involvement during confinement, and (5) aftercare.

a tool to understand the business of working with juvenile delinquents, by articulating the process, and by providing time frames to get things done—intake procedures, juvenile offender classification, and reporting on case outcomes" (p. 61).

In sum, states and other units of government should build a forward-looking administrative model, a system organized around risk management that supports the development of individualized disposition plans for offenders. Placements should be guided by a disposition matrix. The program continuum should be populated with effective, evidence-based intervention programs and integrated with a graduated sanctions framework. Structured decision-making tools should be used to increase system capacity for (1) better matching of offender treatment needs with effective services in comprehensive treatment plans, (2) targeting of higher risk offenders, and (3) making improvements in prevention, court, and correctional programs across the entire continuum. Having these structured decision-making tools in place, along with an automated management information system, and using them efficiently is essential for effective system-wide implementation of an evidence-based system.

NOTES

1. Source: National Center for Juvenile Justice, http://www.ncjj.org/Topic/Risk-and-Needs-Assessments.aspx.

2. Hoge, Vincent, and Guy (2012) reviewed several instruments for predicting recidivism of older juvenile offenders in early adulthood.

3. Sites included Arizona, Georgia, Ohio, Indiana, Maryland, Michigan, Missouri, New Mexico, North Carolina, Oklahoma, Rhode Island, Texas, Virginia, and Wisconsin.

4. Percents total more than 100 because of multiple treatment needs.

5. It derives up to twenty-two DSM-IV diagnoses for the past month.

8

Conclusion

The past thirty years have been a tumultuous period for the American juvenile justice system. Although many have claimed that a general "epidemic" of juvenile violence occurred in the United States from the mid-1980s through the early 1990s, research has shown that this did not actually happen. Nevertheless, the widely presumed general epidemic of juvenile violence contributed to a moral panic over juvenile delinquency in the United States and a "get tough" movement that led to unwarranted changes in the juvenile justice system. Large numbers of juvenile offenders were removed from the juvenile justice system and placed in the criminal justice system. Rehabilitation was emphasized far less, and punitive measures came to be used more widely than ever before. New laws designated more juveniles as serious offenders, brought more minor offenders into the system, and extended periods of confinement in juvenile correctional facilities. Juvenile court intake and probation caseloads grew to overwhelming proportions, and many detention centers and juvenile reformatories became—and remain—overcrowded. Minority youth, particularly black youngsters, continue to bear the brunt of the punitive juvenile justice reforms that the panic over juvenile violence wrought, though Latino and Latina youth are now catching up. This is the general context within which juvenile justice systems across the United States currently operate.

Lipsey's numerous meta-analyses cited in this volume have been instrumental in debunking the "nothing works" myth with respect to juvenile rehabilitation programs. His initial meta-analysis included nearly 400 controlled studies of general delinquency prevention and treatment.

Contrary to the myth, Lipsey found that juveniles in treatment programs had recidivism rates about 10 percent lower, on average, than those of untreated juveniles. The best intervention programs produced up to a 37 percent reduction in recidivism rates and similar improvements in other outcomes. After completing his review, Lipsey (1995) issued a clarion call to JJ systems.

> It is no longer constructive for researchers, practitioners, and policymakers to argue about whether delinquency treatment and related rehabilitative approaches "work," as if that were a question that could be answered with a simple "yes" or "no." As a generality, treatment clearly works. We must get on with the business of developing and identifying the treatment models that will be most effective and providing them to the juveniles they will benefit. (p. 78)

In 2005, Lipsey operationalized evidence-based criteria in a program rating scheme called the Standardized Program Evaluation Protocol (SPEP) that can be used by service providers and juvenile justice systems to assess their programs for juvenile offenders. The SPEP applies to any therapeutic program type for which there is a sufficient body of supporting research in the associated meta-analytic database. Presently eight states and one county are engaged in a pioneering effort in using the SPEP as a centerpiece for integrating model program implementation and improvement of established local programs. These efforts have been combined with management tools that enable these state systems to adapt the OJJDP Comprehensive Strategy for Serious, Violent, and Chronic Juvenile Offenders to their own circumstances. The Comprehensive Strategy provides a preventive risk-management model of juvenile justice (Slobogin, 2013; Slobogin and Fondacaro, 2011) that determines program placement and supervision levels on the basis of objective risk and needs assessments and promotes system-wide data-driven management of juvenile offenders, services, and resources. The necessary tools are available to make system-wide improvements and to perform statewide evaluations of all service programs against research-based guidelines.

Each state should assess the performance of its juvenile justice system with a focus on consistency with the framework and principles of the Comprehensive Strategy. In this assessment, particular attention should be given to the quality of structured decision-making tools, their adequacy for classifying offenders by risk level, building a continuum of evidence-based services, and matching offender characteristics with the programs that will benefit them most. The Comprehensive Strategy mantra applies: Juvenile justice systems must deliver "the right service, to the right kid at the right time" (J. J. Wilson, cited in Howell, 2009, p. 309).

Appendix:
Needed Juvenile Justice
System Reforms

IN BRIEF

Several reforms are needed to improve justness, fairness, and effectiveness of juvenile justice systems across the United States. Each of the needed reforms discussed here presently impedes implementation of evidence-based programs. Zero tolerance policies have the effect of clogging JJ systems with low risk offenders, and thus should be eliminated. Provision of due process and the effective assistance of counsel to all juveniles would help reduce adjudication and detention of low risk offenders, and in turn, overuse of confinement. Assiduous detention screening would have the same benefits and also reduce system penetration of low risk offenders. Minority youth are over-represented at all stages of JJ system processing. Improvements in each of these areas would have the net effect of increasing JJ systems' capacity to serve juveniles presently transferred to adult criminal justice systems. Similarly, the elimination of misuse of confinement and associated costs would support more placements in less costly and more effective community services. Sufficient treatment opportunities for girls are not readily available and options for meeting their needs are lacking. Last, addressing community-wide gang problems would help reduce recidivism across JJ systems. Each of these recommendations is discussed below.

133

ELIMINATE ZERO TOLERANCE
POLICIES IN SCHOOL SYSTEMS

In an unprecedented study of nearly 1 million Texas public secondary school students that were followed for more than six years beginning in 2000, nearly 60 percent were suspended or expelled from school (Fabelo, Thompson, Plotkin et al., 2011). About 15 percent were suspended or expelled eleven times or more; nearly half of these students with eleven or more disciplinary actions were involved in the juvenile justice system. But only 3 percent of the total disciplinary actions were in response to conduct for which state law mandated suspensions and expulsions; virtually all were made at the discretion of school officials, presumably in response to violations of local schools' conduct codes (see Teske and Huff, 2011, for judicial perspectives).

Equally incredible, more than 5,000 children ages three to four years old are expelled from state-funded *pre-kindergarten* school systems each year across the country (Gilliam, 2005). The pre-kindergarten expulsion rate in the 2003–2004 school year was more than three times the national rate for K–12 grades. There is no obvious explanation for such high pre-kindergarten expulsion rate except an insidious spread of a "zero tolerance" mentality throughout all types of organized schooling that originated in the moral panic over delinquency that occurred in the 1990s (Howell, 2003b). To be sure, the spate of school shootings that occurred during the 1997–1998 school year was a contributing factor.

Zero tolerance policies can have a cumulative effect, as follows (Howell, 2012). The "difficult schools," those with inflexible zero tolerance policies, can increase future delinquency by imposing more severe sanctions. School suspension correlates moderately well with delinquency (Hemphill, McMorris, Toumbourou et al., 2007). Suspensions and expulsions from school often mean that students are removed from adult supervision, and, in turn, experience more exposure to delinquent peers, which can lead to delinquency onset. To complete the process, delinquency involvement can increase gang membership and court referral.

Many public schools "have turned into feeder schools for the juvenile and criminal justice systems" (Advancement Project, 2005, p. 11). The Civil Rights Division of the U.S. Department of Justice recently filed a lawsuit charging that Meridian, Mississippi, officials are running a "school-to-prison pipeline" in violation of the constitutional rights of students who are wrongfully reported to law enforcement for minor disobedience by public schools. To reduce unwarranted court referrals, a comprehensive school resource officer (SRO) study (Langberg, Fedders, and Kukorowski, 2011) made the following recommendations:

- Teachers and administrators should have readily available, high-quality alternatives to suspensions, arrests, and court referrals, such as mediation, community service, restitution, and mental health programs.
- All SROs, security investigators, and other security personnel should be required to undergo mandatory, intensive, ongoing trainings, including instruction on:
  - Legal standards for searches and seizures of students in schools
  - Adolescent development science
  - Working with students who have disabilities and other special needs
  - Cultural competency
  - De-escalating student misbehavior without using physical force
  - Using safe restraint techniques
  - Long-term consequences of court involvement and arrests
  - Clear limitations reflecting SROs' status as fully authorized and armed law enforcement personnel should be adhered to by school administrators and school police.
  - SROs should be prohibited from carrying guns and TASERs on school campuses.
  - Students who commit minor offenses in schools should not be routinely arrested and referred to court; court referrals should occur only as a last resort.
- Clear, standardized, well-publicized complaint procedures should be established for students, parents, teachers, and administrators to use when SROs act inappropriately.
- The public should have access to more complete, easy-to-understand data about SROs.

Judge Teske's Georgia Clayton County School Referral Reduction Protocol (reviewed earlier) is an ideal solution to excessive school suspension and expulsions.

FULFILL THE PROMISE OF *IN RE GAULT* BY PROVIDING DUE PROCESS AND EFFECTIVE ASSISTANCE OF COUNSEL

A major juvenile justice system reform, and one that can be expected to have a significant impact on all of the reform efforts detailed in this section, would be to fulfill the promise of *In re Gault*, 387 U.S. 1 (1967), by providing a full measure of due process protections and the effective assistance of counsel to all juveniles subject to the juvenile offender jurisdiction of the juvenile court.

The Supreme Court's decision in *Gault* established that juvenile court hearings that could result in a juvenile's commitment to an institution require that the juvenile be provided the same fundamental due process rights and privileges that are provided in state criminal court proceedings under the Fourteenth Amendment to the U.S. Constitution, including: (1) a right to timely notice of the charges; (2) the right to counsel; (3) the right to present and cross-examine witnesses; and (4) the privilege against self-incrimination. The Court encouraged states to also provide a right to a transcript of the proceedings and to appellate review. The Court's majority opinion, written by Chief Justice Abe Fortas, was based on the fact that Gerald Gault was being punished, not helped, by the juvenile court and that the doctrine of *parens patriae*, the original foundation for the establishment of the juvenile court in 1899, is no longer relevant to contemporary standards of justice. Fortas called the court in this case no better than a "kangaroo court" and opined that "Juvenile court history has again demonstrated that unbridled discretion, however benevolently motivated, is frequently a poor substitute for principle and procedure."

Unfortunately, the promise of the right to counsel remains far from being fully realized in juvenile court policy and practice and, without it, the constitutional rights guaranteed in juvenile court proceedings by *Gault* and its progeny are, too often, simply not exercised.

Twenty-five years after *Gault*, Congress directed the Federal Office of Juvenile Justice and Delinquency Prevention to examine the status of juveniles' access to counsel and the quality of their representation. The resulting assessment, *A Call for Justice: An Assessment of the Right to Counsel and Quality of Representation in Delinquency Proceedings* (1995), conducted by the American Bar Association's Juvenile Justice Center, the Juvenile Law Center, and the Youth Law Center, identified serious concerns that the rights of many young people in the juvenile justice system continued to be significantly compromised due to a variety of factors, including:

- Large numbers of waivers of the right to counsel
- High caseloads, particularly for public defenders
- Delays in the appointment of counsel
- Inadequate trial preparation and trial performance
- Deficient representation at the dispositional stage
- Infrequency of appeals and lack of post-dispositional representation
- Lack of training
- Inadequate resources, including basic defender office needs and staff support, and
- Lack of effective supervision.

The reasons why the promise of *Gault* has not been kept are numerous. They include a lingering belief that defense counsel is not necessary and, perhaps, keep the court from acting in the best interests of the child. Also, there is a lack of resources to provide competent counsel for indigent juveniles, whether through often overwhelmed public defenders or underpaid and unqualified court appointed counsel. Even when competent counsel is available, they often do not have the support staff and resources needed to mount a proper defense.

A related issue is delay in the appointment of counsel, particularly in jurisdictions that require proof of indigence, often resulting in counsel not being appointed until after the initial detention hearing or of a plea bargain being reached even before the juvenile has had an opportunity to consult with counsel. In either case, detention/or confinement becomes more likely. Research demonstrates that juveniles held pending a hearing have a greater chance of being adjudicated and being incarcerated as a result. Juvenile courts are often underfunded and understaffed, leading to a reliance on plea bargaining and assembly-line justice. In many jurisdictions, juveniles are encouraged to waive their right to counsel, either directly or with the consent or under the authority of a parent. While a few jurisdictions require counsel for all juveniles or restrict waivers to situations where waiver occurs following consultation with counsel, this remains a distinct minority of jurisdictions.

These issues are compounded by the fact that juvenile defense requires a skill set that, in many ways, must be greater than that of an adult defender. Juvenile defenders must be able to relate to children, understand adolescent development and neurology (including brain science), explain the proceedings in a way that the juvenile can understand and zealously advocate their wishes, be learned in the social work aspects of their needs, including school, parental relationships, mental health and substance abuse, and placement options.

These issues and others that continue to impact juveniles' right to counsel and the quality of representation are documented in a series of twenty-one state-based assessments conducted by the National Juvenile Defender Center (NJDC) (http://www.njdc.info/assessments.php). According to the NJDC Web site:

> The assessments provide comprehensive examinations of the systemic and institutional barriers that prevent lawyers from providing adequate legal services to indigent (and other) children within a particular state legal system. In addition to gathering general data and information about the structure of the juvenile indigent defense system, assessments examine issues related to the timing of appointment of counsel, the frequency with which children waive their right to counsel and under what conditions they do so, resource allocation, attorney compensation, supervision and training, and access to investigators, experts, social workers and support staff. Assessments also highlight promising approaches and innovative practices within the state and offer recommendations to improve weak areas.

NJDC's assessments are ongoing and provide excellent insights into the state of juvenile defender services across America.

ELIMINATE THE OVERUSE OF DETENTION

U.S. detention centers held 40 percent of all juvenile offenders in residential placement on the census date in 2008 (approximately 32,000 on a given day) (Hockenberry et al., 2011). However, *admissions* to detention centers actually total approximately 500,000 annually in the United States (Holman and Ziedenberg, 2006). Several studies show that the detention of juveniles is associated with a number of negative outcomes, including an increased likelihood of subsequent delinquency and higher rates of future offending (Benda and Tollett, 1999; Green, Carlson, and Colvin, 2004; Holman and Ziedenberg, 2006; Soler, Shoenberg, and Schindler, 2009). Over the long term, the risk of recidivism increases significantly when detention is imposed at a young age (Van der Put et al., 2011). In addition, lengthy periods of detention tend to wipe out the positive effects of court rehabilitation programs (Wooldredge, 1988). Given that detention is expensive, increases recidivism, and decreases positive outcomes for youth, it makes sense to restrict the use of detention and increase prevention initiatives which are cost effective and successful interventions (Mallett, Stoddard-Dare, and Seck, 2011). As an example, in Mallett and colleagues' study, mental health counseling that occurred prior to juvenile court involvement was associated with decreased detention stays.

A model Detention Assessment Instrument (DAI) was developed more than a decade ago based on a review of DAI's in use throughout the country (Wiebush, 2002). In developing the model instrument, NCCD compared a wide range of DAI's and identified those factors—and their associated weights—that appeared consistently across the scales. The model DAI (p. 80) includes these items:

- Measures concerned with the nature of the referral offense (severity and number of charges) and any outstanding warrants;
- Measures of the number and nature of other pending petitions and previous adjudicated offenses;
- The youth's supervision status at the time of the referral; and
- Two stability measures including prior failures to appear and previous escapes/runaways.

An empirically generated detention screening tool, developed by New York City stakeholders, includes only those risk factors that statistically correlated with absconding and rearrests in the city during the period between the initial arrest and sentencing (Fratello, Salsich, and Mogulescu, 2011). The statistical analysis determined the strength of correlations between specific factors and the risk of either rearrest or failure to appear. The four items that predicted absconding are:

- An open warrant for a previous juvenile delinquency case;
- No parent or responsible adult present at probation intake;
- School attendance of less than 30 percent in the last full semester of school; and
- A prior warrant for a juvenile delinquency or Persons in Need of Supervision (PINS) case (pp. 7–8).

The five items that predicted rearrest while a case is pending are:

- Prior arrest(s) at the time of probation intake;
- Prior juvenile delinquency adjudication(s);
- Prior arrest(s) for a felony offense at the time of probation intake;
- Previous adjudication(s) for a designated felony offense; and
- Being on probation for a previous adjudication at the time of probation intake.

Once the factors that signal a risk of failure to appear or rearrest were identified, the stakeholders developed a numeric system to determine an overall risk score for each youth. A risk score matrix was then developed, comprised of the two sets of predictors for either rearrest or failure to appear. The intersection of these two axes represents the youth's overall risk score, which a judge can consider in deciding whether a youth should be released without court-ordered supervision, released to a detention alternative, or detained while his or her case is pending. Next, a continuum consisting of three tiers was developed. The first and least restrictive level is community monitoring. At this level, youth receive regular curfew checks and must make phone check-ins. The second level, after-school supervision, requires youth to attend a site-based program between 3:00 and 7:00 p.m. and to participate in activities that develop social skills, such as tutoring, community service, and recreation. The third and most restrictive level is managed by the probation department: intensive community monitoring and enforcement of a contractual agreement with the parent or guardian. Preliminary outcomes are positive (Fratello et al., 2011). Information from the Juvenile Justice Research Database—the database used to monitor and assess implementation—"suggests that the city's reform effort is being adopted successfully by staff and is generating positive outcomes for youth on a variety of measures" (p. 11).

A large-scale illustration of how juvenile detention alternatives have reduced detention use is reflected in the Annie E. Casey JDAI (Juvenile Detention Alternatives Initiative). The best metric of detention utilization is the average daily population, because it reflects both of the key system flow indicators, the number of youth admitted to detention and the length of time those youth remain in detention. "By this indicator, JDAI sites had reduced their use of detention by 41 percent in the aggregate as of 2011" (Annie E. Casey Foundation, 2013, p. 6). Juvenile justice systems can also benefit by forming local partnerships with law enforcement, schools, and community members to address the overuse of detention.

REDUCE DISPROPORTIONATE MINORITY CONTACT

Reducing disproportionate minority confinement of juveniles became federal policy in the United States with the 1992 amendments to the Juvenile Justice and Delinquency Prevention Act (JJDPA) of 1974 (P.L. 93–415). Later amendments to the JJDPA changed the emphasis from "disproportionate minority confinement" to "disproportionate minority contact (DMC)," requiring an examination of possible disproportionate representation of minority youth at all decision points in the juvenile justice system.

The acid test of DMC rests on the presumption of disparities in actual delinquent behaviors between children of color and Caucasian youth. Actually, large disparities do not exist. In other words, studies have not revealed large Black-White differences in age-specific prevalence rates nationwide for serious and violent offenses during the adolescent period (Elliott, 1994). It is in adulthood that self-reported serious and violent offense rates for Black persons greatly exceed the rates for Whites. Recent studies confirm these findings in Pittsburgh, Rochester, and Denver (Huizinga, Thornberry, Knight et al., 2007). In these three cities, racial/ ethnic disparities in JJ system processing were not explained either by different levels of offending behavior or the presence of other risk factors. Yet one of the most transparent nationwide disparities is that Black youths are disproportionately processed in the juvenile and criminal justice systems for drug offenses, even though their drug use rates are no higher than those of White youngsters (Centers for Disease Control and Prevention, 2006). Hence, it is very important to use adolescent self-report surveys of delinquency and other problem behaviors as a baseline for calculating the DMC Relative Rate Index (RRI).

As demonstrated in this handbook, it is more beneficial to use self-reports of delinquency to get a better picture of offending. However, a useful tool has been developed by OJJDP, entitled the Relative Rate Index (RRI) which calls for calculation of DMC rates through racial/ethnic population considerations paired with official records (court referrals, approvals to court, detention admissions, long-term confinement, etc.)[1]

The RRI is a standard measure that points to where problems may exist. In a presentation supported by OJJDP, it was stated that "Measuring DMC is like taking vital signs in a hospital emergency room. It doesn't identify the illness or tell you how to treat it [but] it alerts you to potential problems and tells you where to focus your diagnostic efforts" (Feyerherm and Butts, 2003, p. 7).

High RRI rates are very common (Hawkins and Kempf-Leonard, 2005; Leiber and Brubaker, 2010; Leiber and Rodriguez, 2011; Puzzanchera et al., 2012; Rodriguez, 2010; Snyder and Sickmund, 2006). Moreover, Latino and Latina youth appear to be reducing the gap relative to Black youth as victims of disproportionate minority representation (Snyder and Sickmund, 2006, p. 211; Villarruel and Walker, 2002). Rodriguez (2010, p. 392) succinctly states the current national situation:

> Over the past twenty-five years, prior work has established several key findings regarding racial biases in juvenile court outcomes. These findings can be summarized in the following: (1) race directly and indirectly influences court outcomes (through gender, age, and community context), (2) racial biases are more common in front-end court processes than back-end processes, and (3) racial disparities accumulate as youth are processed further into the system.

Minority youth overrepresentation is highest in the arrest, detention, and waiver decisions (Leiber and Rodriguez, 2011). In the first study to include White, Black, Latino/a, and American Indian youth in a study of minority overrepresentation across multiple stages of juvenile court processing, Rodriguez (2010) found that, although disparities were evident statewide in one southwestern state from intake to secure confinement, inequities varied from one processing stage to another. In addition, the research supported an important finding in prior studies, that "youth who were detained were more likely to have a petition filed, less likely to have petitions dismissed, and more likely to be removed from the home and ordered to the juvenile state correctional institution" (p. 406). This finding is consistent with prior studies showing that even short-term incarceration of youth can lead to more severe treatment of youth. In many situations, it is apparent that a broader and historical framework of racism applies (Hawkins, 2011; West, 1993). To be sure, both school and JJ system pipelines exist in many jurisdictions, typically beginning with either inappropriate school referrals or unwarranted arrests.

DMC typically begins at the point of arrest. Black youth are seriously overrepresented in juvenile arrests (Puzzanchera and Adams, 2011). "Of all juvenile arrests for violent crimes in 2009, 47 percent involved White youth, 51 percent involved Black youth, 1 percent involved Asian youth, and 1 percent involved American Indian youth" (p. 6). RRI calculations should never begin later than the point of arrest. However, the ideal baseline would be a comparison of racial/ethnic disparities in arrests versus differences in self-report measures of delinquency.

Collectively, DMC studies underscore the need to examine closely arrests and juvenile justice decision making for unintended bias, and to ensure that needed services are available and accessible on geographic and other important eligibility criteria. It also is imperative that objective risk and needs assessments are used to guard against the perception that minority youth are more violent (Chapman, Desai, Falzer et al., 2006) and less amenable to treatment than White offenders (Leiber and Brubaker, 2010).

The priority goal should be DMC reductions in secure detention and confinement. There is some good news with respect to progress on the latter front. Based on confinement rates reported in the Census of Juveniles in Residential Placement, the data suggest a decline in Black versus White racial disproportionality in juvenile placement rates in the United States over the period 1997–2006 (Davis and Sorensen, 2013). "The results show a decrease in the disproportionate Black:White ratio of juvenile placements, controlling for the groups' rate of arrests from the baseline in 1997, which indicates partial support for the effectiveness of the federal DMC initiative" (p. 132).

ELIMINATE THE TRANSFER OF
JUVENILES TO THE CRIMINAL JUSTICE SYSTEM

Every U.S. state uses one or more statutory approaches to prosecute some juveniles as adult criminals (Griffin, 2012). Although the details of states' transfer laws differ, all rely on variations of three general strategies—judicial waiver, legislative offense exclusion, and prosecutorial direct-file—to prosecute children in adult criminal courts. Transfer has served as a central focus of juvenile justice reforms in recent decades. Analysts estimate that more than 200,000 juveniles are transferred annually to adult criminal courts under these three methods and including states with juvenile court jurisdiction that ends before age seventeen (Adams and Addie, 2009; Howell, Feld, and Mears, 2012). Although the upper age of original juvenile court jurisdiction for delinquency is seventeen (eight states) or eighteen (forty states and D.C.) for all states except New York and North Carolina (age sixteen), statutes in many jurisdictions require mandatory transfer to adult court for certain offenses committed by children as young as ten years of age. For example, youths in Kansas can be waived to adult court for any criminal offense at ten years of age, in Mississippi the age is thirteen, and in Florida the age is fourteen (Griffin, Addie, Adams, and Firestine, 2011).

The U.S. Supreme Court's decision in *Roper v. Simmons* (2005) to abolish executions of juvenile offenders in the United States provides the backdrop for discussion of the reduced criminal responsibility of young people (Farrington, Loeber, and Howell, 2012). Culpability focuses on a person's blameworthiness and the degree of deserved punishment. "The diminished responsibility of young people for offending is thought to require mitigated sanctions to avoid permanently life-changing penalties and provide room for reform. Compared with adults, youths' immature judgment reflects differences in appreciation of risk, appraisal of short- and long-term consequences, self-control, and susceptibility to negative peer influences" (p. 731). Until recently, developmental psychologists focused on logical reasoning capacity as the linchpin of maturity. However, recent research shows that although physical maturity (the completion of puberty) typically occurs by age twelve or thirteen, intellectual maturity ordinarily is completed by age eighteen. But the higher level executive functions of the brain (such as impulse control, emotion regulation, delay of gratification, planning, and resistance to peer influence) may not be fully developed until age twenty-five (Prior, Farrow, Hughes et al., 2011). Thus analysts have called for an "immaturity discount" that should be implemented for juvenile and young adult offenders: a decrease in the severity of penalties that takes account of young persons' lesser culpability and diminished responsibility (Howell, Feld, and Mears, 2012). The recent adolescent brain research also suggests that death sentences and life without parole sentences should be abolished for young adult offenders (Farrington et al., 2012).

There is yet another scientific basis for this recommendation. A systematic review of transfer studies conducted by the Task Force on Community Preventive Services (2007) of the Centers for Disease Control and Prevention (Hahn, McGowan, Liberman et al., 2007) found that transferring juveniles to the adult criminal justice system generally increased, rather than decreased, rates of violence. Transferred juveniles are 34 percent more likely to be rearrested for violent or other crimes than are juveniles retained in the JJ system, an iatrogenic effect (Tonry, 2007).

Juveniles should never be placed in adult prisons for another reason: It is inhumane. After conducting many studies of confinement conditions and practices around the world, Human Rights Watch (2012, p. 91) insists that the United States should "end the practice of trying, sentencing, and incarcerating youth under eighteen in the adult criminal justice system; where this is not immediately feasible, mandate that all people under age eighteen be held in the juvenile justice system—before trial and after conviction or adjudication—no matter how they are charged; and appropriate funds, as necessary, to provide for changes in population in juvenile facilities." Considerable progress has been seen recently in this direction. Over the past eight years (2006–2013), twenty-three states have enacted forty pieces of legislation designed to reduce the prosecution of youth in adult criminal courts and end the placement of youth in adult jails and prisons (Campaign for Youth Justice, 2013).

The U.S. criminal justice system has demonstrated that it is unqualified as a model that should be used for juvenile offenders (Howell, 2009, pp. 296–97; Howell et al., 2012; Howell and Howell, 2007; Kurlychek and Johnson, 2010; Liebman, Fagan, and West, 2000; Tonry, 2007). Adult court processing makes offenders worse; convictions are followed by an increase in offending, juveniles who are dealt with in adult criminal court are more likely to reoffend than other juveniles, and sending young people to adult prisons leads to an increase in recidivism. Neither short nor long prison terms reduce recidivism (Lipsey and Cullen, 2007). Moreover, the average net cost benefit of the top five evidence-based programs in JJ systems is nearly four times greater ($41,000) per offender compared with the five best programs in the criminal justice system ($11,270) (Aos et al., 2006, p. 9). Thus large cost savings can be realized from retaining juvenile offenders in JJ system programs.

Older dangerous juvenile offenders who require secure confinement should be placed in youthful offender facilities. Some existing prisons and juvenile correctional facilities could be made available for this purpose if juvenile and adult correctional systems were to rigorously apply risk assessment and classification procedures and reduce current excessive populations in prisons and juvenile correctional facilities. The cost savings should be reinvested in expanded and improved rehabilitative services in JJ systems where the benefits would be greater. Importantly, incarcerated youth have a higher incidence of mental health, health, and educational needs than the general population, but services are inadequate relative to the risks and needs of these youth (Sedlak and McPherson, 2010). Providing evidence-based services surely would reduce recidivism and improve the overall effectiveness of JJ systems.

As in some European countries, older adolescent and young adult offenders eighteen to twenty-four years of age should be recognized as a distinct category. After studying offender careers that persist from juvenile to adult status and desistance measures, an international study group of scholars (Loeber and Farrington, 2012) recommend increasing the minimum age for adjudication in the adult court system, applying an "immaturity discount" for this age group in conjunction with individual risk/needs assessments, modifying sentencing guidelines accordingly, establishing special courts and/or correctional facilities, and providing access to evidence-based treatment (Farrington, Loeber, and Howell, 2012).

ELIMINATE MISUSE OF CONFINEMENT

Owing partly to the 17 percent drop in the number of juvenile arrests between 2000 and 2009, there was a 34 percent decrease in the number of juvenile offenders in residential placement during this period (Hockenberry, 2013). In addition, residential placement reform efforts have resulted in the movement of many juveniles from secure, large public facilities to less secure, small private facilities. Also, economic factors have prompted a shift from committing juveniles to high-cost residential facilities to providing lower-cost options, such as probation, day treatment, or other community-based sanctions (p. 5). But it appears that this decreased reliance on residential placements has not led to improvements in conditions of confinement. In 2010, the Office of Juvenile Justice and Delinquency Prevention published findings from the Survey of Youth in Residential Placement in a bulletin entitled *Conditions of Confinement*. Briefly, the survey revealed that:

- 50 percent of youth reported that staff applied punishment without cause,
- More than 33 percent of youth reported that staff used unnecessary force in interactions with residents,
- 28 percent of youth reported that staff used some method of restraint on them,
- 35 percent of youth reported being placed in isolation (half of whom said the period of isolation exceeded twenty-four hours), and
- 28 percent of youth reported that their families had to travel 3 hours or longer to visit them.

Several federal investigations of juvenile correctional facilities have revealed inhumane and unsafe conditions of confinement. Between 2000 and 2007, twenty CRIPA[2] investigations were made of twenty-three juvenile justice facilities in more than a dozen states (U.S. Department of Justice, 2007). During Fiscal Year 2011, a total of eleven such investigations were active in nine states and Puerto Rico (U.S. Department of Justice, 2012). The OJJDP Performance-based Standards (PbS) program[3] has been in place for more than twenty years. This is a program developed by the Council of Juvenile Correctional Administrators (CJCA) to specifically address safety, health, and quality of life issues in youth facilities—unhealthy and dangerous conditions of confinement. PbS sets national standards that establish the highest expectations for facility conditions and services and measures practices impacting the quality of life. PbS trains and supports participants to collect data, analyze the results, and change practices to best serve youths, staff, families, and communities.

Participating PbS facilities have worked to cut in half the time youths are isolated and confined to their rooms, an ineffective practice in managing youths' behavior, and also one which research has shown to be dangerous, increasing youths' risk for suicide. Facilities implementing PbS as intended will meet standards at very high operational expectation levels, greater than constitutional minimum requirements and, therefore, not be significantly at risk for CRIPA violations.

The Justice Policy Institute recently singled out five states that have made significant progress in reducing confinement of juvenile offenders (Arizona, Connecticut, Louisiana, Minnesota, and Tennessee). Two even higher achieving states were overlooked in this review: North Carolina (M.Q. Howell, Lassiter, and Anderson, 2012) and California (Males and Macallair, 2010), both of which have reduced confinement by more than two-thirds since 2000. North Carolina reduced the number of offenders placed in correctional facilities by two-thirds in the past decade—attributable, in large part, to implementation of the Comprehensive Strategy and use of a disposition matrix that restricted confinement to only SVC offenders and saving more than $30 million. Juvenile delinquency also decreased along with reduced confinement, as court referrals dropped by 27 percent during the period 2000–2011 (M. Q. Howell et al., 2012, p. 2).

In the past decade, state legislatures have promoted a shift from confinement to community-based programming (Brown, 2012). The main theme of these initiatives is a reinvestment strategy. In 2004, major reform legislation was passed in Illinois to establish "Redeploy Illinois," which has become a model for other states (p. 8). In addition to encouraging counties to develop community-based programs for juveniles rather than confine them in state correctional facilities, the new law mandated that savings from the reduced commitments must be reallocated to the counties for development of community-based treatment programs. "In at least half a dozen states today, other realignment strategies are moving fiscal resources from state institutions to community-based services" (p. 8). Similar reform measures were enacted into law in Ohio and Texas. In California—long recognized as having the most deplorable youth corrections facilities in the United States—the Hoover Commission recommended that the state eliminate its juvenile justice operations and create regional rehabilitative facilities for high-risk, high-need offenders to be leased to and run by the counties, which proved to be cost-effective (Males and Macallair, 2010).

An effective alternative to confinement, the Teaching-Family Home model, has been overlooked in program-by-program reviews, even though at least 700 replications were reported by 2000 (Fixsen, Blasé, Timbers, and Wolf, 2001). Originally developed in the 1970s, the Teaching-Family Home model is a behaviorally-oriented approach that integrates family-style living, youth self-government, and a token economy for teaching social skills. The model engages a married couple or other "teaching parents" to offer a family-like environment in the residence, a model broadly characterized as "teaching family care." In a modified version, structured group care, trained therapists implement the Teaching-Family Home Model. To illustrate, the North Carolina structured group care provided by Methodist Home for Children in multipurpose residential juvenile homes incorporates the Teaching-Family Home Model and integrates therapeutic teaching and reinforcement for youth based on the service plan and their learning levels. This model reduced recidivism and secure confinement (Strom, Colwell, Dawes et al., 2010). In a meta-analysis of programs for serious and violent offenders, Lipsey and Wilson (1998) found that the Teaching-Family Home Model reduces recidivism for this target group. Importantly, this program can be used in either format, residential foster care or community group care (Lee and Thompson, 2008).

ADDRESS THE TREATMENT NEEDS OF GIRLS IN A BALANCED APPROACH

Contrary to some reports, the juvenile justice system is not currently flooded with girls, although an increase in court-referred females clearly has occurred in recent years (Snyder and Sickmund, 2006; Steffensmeier et al., 2006). Consequently, girls now represent a larger proportion of JJ system clients than in the past (Puzzanchera et al., 2012). Hubbard and Matthews (2008) observe that the increases in girls' violent delinquency arrests reported in the FBI Uniform Crime Report are mainly attributable to changes in the laws and the actions of officials rather than from changes in the behavior of girls. As one example, "what were once considered normal fights between family members are now classified as assaults that attract formal police intervention and more frequently result in arrest" (p. 228; see also Chesney-Lind and Sheldon, 2004; Stevens, Morash, and Park, 2011). Indeed, "comparisons of juvenile court dispositions for boys and girls . . . suggest that in recent years, girls have experienced harsher penalties for less serious crimes" (Hubbard and Matthews, 2008, p. 228). Several examples of unjust handling of girls in JJ systems are disturbing (Howell, 2009; Hubbard and Matthews, 2008):

- Locking girls up may worsen some of the very problems that got them into trouble in the first place (e.g., disruptions in relationships, depression, sexual abuse, violent victimization).
- Girls have a greater likelihood than boys of being arrested and detained for running away.

- Girls are far more likely than boys to be held in detention centers for minor offenses.
- Girls are also more likely than boys to be detained for contempt of court, increasing the likelihood of their return to detention centers, providing more opportunities for victimization.
- Once girls are placed on probation—typically for status offenses—any subsequent offense becomes "a vector" for their greater involvement in the juvenile justice system through probation violations and new offenses (Acoca, 2005).
- Alternatives to JJ system processing for girls are lacking.

Fortunately, much more is now known about girls' mental health status and service needs (McReynolds et al., 2010; Teplin, Abram, McClelland et al., 2006; Wasserman et al., 2005). To be sure, studies show that certain treatment needs of girls are elevated, warranting the tailoring of certain services for them (Hipwell and Loeber, 2006; Hubbard and Matthews, 2008; McReynolds et al., 2008; Wasserman et al., 2005). In general, girls are at significantly higher risk (80 percent) than boys (67 percent) for a mental health disorder, with girls demonstrating higher rates than boys of internalizing disorders (Shufelt and Cocozza, 2006). Other research shows that among youths at JJ system intake, as many as 45 percent of boys and 50 percent of girls have at least one diagnosable psychiatric disorder (Wasserman et al., 2005). "Concern over these recent statistics is making the development of effective girls' programming a priority with juvenile justice agencies that have traditionally neglected this population of offenders" (Hubbard and Matthews, 2008, p. 226).

Two treatment philosophies are widely promoted: the "female-responsive" philosophy (that girls have unique treatment needs) and the "what works" philosophy (that gender-neutral services are equally effective with girls and boys) (Hubbard and Matthews, 2008). Even though there is research support for both philosophies, Hubbard and Matthews insist the two can be integrated to the greater benefit of girls. Thus these scholars provide a blueprint for working effectively with girls in this dual approach that is outlined below.

Advocates of the "female-responsive" philosophy are concerned that bringing low risk girls into the JJ system could well exacerbate their delinquency and bring other unintended harm to them. "What girls need, these advocates argue, are services in the community" (Hubbard and Matthews, 2008, p. 234). These advocates also argue that although girls may have elevated treatment needs, this does not necessarily mean that they are "high risk" (Hubbard and Matthews, 2008). Another contentious issue is the notion of "criminogenic needs." First, some advocates suggest that this framework places excessive blame on individuals instead of society. Second, they assert that limiting the targets of intervention to a select number of criminogenic needs is myopic and ignores the full range of problems that precipitate girls' delinquent behavior and the broader social context in which they live—in families, schools, communities, and so on.

In turn, advocates of the "what works" philosophy respond to the risk issue in two ways. First, these advocates argue that, for both boys and girls, a youth's level of risk indicates his or her likelihood of recidivism, and this information can be used properly to determine the appropriate level of supervision needed to protect the public and the child, for program placement, and to gauge the intensity and duration of services that the youth needs. Second, these advocates are emphatic that low risk offenders should not be placed in intensive sanctions or services. On the notion of criminogenic needs, the "what works" philosophy proponents insist that treatable risks exist within five broad domains including individual, family, school, peers, and community context and that this encompassing framework can be used to organize service delivery.

As Hubbard and Matthews (2008) suggest, an overriding goal of the JJ system—to reduce the recidivism of youth under its care—is common ground for uniting the gender-responsive and what works advocates. It has become apparent that girls are disproportionately "high need" and "low risk," meaning they have a critical need for services, but do not pose as large a threat to public safety as boys. The service "blueprint" these scholars propose consists of the following protocols (pp. 246–247). First, agencies should use a validated, actuarial risk assessment instrument to measure girls' risk of recidivism. These instruments must be normed on female offenders and appropriate cutoff levels should be established that distinguish low, medium, and high risk offenders. Low risk offenders should be diverted outright, along with many of the moderate and high risk offenders who may have treatment needs that can be met in community programs. Second, it is recommended that agencies conduct other standardized, objective measures of problem areas known to be prevalent among girls. Statewide implementation of the Voice Diagnostic Interview Schedule for Children would serve to identify the mental health and substance use treatment needs of girls and boys alike (McReynolds et al., 2010). Third, intake staff should conduct an in-depth interview with each girl at court or assessment center intake. Fourth, a thorough treatment needs assessment should measure girls' strengths and assets. Last, services should be matched with each girl's specific treatment needs in comprehensive service plans.

Female-Responsive Programs

Proponents of the female-responsive philosophy strongly oppose singling girls out for intensive treatment because, in their view, the main source of their problems is not individual flaws. Rather, it is predominantly societal and system overreactions to girls' minor forms of delinquency that need repair. Hence, Hubbard and Matthews (2008, p. 238) propose strengths-based supports, "a therapeutic model that allows girls to explore common problems in their lives and develop a sense of self-worth through intimate communication with others." More specifically, they support treatment approaches that are (a) based on the relational model and (b) trauma informed.

In the female-to-female relational arena, "positive change for girls is dependent on developing mutually trusting and empathetic relationships that prevent them from undergoing the same experiences again" (Hubbard and Matthews, 2008, p. 239). In a facilitative manner, "trauma-informed services conduct universal screening on intake to identify [girls] with a history of abuse, use a strengths-based approach to help consumers recognize the skills that have helped them survive their abuse, and help them transfer these skills to achieve important treatment goals (e.g., improved decision making, reduced substance abuse)" (pp. 238–239). These two service delivery requirements of gender-responsive programming can be integrated with CBT in a "therapeutic helping alliance" with girls that Hubbard and Matthews (2008) insist is particularly relevant when working with them.

A continuum of programs for girls should emphasize the importance of building positive connections in the domains of family, peers, school, and community. In each of these developmental domains, "the goal is to surround girls with social support that insulates them from adverse circumstances that may lead to risky or antisocial behavior. Studies show that social support protects youth from adverse circumstances by providing them with a sense of felt security and counteracting psychological and physical consequences of stress" (Hubbard and Matthews, 2008, p. 248). Victimized and "beyond risk" girls also could benefit from treatment for traumatic victimization, posttraumatic stress disorder, and other mental health services; health screening, health education, and basic health services; substance abuse services, and a full spectrum of on-grounds experiential learning and educational services. In constructing such a continuum it is important to be mindful that girls' access to needed services is often problematic (for a variety of program options for girls, see Chesney-Lind, Morash, and Stevens, 2008; and the Center for the Promotion of Mental Health in Juvenile Justice's Guidelines for Child and Adolescent Mental Health Referral, 2003). Both Connecticut and Florida have made major strides in providing female-responsive services for girls (Watson and Edelman, 2012). A Girls Health Screen (GHS) instrument has been developed for girls between the ages of eleven and seventeen who are in detention (Acoca, 2005). The screening allows for the immediate detection of health conditions for girls entering the system and helps guide proper treatment.

Farrington and Painter (2004) suggest that parent training and parent education techniques, which target parental discipline, parental supervision, parental reinforcement of children (e.g. praising) and parental interest in children are likely to have proportiona,lly more impact in reducing female offending than in reducing male offending (especially early onset of delinquency). Early intervention with female child delinquents, particularly aggressive girls, is the recommended best practice. Intervention at this level necessarily includes parents or guardians. Augimeri's team discovered that more than half of the child delinquent girls displayed aggressive behavior problems before age seven, that they tended to come from chaotic families with high levels of mother-daughter conflict and experienced multiple separations from their primary caregivers (Augimeri and Koegel, 2012; Augimeri, Walsh, Liddon et al., 2011). SNAP® Girls is an evidence-based gender-sensitive cognitive-behavioral program for young aggressive girls and their parents (Pepler, Walsh, Yuile et al., 2010). In fact, this is the first evidence-based *gender-specific* intervention for girls under age 12 with disruptive behavior problems. Therapy includes social learning, self-control, problem solving, and feminist perspectives with a growing emphasis on trauma and attachment disorders (Pepler et al., 2010). (http://www.stopnowandplan.com/girl_program.php). This program lowers aggressive, bullying, and delinquent behaviors in the short term, with good evidence that these effects can be sustained over the intermediate future.

Gender-Neutral Programs

While female-specific or female-responsive approaches can be effective in reducing delinquency, gender-neutral programs can also be effective. Until recently, common knowledge in the juvenile justice field held that nothing had proven effective in addressing girls' delinquency involvement, attributable in large part to the fact that few female-specific programs had been developed and only a handful of these had been rigorously evaluated (Zahn, Agnew, Fishbein et al., 2010). At the insistence of outside observers, the Office of Juvenile Justice and Delinquency Prevention (OJJDP) Study Group on Girls broadened its lens to consider evidence-based programs that are not female-specific, and the Study Group identified two programs that appear to be effective with girls as well as boys (Zahn, Day, Mihalic et al, 2009), Multisystemic Therapy (MST) and Multidimensional Treatment Foster Care (MTFC), both of which use behavioral management approaches.

In his meta-analysis of all program types (reviewed earlier) Lipsey (2009) found no difference in effectiveness for girls and boys, though he cautions that there are too few studies with female samples to have confidence in this conclusion. It is encouraging, however, that several evidence-based services identified in Lipsey's meta-analyses are commonly used in some of the effective programs identified for girls and discussed in this section, particularly CBT, family therapy, counseling, and interpersonal skills development. In an important new study, family therapy and mixed and group counseling are very effective treatments for substance abuse for girls and boys (Tanner-Smith, Wilson, and Lipsey, 2013b). Effective programs for male serious and violent adolescent offenders also may produce positive results for girls (Lipsey and Wilson, 1998). In particular, Aggression Replacement Training (ART) that targets violent youth appears effective for females as well as for males. ART consists of a ten-week, thirty-hour cognitive-behavioral program administered to groups of eight to twelve adolescents ages eleven to seventeen (Goldstein and Glick, 1994). During these ten weeks, youth typically attend three one-hour sessions per week on skill streaming, anger control, and moral reasoning training. A condensed version of ART for adolescents placed temporarily in a short-term residential facility (a runaway shelter) who had exhibited signs of antisocial behavior also was effective with girls (Nugent, Bruley, and Allen, 1999).

Strengthening Families Program: For Parents and Youth 10–14 (SFP 10–14) is a gender-neutral program for parents and their adolescent children. The adapted program aims to reduce substance use and behavior problems during adolescence through improved skills in nurturing and child management by parents and improved interpersonal and personal competencies among youths. Parent group sessions teach appropriate disciplinary practices, effective communication skills for dealing with their youths. Youth group sessions teach refusal skills for dealing with peer pressure and personal skills such as dealing with stress. The program led to a significant increase in parenting competencies, reduced student substance-related risk, and led to significant increases in school engagement (http://www.crimesolutions.gov/ProgramDetails.aspx?ID=190).

Safe Dates is an exemplary program for preventing dating violence that can help reduce girls' violent sexual victimizations. The goals of this program are to change adolescent dating violence norms, change adolescent gender-role norms, improve conflict resolution skills for dating relationships, promote victims' and perpetrators' beliefs in the need for help and awareness of community resources for dating violence, promote help-seeking by victims and perpetrators, and improve peer help-giving skills. Foshee and colleagues (2005) found program effectiveness in the areas of psychological abuse perpetration, moderate physical violence perpetration, and sexual violence perpetration. Intended for middle and high school students, the Safe Dates program can stand alone or fit easily within health education, family, or general life-skills curriculum.

ADDRESS COMMUNITY-WIDE GANG PROBLEMS

Nationwide, about one-third of law enforcement agencies report gang activity each year (Egley and Howell, 2013). Reported gang problems declined steeply in the late 1990s, surged in the early 2000s, and stabilized in recent years. The three commonly used gang-seriousness indicators—number of gangs, gang members, and gang-related homicides—show that gang activity is concentrated primarily in urban areas, especially in very large cities (Howell, Egley, Tita, and Griffiths, 2011). More than half of all gangs, 75 percent of gang members, and 87 percent of gang-related homicides are located in metropolitan areas (cities with populations greater than 100,000 and adjacent suburban counties) (Egley and Howell, 2013). Moreover, each of these three gang-seriousness indicators shows increases in gang-related homicides within metropolitan areas from 2002 to 2011, in contrast with the historical drop in violent and property crime rates over the past decade. Two-thirds of the cities with populations of 50,000 or more also report persistent gang problems. Thus cities this size and larger should be alert to possible gang activity—particularly if the given city is near a large metropolitan area with a long history of gang activity. Gang member homicide rates are approximately 100 times greater than in the broader population (Decker and Pyrooz, 2010). The strongest predictors of homicide are prior serious delinquency, selling hard drugs, gun carrying, cruelty to people, and gang membership (Loeber and Farrington, 2011). Prevention of gang joining is paramount, especially in schools and communities (Howell, 2010, 2013b), while addressing research-based risk factors (Howell and Egley, 2005).

It also is important to address gang involvement of juvenile offenders at all stages of system processing. Because of their heightened and prolonged involvement in crime, active gang members invariably penetrate JJ systems more deeply. This systematic progression in multiple system stages was first documented statewide in North Carolina, where gang members represent:

- 7 percent of all juveniles on whom delinquent complaints are filed,
- 13 percent of juveniles adjudicated,
- 21 percent of juveniles admitted to short-term detention, and
- 38 percent of juveniles committed to secure residential facilities (M.Q. Howell and Lassiter, 2011).

This latter statistic is concordant with nationwide data on perceptions of incarcerated juvenile offenders. About one in three youth in residential juvenile detention or correctional facilities professes some gang affiliation, and nearly two-thirds (60 percent) of confined youth report the presence of gangs in the facility in which they are confined (Sedlak and McPherson, 2010). Most youth (64 percent) are living in units where one-fifth or fewer of the residents are gang members, less than one-third (30 percent) are in living units where between one-fifth and one-half of youth are gang members, and just 6 percent are living in units with a majority of gang members. This research suggests that the presence of gangs can negatively affect the custody environment for all youth residing within facilities. For example, the presence of gangs in detention or correctional facilities is associated with the percentage of youth who say they have been offered contraband (24 percent versus 8 percent) and also with the percentage of youth who are in living units characterized by poor youth-staff relations (51 percent versus 30 percent). "Certain problematic conditions tend to cluster in custody environments. When problems escalate, facilities sometimes engage in last-resort control methods. For instance, when there are gangs in a facility, significantly more youth are in living units where one or more residents say that staff sprayed them with pepper spray (38 percent versus 18 percent)" (Sedlak and McPherson, 2010, p. 8).

Thus it is important to target SVC gang members with intensive services and graduated sanctions. But this is a formidable challenge. The North Carolina research (M.Q. Howell and Lassiter, 2011) shows that there are more than seven times as many high risk offenders among gang members than among non-gang youth (52 percent vs. 7 percent) (Figure A.1). Appendix Table A.1 provides specific research-supported risk fac-

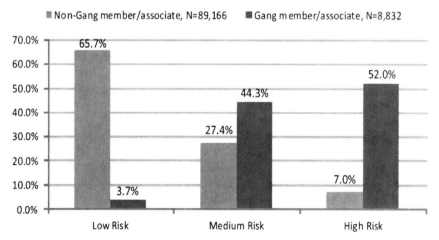

Figure A.1.   **Average Risk Levels of Gang and Non-Gang Juvenile Offenders in North Carolina**

Table A.1.   Risk Factors for Recidivism among Gang Members (With Greater Certainty for Males than Females)

Very strong research support:
  Offense history: Frequency of violent assaults
  Individual: Degree of gang embeddedness
  Individual: Low self-control
  Peer: Frequency of associations with fellow gang members
Strong research support:
  Offense history: Prior referrals to juvenile court
  Individual: Substance use/abuse history
  Family: Have run away from home or program placement
  Family: Have parents that are willing but unable to supervise them
  Family: Family transitions
  Family: Low parent education
  Peer: Early dating
  School: Serious school problems (drop out, expulsion, long-term suspension)
Good research support:
  Family: Family disadvantage
  Family: Poverty income level

Sources: Howell, 2012; Howell and Egley, 2005; M.Q. Howell and Lassiter, 2011; Pyrooz et al., 2013; Thornberry et al., 2003

tors for recidivism among gang members who had been adjudicated delinquent. The risk factors with very strong research support are frequency of violent assaults, degree of gang embeddedness, low self-control, and frequency of associations with fellow gang members.

In the late 1980s, OJJDP supported a comprehensive nationwide assessment of organized agency and community group responses to gang problems in the United States. It remains the only national assessment of efforts to combat gangs. Based on this assessment, the Comprehensive Gang Prevention, Intervention, and Suppression Model was developed (called the Comprehensive Gang Program Model, or CGM for short). The CGM provides a flexible framework for locally appropriate activities based on five integrated strategies: (1) *Social intervention* and (2) *opportunities provision* activities are primarily delivered within the context of a multidisciplinary intervention team composed of personnel from several agencies including street outreach, law enforcement, social services, probation/parole, and education. (3) *Community mobilization* engages members of the community in addressing local gang issues. (4) *Suppression* activities emphasize accountability and community safety. (5) *Organizational change and development* activities seek to improve information sharing between agencies and the delivery of services to gang members and their families.

Evaluations of the CGM have found reductions in gang violence and drug-related offenses (Spergel, Wa, and Sosa, 2006), and reductions in gang involvement and gang crime (Cahill and Hayeslip, 2010; Hayeslip and Cahill, 2009). Spergel and colleagues (2006) found that, in the three sites in which the program was implemented with high fidelity (Chicago, Illinois; Riverside, California; Mesa, Arizona), there were statistically significant reductions in gang violence when compared with control groups of youth and neighborhoods; in two of the sites, there were statistically significant reductions in drug-related offenses. The Cahill and Hayeslip evaluation focused on four cities (Los Angeles, California; Richmond, Virginia; Milwaukee, Wisconsin; and North Miami Beach, Florida), and found reductions in one or more crime reduction indicators, though not in all sites.

Multiple replications of this Model have provided insight into CGM best practices. Core elements crucial to successful implementation of the Model include the following (National Gang Center, 2010):

- An effective Steering Committee convened by community leaders and policymakers to share responsibility for addressing local gang problems.
- A methodical and comprehensive community gang assessment for the purpose of identifying the unique social contexts in which gangs form, the risk factors associated with gang involvement, and an inventory of existing programs appropriate for reducing gang activities in the specific location. This step is critical to efficient and effective targeting of activities and strategies.
- A multidisciplinary Intervention Team which manages cases for the coordinated delivery of targeted services to gang members who have been identified through screening criteria drawn from the assessment.
- Once the Intervention Team has been convened, street outreach workers play an active role in connecting gang members to necessary services. Outreach workers are not only the primary source of program referrals, but they often play an active role in delivering services and working closely with community service providers. In addition, outreach workers are the Intervention Team's "eyes and ears" on the street, giving the team perspective on the personal aspects of gang conflicts and violence and how these affect the team's clients (Arciaga and Gonzalez, 2012). Evaluations have substantiated that well-implemented outreach work is essential for success (Hayeslip and Cahill, 2009; Spergel et al., 2006).
- A project coordinator who can serve as liaison between the Steering Committee and the Intervention Team. Sustained leadership is critical for long-term program success and to ensure the effectiveness of the program coordinator (Hayeslip and Cahill, 2009).

The states of Massachusetts (Gebo and Bond, 2012) and North Carolina (M.Q. Howell and Lassiter, 2011) have implemented the CGM in multiple sites covering most of the state population affected by gangs. In Massachusetts, all cities with populations greater than 100,000 were supported, whereas in North Carolina, counties were invited to participate. In both cases and in other states that are able to implement the CGM, the model allows for local decision making based on the community gang assessment as to which evidence-based programs are best suited to prevent further escalation and reduce gang involvement among youth (https:// www.nationalgangcenter.gov/SPT).

NOTES

1. http://www.ojjdp.gov/dmc/pdf/StepsinCalculatingtheRelativeRate Index.pdf.

2. Since its enactment in 1980, the Civil Rights of Institutionalized Persons Act (CRIPA), 42 U.S.C. § 1997a *et seq.*, has allowed the Civil Rights Division of the U.S. Department of Justice to investigate possible civil rights violations pertaining to persons in publicly operated institutions and to bring consequent legal actions against state or local governments. Accessed at: http://www.justice.gov/crt/about/spl/juveniles.php.

3. Accessed at: http://pbstandards.org/.

References

Abrams, D. E. (2003). *A very special place in life: The history of juvenile justice in Missouri*. Jefferson City, MO: The Missouri Juvenile Justice Association.

Acoca, L. (2005). Introduction to the National Girls Health Screen Project. Philadelphia, PA: Stoneleigh Foundation. Available at http://stoneleighfoundation .org/content/national-girls-health-screen-project.

Adams, B., and Addie, S. (2009). Delinquency cases waived to criminal court, 2005. *Fact Sheet*. Washington, DC: Office of Juvenile Justice and Delinquency Prevention.

Advancement Project. (2005). Education on lockdown: *The schoolhouse to jailhouse track*. Washington, DC: Advancement Project.

Ægisdóttir, S., White, M. J., Spengler, P. M. Maugherman, A. S., Anderson, L. A., Cook, R. S., et al. (2006). The meta-analy,sis of clinical judgment project: Fifty-six years of accumulated research on clinical versus statistical prediction. *The Counseling Psychologist*, 34, pp. 341–382.

Andrews, D. A. (2006). Enhancing adherence to risk-need-responsivity. *Criminology and Public Policy*, 5, 595–602.

Andrews, D. A., and Bonta, J. (2006). *The psychology of criminal conduct*, 4th ed. Cincinnati, OH: Anderson/LexiNexis.

———. (2010a). Rehabilitating criminal justice policy and practice. *Psychology, Public Policy and Law*, 16, 39–55.

———. (2010b). *The psychology of criminal conduct* (Fifth ed.). New Providence, NJ: LexisNexis Matthew Bender.

Andrews, D., Bonta, J., and Hoge, R. D. (1990). Classification for effective rehabilitation: Rediscovering psychology. *Criminal Justice and Behavior*, 17, 19–52.

Andrews, D., Bonta, J., and Wormith, S. (2006). The recent past and near future of risk and/or need assessment. *Crime and Delinquency*, 52, 7–27.

Andrews, D. A., Zinger, I., Hodge, R. D., Bonta, J., Gendreau, P., and Cullen, F. T. (1990). Does correctional treatment work? A clinically-relevant and psychologically informed meta-analysis. *Criminology*, 28, 369–404.

Annie E. Casey Foundation. (2013). *Juvenile Detention Alternatives Initiative: 2011 annual results report*. Baltimore, MD: Annie E. Casey Foundation.

Aos, S., Miller, M., and Drake, E. (2006). *Evidence-based public policy options to reduce future prison construction, criminal justice costs, and crime rates*. Olympia: Washington State Institute for Public Policy. (http://www.wsipp.wa.gov/).

Aos, S., Lee, S., Drake, E., Pennucci, A., Klima, T., Miller, M., Anderson, L., Mayfield, J., and Burley, M. (2012). *Return on investment: Evidence-based options to improve statewide outcomes*. Olympia: Washington State Institute for Public Policy. (http://www.wsipp.wa.gov/).

Arciaga, M., and Gonzalez, V. (2012). Street outreach and the Comprehensive Gang Model. *NGC Bulletin No. 7*. Tallahassee, FL: National Gang Center.

Arthur, M. W., Hawkins, J. D., Pollard, J. A., Catalano, R. F., and Baglioni, A. J. (2002). Measuring risk and protective factors for substance use, delinquency, and other adolescent problem behaviors: The Communities That Care Survey. *Evaluation Review*, 26, 575-601.

Augimeri, L. K., Enebrink, P., Walsh, M. M., and Jiang, D. (2010). Gender specific childhood risk assessment tools. Early assessment risk lists for boys (EARL-20B) and girls (EARL-21G). In R. K. Otto and K. S. Douglas (eds.), *Handbook of violence risk assessment* (pp. 43–62). New York: Routledge, Taylor and Francis Group.

Augimeri, L. K., and Koegel, C. J. (2012). Raising the bar: Transforming knowledge to practice for children in conflict with the law. In R. Loeber and B. C. Welsh (eds). *The Future of Criminology* (pp. 204–210). Oxford, NY: Oxford University Press.

Augimeri, L. K., Koegl, C. J., Webster, C. D., and Levene, K. (2001). *Early assessment risk list for boys: EARL-20B, Version 2*. Toronto: Earlscourt Child and Family Centre.

Augimeri, L. K., Walsh, M. M., Jiang, D., Koegl, C. J., and Logue L. (2010). Early Assessment Risk List – Pre Checklist: EARL-PC (Pilot Checklist). Toronto, ON: Child Development Institute.

Augimeri, L. K., Walsh, M., Liddon, A. D., and Dassinger, C. R. (2011). From risk identification to risk management: A comprehensive strategy for young children engaged in antisocial behavior. In D. W. Springer and A. Roberts, (eds.), *Juvenile justice and delinquency* (pp. 117–140). Sudbury, MA: Jones and Bartlett.

Augimeri, L. K., Walsh, M. M., and Slater, N. (2011). Rolling out SNAP, an evidence-based intervention: A summary of implementation, evaluation and research. *International Journal of Child, Youth and Family Studies*, 2, 330–352.

Austin, J. (2006). How much risk can we take? The misuse of risk assessment in corrections. *Federal Probation*, 70, 58–63.

Backer, T. E. (1993). Information alchemy: Transforming information through knowledge utilization. *Journal of the American Society for Information Science*, 44, 217–221.

Baglivio, M. (2009). The assessment of risk to recidivate among a juvenile offending population. *Journal of Criminal Justice*, 37, 596–607.

———. (2013a). Serious, violent, chronic analysis. *Briefing Report*. Tallahassee, FL: Florida Department of Juvenile Justice, February 13.

———. (2013b). The risk principle. *Briefing Report*. Tallahassee, FL: Florida Department of Juvenile Justice, March 21.

———. (2013c). Serious, violent, and chronic (SVC) offenders: How much crime are they responsible for? *Briefing Report*. Tallahassee, FL: Florida Department of Juvenile Justice, December 21.

Baglivio, M. T., and Jackowski, K. (2013). Examining the validity of a juvenile offending risk assessment instrument across gender and race/ethnicity. *Youth Violence and Juvenile Justice*, 11, 26–43.

Baglivio, M. T., Jackowski, K., Greenwald, M.A., and Howell, J.C. (2014). Serious, violent, and chronic juvenile offenders: A statewide analysis of prevalence and prediction of subsequent recidivism using risk and protective factors. *Criminology and Public Policy*, 13, 83–116.

Baird, C. (2009). A question of evidence: A critique of risk assessment models used in the justice system. *A special report*. Oakland, CA: National Council on Crime and Delinquency.

Baird, C., Johnson, K., Healy, T., Bogie, A., Dankert, E. W., and Scharenbroch, C. (2013). *Risk and needs assessments in juvenile justice: A comparison of widely available risk and needs assessment systems*. Oakland, CA: National Council on Crime and Delinquency.

Baird, S., Storrs, G. M., and Connelly, H. (1984). *Classification of juveniles in corrections: A model systems approach*. Washington, DC: Arthur D. Little, Inc.

Barnoski, R. (2002). Washington State's implementation of Functional Family Therapy for juvenile offenders: Preliminary results. Olympia: Washington State Institute for Public Policy. Retrieved from wsipp.wa.gov/.

———. (2004a). *Assessing risk for re-offense: Validating the Washington state juvenile court assessment*. Olympia, WA: Washington State Institute for Public Policy. Retrieved from wsipp.wa.gov/.

———. (2004b). *Outcome Evaluation of Washington State's research-based programs for juvenile offenders*. Olympia: Washington State Institute for Public Policy. Retrieved from wsipp.wa.gov/.

———. (2005). *Washington State's experience with research-based juvenile justice programs*. Olympia, WA: Washington State Institute for Public Policy. Retrieved from wsipp.wa.gov/.

———. (2009). *Providing evidence-based programs with fidelity in Washington State juvenile courts: Cost analysis*. Olympia: Washington State Institute for Public Policy. Retrieved from wsipp.wa.gov/.

Bechard, S., Ireland, C., Berg, B., and Vogel, B. (2011). Arbitrary arbitration: Diverting juveniles into the justice system—a reexamination after 22 years. *International Journal of Offender Therapy and Comparative Criminology*, 55, 605–625.

Bell, K. (2009). Gender and gangs: A quantitative comparison. *Crime and Delinquency*, 55, 363-387.

Benda, B. B., and Tollett, C. L. (1999). A study of recidivism of serious and persistent offenders among adolescents. *Journal of Criminal Justice*, 27, 111–126.

Berkel, C., Mauricio, A. M., Schoenfelder, E., and Sandler, I. N. (2011). Putting the pieces together: An integrated model of program implementation. *Prevention Science*, 12, 23–33.

Bernard, T. J. (1992). *The cycle of juvenile justice.* New York: Oxford University Press.

Blumstein, A. (1995). Youth violence, guns, and the illicit drug industry. *Journal of Criminal Law and Criminology,* 86, 10–36.

Borduin, C. M., and Ronis, S. T. (2012). Individual, family, peer, and academic characteristics of female serious juvenile offenders. *Youth Violence and Juvenile Justice,* 10, 386–400.

Brown, J., and Langan, P. (1998). *State court sentencing of convicted felons, 1994.* Washington, DC: U.S. Department of Justice, Bureau of Justice Statistics.

Brown, L. M. (2003). *Girlfighting: Betrayal and rejection among girls.* New York: New York University Press.

Brown, S. A. (2012). *Trends in Juvenile Justice State Legislation: 2001–2011.* Denver, CO: National Conference of State Legislators.

Bumbarger, B. K. (2012). Pennsylvania's statewide strategy for promoting blueprint programs. Paper presented at the Annual Blueprints Conference. April. San Antonio, TX.

Burke, C., and Pennell, S. (2001). *Breaking Cycles evaluation: A comprehensive approach to youthful offenders.* San Diego, CA: San Diego Association of Governments.

Burns, B. J., Landsverk, J., Kelleher, K., Faw, L., Hazen, A., and Keeler, G. (2001). Mental health, education, child welfare, and juvenile justice service use. In R. Loeber and D.P. Farrington (eds.). *Child Delinquents: Development, Intervention, and Service Needs* (pp. 273–304). Thousand Oaks, CA: Sage.

Bushway, S. D., Krohn, M. D., Lizotte, A. J., Phillips, M. D., and Schmidt, N. M. (2013). Are risky youth less protectable as they age? The dynamics of protection during adolescence and young adulthood. *Justice Quarterly,* 30, 84–116.

Bushway, S. D., Thornberry, T. P., and Krohn, M. D. (2003). Desistance as a developmental process: A comparison of static and dynamic approaches. *Journal of Quantitative Criminology,* 19, 129–15.

Butts, J. A., and Evans, D. N. (2011). Resolution, reinvestment, and realignment: Three strategies for changing juvenile justice. New York, NY: Research and Evaluation Center, John Jay College of Criminal Justice, City University of New York.

Cahill, M., and Hayeslip, D. (2010). Findings from the Evaluation of OJJDP's Gang Reduction Program. Juvenile Justice Bulletin. Washington, DC: U.S. Department of Justice, Office of Juvenile Justice and Delinquency Prevention.

California Department of Corrections and Rehabilitation. (2010). Juvenile justice outcome evaluation report: Youth released from the Division of Juvenile Justice in Fiscal Year 2004–05. Sacramento, CA: Office of Research.

Campaign for Youth Justice. (2013). State Trends: Legislative Victories 2011–2013. Washington, DC: Campaign for Youth Justice.

Centers for Disease Control and Prevention. (2006). Youth risk behavior surveillance: United States, 2005. *Prevention Morbidity and Mortality Weekly Report,* 55 (SS-5), 1–108.

Center for the Promotion of Mental Health in Juvenile Justice. (2003). *Guidelines for Child and Adolescent Mental Health Referral.* New York: Columbia University Department of Child and Adolescent Psychiatry.

Chapman, J. J., Desai, R. A., Falzer, P. R., and Borum, R. (2006). Violence risk and race in a sample of youth in juvenile detention: The potential to reduce disproportionate minority confinement. *Youth Violence and Juvenile Justice: An Interdisciplinary Journal*, 4, 170–184.

Chesney-Lind, M., and Sheldon, R. (2004). *Girls, delinquency, and juvenile justice* (Third ed.). Belmont, CA: Wadsworth.

Chesney-Lind, M., Morash, M., and Stevens, T. (2008). Girls' troubles, girls' delinquency, and gender responsive programming: A review. *Australian and New Zealand Journal of Criminology*, 41, 162–189.

Chung, H. L., Schubert, C. A., and Mulvey, E. P. (2007). An empirical portrait of community reentry among serious juvenile offenders in two metropolitan cities. *Criminal Justice and Behavior*, 34, 1402–1426.

Cocozza, J. J., Veysey, B. M., Chapin, D. A., Dembo, R., Walters, W., and Farina, S. (2005). Diversion from the juvenile justice system: The Miami-Dade juvenile assessment center post-arrest diversion program. *Substance Use and Misuse*, 40, 935–951.

Cohen, M. A., Piquero, A. R., and Jennings, W. G. (2010). Estimating the costs of bad outcomes for at-risk youth and the benefits of early childhood interventions to reduce them. *Criminal Justice Policy Review*, 21, 391–434.

Cook, P. J., and Laub, J. H. (1998). The unprecedented epidemic of youth violence. In M. Tonry and M. H. Moore (eds.), *Youth violence* (pp. 27–64). Chicago: University of Chicago Press.

Crosnoe, R., Erickson, K. G., and Dornbusch, S. M. (2002). Protective functions of family relationships and school factors on the deviant behavior of adolescent boys and girls: Reducing the impact of risky friendships. *Youth and Society*, 33, 515-544.

Cullen, F. T. (2005). The twelve people who saved rehabilitation: How the science of criminology made a difference. *Criminology*, 43, 1–42.

Davis, J., and Sorensen, J. R. (2013). Disproportionate minority confinement of juveniles: A national examination of black–white disparity in placements, 1997–2006. *Crime and Delinquency*, 59, 115–139.

Decker, S. H., and Pyrooz, D. C. (2010). Gang violence worldwide: Context, culture, and country. Small Arms Survey 2010. Geneva, Switzerland: Small Arms Survey.

Dedel-Johnson, K., and Hardyman, P. L. (2004). How do you know if the risk assessment instrument works? National Institute of Corrections. In *Topics in community corrections: Assessment issues for managers* (pp. 20–26). Washington, DC: U.S. Department of Justice, National Institute of Corrections.

Dembo, R., Schmeidler, J., and Walters, W. (2004). Juvenile assessment centers: An innovative approach to identify and respond to youths with substance abuse and related problems entering the justice system. In A. R. Roberts (ed.), *Juvenile justice sourcebook: Past, present and future* (pp. 512–536). New York, NY: Oxford University Press.

DiIulio, J. J., Jr. (1995, November 27). The coming of the super-predators. *Weekly Standard*, pp. 23–28.

Dishion, T. J., McCord, J., and Poulin, F. (1999). When interventions harm: Peer groups and problem behavior. *American Psychologist*, 54, 755–764.

Dodge, K. A., Dishion, T. J.,and Lansford, J. E. (eds.). (2006). *Deviant Peer influences in programs for youth: Problems and solutions.* New York: Guilford Press.

Drake, E. K. (2012). Reducing crime and criminal justice costs: Washington State's evolving research approach. *Justice Research and Policy,* 14, 97–115.

Drake, E. K., Aos, S., and Miller, M. G. (2009). Evidence-based public policy options to reduce crime and criminal justice costs: Implications in Washington State. *Victims and Offenders,* 42, 170–196.

Egley, A., Jr., and Howell, J. C. (2013). *Highlights of the 2011 National Youth Gang Survey.* Washington, DC: U.S. Department of Justice, Office of Justice Programs, Office of Juvenile Justice and Delinquency Prevention.

Elliott, D. S. (1994). Serious violent offenders: Onset, developmental course, and termination. *Criminology,* 32, 1–21.

Elliott, D. S., ed. (1998). *Blueprints for violence prevention.* Denver, CO: C and M Press.

Esbensen, F., Osgood, D. W., Peterson, D., Taylor, T. J., and Carson, D. C. (2013). Short and long term outcome results from a multi-site evaluation of the G.R.E.A.T. Program. *Criminology and Public Policy,* 12, pp. 375–411.

Esbensen, F., Peterson, D., Taylor, T. J., and Freng, A. (2010). *Youth violence: Sex and race differences in offending, victimization, and gang membership.* Philadelphia, PA: Temple University Press.

Ezelle, M. E. (2007). Examining the overall and offense-specific criminal career lengths of a sample of serious offenders. *Crime and Delinquency,* 53, 3-37.

Fabelo, T., Thompson, M. D., Plotkin, J. D., Carmichael, D., Marchbanks, M. P., and Booth, E. A. (2011). Breaking school rules: A statewide study of how school discipline relates to students' success and juvenile justice system involvement. New York: Council of State Governments Justice Center.

Fagan, A. A., Hanson, K., Hawkins, J. D., and Arthur, M. W. (2008). Implementing effective community-based prevention programs in the community youth development study. *Youth Violence and Juvenile Justice,* 6, 256–278.

Fagan, A., Van Horn, M. L., Hawkins, J.D., Arthur, M.W. (2007). Gender similarities and differences in the association between risk and protective factors and self-reported serious delinquency. *Prevention Science,* 8, 115-124.

Farrell, J. L., Young, D. W., and Taxman, F. S. (2011). Effects of organizational factors on use of juvenile supervision practices. *Criminal Justice and Behavior,* 38, 565–583.

Farrington, D. P., Loeber, R., and Howell, J. C. (2012). Young adult offenders: The need for more effective legislative options and justice processing. *Criminology and Public Policy,* 11, 729–750.

Farrington, D. P., Loeber, R., Jolliffe, D., and Pardini, D.A. (2008). Promotive and risk processes at different life stages. In R. Loeber, D. P. Farrington, M. Stouthamer-Loeber, et al., *Violence and serious theft: Development and prediction from childhood to adulthood* (pp. 169–229). New York: Routledge.

Farrington, D. P., Loeber, R., and Joliffe, D. (2008). The age-crime curve in reported offending. In R. Loeber, D. P. Farrington, M. Stouthamer-Loeber, et al., *Violence and serious theft: Development and prediction from childhood to adulthood* (pp. 77–104). New York: Routledge.

Farrington, D., and Painter, K. (2004). *Gender differences in risk factors for offending.* Research, Development and Statistics Directorate, UK. (Home Office RDS

Online Report OLR09/04) Retrieved October 20, 2012, from http://webarchive. nationalarchives.gov.uk/20110218135832/http://rds.homeoffice.gov.uk/rds/ onlinepubs1.html.

Farrington, D. P., and Welsh, B. C. (2007). *Saving children from a life of crime: Early risk factors and effective interventions.* New York: Oxford University Press.

Feyerherm, W., and Butts, J. (2003). Proposed methods for measuring disproportionate minority contact. Washington, DC: Office of Juvenile Justice and Delinquency Prevention.

Fixsen, D. L., Blasé, K. A., Naoom, S. F., and Wallace, F. (2009). Core implementation components. *Research on Social Work Practice,* 19, 531–540.

Fixsen, D. L., Blasé, K. A., Timbers, G. D., and Wolf, M. M. (2001). In search of program implementation: 792 replications of the Teaching-Family Model. In G. A. Bernfeld, D. P. Farrington, and A. W. Leschied (eds.), *Offender rehabilitation in practice: Implementing and evaluating effective programs* (pp. 149–166). London: Wiley.

Fixsen, D. L., Naoom, S. F., Blasé, K. A., Friedman, R. M., and Wallace, F. (2005). Implementation research: A synthesis of the literature. Tampa, FL: University of South Florida, Louis de la Parte Florida Mental Health Institute, The National Implementation Research Network (FMHI Publication #231).

Flinchum, T., and Hevener, G. (2011). Juvenile recidivism study: FY 2006/07 juvenile sample. Raleigh, NC: North Carolina Sentencing and Policy Advisory Commission.

Florida Department of Juvenile Justice. (2012). *2011 Comprehensive Accountability Report (CAR), Probation and Community Intervention.* Tallahassee, FL.

Foshee, V. A., Bauman, K. E., Ennett, S. T., Suchindran, C., Benefield, T., and Linder, G. R. (2005). Assessing the effects of the dating violence prevention program "Safe Dates" using random coefficient regression modeling. *Prevention Science,* 6, 245-258.

Fowler, J. (2013). An exploratory statewide analysis of serious, violent, and chronic offenders among delinquent youth in Pennsylvania. Paper presented at the annual meeting of the American Society of Criminology, Atlanta, November.

Fox, J. A. (1996). *Trends in juvenile violence: A report to the United States attorney general on current and future rates of juvenile offending.* Washington, DC: Bureau of Justice Statistics.

Fraser, M. W., Day, S. H., and Schwalbe, C. (2002). *Risk assessment in juvenile justice: The reliability and validity of a risk assessment instrument protocol.* Chapel Hill, NC: Jordan Institute for Families, School of Social Work, University of North Carolina.

Fratello, J., Salsich, A., and Mogulescu, S. (2011). Juvenile detention reform in New York City: Measuring risk through research. New York: Vera Institute of Justice, Center on Youth Justice.

Gatti, U., Tremblay, R. E., and Vitaro, F. (2009). Iatrogenic effect of juvenile justice. *Journal of Child Psychology and Psychiatry,* 50, 991–998.

Gebo, E., and Bond, B. J. E. (2012). *Beyond suppression: Community strategies to reduce gang violence.* Lanham, MD: Lexington Books.

Gebo, E., Stracuzzi, N. F., and Hurst, V. (2006). Juvenile justice reform and the courtroom workgroup: Issues of perception and workload. *Journal of Criminal Justice,* 34, 425–433.

Gendreau, P. (1981). Treatment in corrections: Martinson was wrong. *Canadian Psychology, 22,* 332-338.

Gilliam, W. S. (2005). *Prekindergartners left behind: Expulsion rates in state pre-kindergartner programs.* New York: Foundation for Child Development.

Gilman, A. B., Hill, K. G., and Hawkins, J. D. (2014). Long-term consequences of adolescent gang membership for adult functioning. *American Journal of Public Health,* 104 (5), 938-945. Published online ahead of print March 13, 2014: e1–e8. doi: 10.2105/AJPH.2013.301821

Glesmann, C., Krisberg, B., and Marchionna, S. (2009). *Youth in gangs: Who is at risk? Focus.* Oakland, CA: National Council on Crime and Delinquency.

Goldstein, A. P., and Glick, B. (1994). *The prosocial gang: Implementing Aggression Replacement Training.* Thousand Oaks, CA: Sage.

Gorman-Smith, D., and Loeber, R. (2005). Are developmental pathways in disruptive behaviors the same for girls and boys? *Journal of Child and Family Studies,* 14, 15–27.

Gottfredson, D. C., Cross, A., and Soule, D. A. (2007). Distinguishing characteristics of effective and ineffective after-school programs to prevent delinquency and victimization. *Criminology and Public Policy, 6,* 289–318.

Gottfredson, D. C., and Gottfredson, G. D. (2002). Quality of school-based prevention programs. *Journal of Research in Crime and Delinquency, 39,* 3–35.

Gottfredson, M. R., and Hirschi, T. (1990). *A general theory of crime.* Stanford, CA: Stanford University Press.

Gottfredson, S. D., and Moriarty, L. J. (2006). Statistical risk assessment: Old problems and new applications. *Crime and Delinquency, 52,* 178–200.

Green, G. S., Carlson, P. M., and Colvin, R. E. (2004). Juvenile accountability and the specific deterrent effects of short-term confinement. *Juvenile and Family Court Journal,* 55, 63–69.

Greenwood, P. W., Model, K. E., Rydell, C. P., and Chiesa, J. (1996). *Diverting children from a life of crime: Measuring costs and benefits.* Santa Monica, CA: Rand.

Greenwood, P. W., and Welsh, B.C. (2012). Promoting evidence-based practice in delinquency prevention at the state level: Principles, progress, and policy directions. *Criminology and Public Policy.* 11, 493–513.

Greenwood, P. W., Welsh, B.C., Rocque, M. (2012). *Implementing proven programs for juvenile offenders.* Downington, PA: Advancing Evidence Based Practice.

Griffin, P. (2004). Aftercare: The sequel. *Pennsylvania Progress: Juvenile justice achievements in Pennsylvania.* Pittsburgh, PA: National Center for Juvenile Justice.

———. (2012). Legal boundaries between the juvenile and criminal justice systems in the United States. In R. Loeber and D. P. Farrington (eds.), *From juvenile delinquency to adult crime: Criminal careers, justice policy and prevention* (pp. 184–199). New York: Oxford University Press.

Griffin, P., Addie, S., Adams, B., and and Firestine, K. (2011). Trying juveniles as adults: An analysis of state transfer laws and reporting. *National Report Series Bulletin.* Washington, DC: Office of Juvenile Justice and Delinquency Prevention.

Grisso, T., Vincent, G., and Seagrave, D. (2005): *Mental health screening and assessment in juvenile justice.* New York: Guilford Press.

Grisso, T., and Underwood, L. A. (2004). *Screening and assessing mental health and substance use disorders among youth in the juvenile justice system: A resource guide for practitioners.* Delmar, NY: National Center for Mental Health and Juvenile Justice, Policy Research Associates, Inc.

Grove, W. M., Eckert, E. D., Heston, L., Bouchard, T. J., Segal, N., and Lykken, D. T. (1990). *Clinical vs. mechanical prediction: A meta-analysis.* Minneapolis, MN: Department of Psychology, University of Minnesota.

Grove, W. M., and Meehl, P. E. (1996). Comparative efficiency of informal (subjective, impressionistic) and formal (mechanical, algorithmic) prediction procedures: The clinical-statistical controversy. *Psychology, Public Policy, and Law, 2,* 293-323.

Hahn, R. A., McGowan, A., Liberman, A., Crosby, A., Fullilove, M., Johnson, R., Moscicki, E., Price, L., Snyder, S., Tuma, F., Lowy, J., Briss, P., Cory, S., and Stone, G. (2007). *Effects on violence of laws and policies facilitating the transfer of youth from the juvenile to the adult justice system.* Atlanta, GA: Centers for Disease Control.

Hallfors, D., and Godette, D. (2002). Will the "principles of effectiveness" improve prevention practice? Early findings from a diffusion study. *Health Education Research, 17,* 461–470.

Hamparian, D. M., Schuster, R., Dinitz, S., and Conrad, J. P. (1978). *The violent few: A study of dangerous juvenile offenders.* Lexington, MA: Lexington.

Hart, J. L, O'Toole, S. K., Price-Sharps, J. L., and Shaffer, T. W. (2007). The risk and protective factors of violent juvenile offending: An examination of gender differences. *Youth Violence and Juvenile Justice, 5,* 367-384.

Hawkins, D. F. (2011). Things fall apart: Revisiting race and ethnic differences in criminal violence amidst a crime drop. *Race and Justice, 1,* 3–48.

Hawkins, D. F., and Kempf-Leonard, K. (2005). *Our children, their children: Confronting racial and ethnic differences in American juvenile justice.* Chicago, IL: The University of Chicago Press.

Hawkins, J. D., Oesterle, S., Brown, E. C., Monahan, K. C., Abbott, R. D., Arthur, M. W., and Catalano, R. F. (2012). Sustained decreases in risk exposure and youth problem behaviors after installation of the Communities That Care prevention system in a randomized trial. *Archives of Pediatrics and Adolescent Medicine, 166,* 140–148.

Hawkins, S. R., Graham, P. W., Williams, J., and Zahn, M. A. (2009). Resilient girls: Factors that protect against delinquency. *Bulletin.* Washington, DC: Office of Juvenile Justice and Delinquency Prevention.

Hayeslip, D., and Cahill, M. (2009). *Community collaboratives addressing youth gangs: Final evaluation findings from the Gang Reduction Program.* Washington, DC: Urban Institute.

Hemphill, S. A., McMorris, B. J., Toumbourou, J. W., Herrenkohl, T. I., Catalano, R. F., and Mathers, M. (2007). Rates of student-reported antisocial behavior, school suspensions, and arrests in Victoria, Australia and Washington state, United States. *Journal of School Health, 77,* 303–311.

Henggeler, S. W., and Schoenwald, S. K. (2011). Evidence-based interventions for juvenile offenders and juvenile justice policies that support them. *Social Policy Report, 25,* 3–26.

Hill, K. G., Howell, J. C., Hawkins, J. D., and Battin-Pearson, S. R. (1999). Childhood risk factors for adolescent gang membership: Results from the Seattle Social Development Project. *Journal of Research in Crime and Delinquency, 36,* 300-322.

Hipwell, A. E., and Loeber, R. (2006). Do we know which interventions are effective for disruptive and delinquent girls? *Clinical Child and Family Psychology Review*, 9, 221–255.

Hipwell, A. E., White, H. R., Loeber, R., Stouthamer-Loeber, M., Chung, T., and Sembower, M. A. (2005). Young girls' expectancies about the effects of alcohol, future intentions and patterns of use. *Journal of Studies on Alcohol*, 66, 630–639.

Hockenberry, S. (2013). Juvenile Residential Facility Census, 2010: Selected findings. *National Report Series Bulletin*. Washington, DC: Office of Juvenile Justice and Delinquency Prevention.

Hockenberry, S., Sickmund, M., and Sladky, A. (2011). Juvenile Residential Facility Census, 2008: Selected findings. *National Report Series Bulletin*. Washington, DC: Office of Juvenile Justice and Delinquency Prevention.

Hoeve, M., McReynolds, L. S., and Wasserman, G. A. (2013). The influence of mental health disorders on severity of reoffending in juveniles. *Criminal Justice and Behavior*, 40, 289–301.

Hoge, R. D., and Andrews, D. A. (2010). *Evaluation for risk of violence in juveniles*. New York: Oxford University Press.

Hoge, R. D., Vincent, G., and Guy, L. (2012). Prediction and risk/needs assessments. In R. Loeber and D. P. Farrington (eds.), *Transition between juvenile delinquency and adult crime* (pp. 150–183). New York: Oxford University Press.

Holman, B., and Ziedenberg, J. (2006). *The dangers of detention: The impact of incarcerating youth in detention and other secure facilities*. Washington, DC: Justice Policy Institute.

Howell, J. C. (2001). Risk-needs assessments and screening devices. In R. Loeber and D. P. Farrington (eds.). *Child delinquents: Development, interventions, and service needs* (pp. 395–404). Thousand Oaks, CA: Sage.

———. (2003a). Diffusing research into practice using the comprehensive strategy for serious, violent, and chronic juvenile offenders. *Youth Violence and Juvenile Justice: An Interdisciplinary Journal*, 1, 219–45.

———. (2003b). *Preventing and reducing juvenile delinquency: A comprehensive framework*. Thousand Oaks, CA: Sage.

———. (2009). *Preventing and reducing juvenile delinquency: A comprehensive framework* (Second ed.). Thousand Oaks, CA: Sage.

———. (2010). Gang prevention: An overview of current research and programs. *Juvenile Justice Bulletin*. Washington, DC: U.S. Department of Justice, Office of Juvenile Justice and Delinquency Prevention.

———. (2012). *Gangs in America's communities*. Thousand Oaks, CA: Sage.

———. (2013a). GREAT results: Implications for PBIS in schools. *Criminology and Public Policy*, 12, pp. 413–420.

———. (2013b). Why is gang membership prevention important? In T. R. Simon, N. M. Ritter, and R. R. Mahendra (eds.). *Changing course: Preventing gang membership* (pp. 7–18). Washington, DC: U.S. Department of Justice, U.S. Department of Health and Human Services.

Howell, J. C., and Egley, A. Jr. (2005). Moving risk factors into developmental theories of gang membership. *Youth Violence and Juvenile Justice*, 3, 334–354.

Howell, J. C., Egley, A., Jr., Tita, G., and Griffiths, E. (2011). *U.S. gang problem trends and seriousness.* Tallahassee, FL: Institute for Intergovernmental Research, National Gang Center.

Howell, J. C., Feld, B. C., and Mears, D. P. (2012). Young offenders and an effective justice system response: What happens, what should happen, and what we need to know. In R. Loeber and D. P. Farrington (eds.), *From juvenile delinquency to adult crime* (pp. 200–244). New York: Oxford University Press.

Howell, J. C., and Howell, M. Q. (2007). Violent juvenile delinquency: Changes, consequences, and implications. In D. Flannery, A. Vazonsyi, and I. Waldman (eds.), *Cambridge handbook of violent behavior* (pp. 501–518). Cambridge, MA: Cambridge University Press.

Howell, J. C., Kelly, M. R., Palmer, J., and Mangum, R. L. (2004). Integrating child welfare, juvenile justice and other agencies in a continuum of services for children, youth and families. *Child Welfare,* 83, 143–156.

Howell, J. C., and Lipsey, M. W. (2012). Research-based guidelines for juvenile justice programs. *Justice Research and Policy,* 14, 17–34.

Howell, M. Q. (2013). Serious, violent and chronic (SVC) offenders in North Carolina. Paper presented at the Annual Meeting of the American Society of Criminology, November. Atlanta, Georgia.

Howell, M. Q. and Bullock, J. (2013). *Juvenile diversion in North Carolina.* Raleigh, NC: North Carolina Department of Public Safety, Rehabilitative Programs and Support Services.

Howell, M. Q., and Lassiter, W. (2011). *Prevalence of gang-involved youth in North Carolina.* Raleigh, NC: North Carolina Department of Juvenile Justice and Delinquency Prevention.

Howell, M. Q., Lassiter, W., and Anderson, C. (2012). *North Carolina Department of Juvenile Justice and Delinquency Prevention Annual Report, 2010.* Raleigh, NC: North Carolina Department of Juvenile Justice and Delinquency Prevention.

Hubbard, D. J., and Matthews, B. (2008). Reconciling the differences between the "gender-responsive" and the "what works" literatures to improve services for girls. *Crime and Delinquency,* 54, 225–258.

Hubbard, D. J., and Pratt, T. C. (2002). A meta-analysis of the predictors of delinquency among girls. *Journal of Offender Rehabilitation,* 34, 1–13.

Huizinga, D. (2010). Who are the long-term gang members? Paper presented at the annual meeting of the American Society of Criminology, San Francisco, November.

Huizinga, D., and Jakob-Chien, C. (1998). The contemporaneous co-occurence of serious and violent offending and other problem behavior. In R. Loeber and D. P. Farrington (eds.). *Serious and violent juvenile offenders: Risk factors and successful interventions* (pp. 46–67). Thousand Oaks, CA: Sage.

Huizinga, D., Loeber, R., and Thornberry, T. P. (1995). *Recent findings from the program of research on causes and correlates of delinquency.* Washington, DC: Office of Juvenile Justice and Delinquency Prevention.

Huizinga, D., Loeber, R., Thornberry, T. P., and Cothern, L. (2000). Co-occurrence of delinquency and other problem behaviors. *Juvenile Justice Bulletin.* Washington, DC: Office of Juvenile Justice and Delinquency Prevention.

Huizinga, D., and Miller, S. (2013). Understanding and responding to girls' delinquency. *Juvenile Justice Bulletin*. Washington, DC: U.S. Department of Justice, Office of Juvenile Justice and Delinquency Prevention.

Huizinga, D., Thornberry, T., Knight, K., Lovegrove, P., Loeber, R., Hill, K., and Farrington, D. P. (2007). Disproportionate minority contact in the juvenile justice system: A study of differential minority arrest/referral to court in three cities. A report to the Office of Juvenile Justice and Delinquency Prevention. Rockville, MD: National Criminal Justice Reference Service.

Human Rights Watch. (2012). *Growing up locked down: Youth in solitary confinement in jails and prisons across the United States*. New York, NY: Human Rights Watch.

Johnson, E. H. (1987). *Handbook on crime and delinquency prevention*. New York: Greenwood Press.

Johnson, K., Lanza-Kaduce, L., and Woolard, J. (2011). Disregarding graduated treatment: Why transfer aggravates recidivism. *Crime and Delinquency, 57*, 756–777.

Johnson, K., Wagner, D., and Matthews, T. (2002). *Missouri juvenile risk assessment re-validation report*. Madison, WI: National Council on Crime and Delinquency.

Justice for Families. (2012). *Families unlocking futures: Solutions to the crisis in juvenile justice*. Oakland, CA: Justice for Families. Retrieved from: www.justice-4families.org.

Kelley, B. T., Loeber, R., Keenan, K., and DeLamatre, M. (1997). Developmental pathways in boys' disruptive and delinquent behavior. *Juvenile Justice Bulletin*. Washington, DC: U.S. Department of Justice, Office of Juvenile Justice and Delinquency Prevention.

Kelly, W. R., Macy, T. S., and Mears, D. P. (2005). Juvenile referrals in Texas: An assessment of criminogenic needs and the gap between needs and services. *The Prison Journal, 85*, 467–489.

Kempf-Leonard, K., Tracy, P. E., and Howell, J. C. (2001). Serious, violent, and chronic juvenile offenders: The relationship of delinquency career types to adult criminality. *Justice Quarterly, 18*, 449–478.

Knitzer, J. (1982). *Unclaimed children: The failure of public responsibility to children and adolescents in need of mental health services*. Washington, DC: The Children's Defense Fund.

Knitzer, J., and Cooper, J. (2006). Beyond integration: Challenges for children's mental health. *Health Affairs, 25*, 670–679.

Krohn, M. D., Lizotte, A. J., Bushway, S. D., Schmidt, N. M., and Phillips, M. D. (2014). Shelter during the storm: A search for factors that protect at-risk adolescents from violence. *Crime and Delinquency, 60*, 379–401.

Krohn, M. D., and Thornberry, T. P. (2008). Longitudinal perspectives on adolescent street gangs. In A. Liberman (ed.), *The long view of crime: A synthesis of longitudinal research* (pp. 128–160). New York: Springer.

Krohn, M. D., Thornberry, T. P., Rivera, C., and Le Blanc, M. (2001). Later careers of very young offenders. In R. Loeber and D.P. Farrington (eds.). *Child delinquents: Development, interventions, and service needs* (pp. 67–94). Thousand Oaks, CA: Sage.

Kroneman, L., Loeber, R., and Hipwell, A. E. (2004). Is neighborhood context differently related to externalizing problems and delinquency for girls compared with boys? *Clinical Child and Family Psychology Review, 7*, 109–122.

Kurlychek, M. C., and Johnson, B. D. (2004). The juvenile penalty: A comparison of juvenile and young adult sentencing outcomes in criminal court. *Criminology*, 42, 485–517.

Kurlychek, M.C., and Johnson, B.D. (2010). Juvenility and punishment: Sentencing juveniles in adult criminal court. *Criminology*, 48, 725–758.

Langberg, J., Fedders, B., and Kukorowski, D. (2011). *Law enforcement officers in Wake County schools: The human, educational, and financial costs.* Durham, NC: Advocates for Children's Services.

Lassiter, W., Clarkson, S., and Howell, M. Q. (2009). *North Carolina Department of Juvenile Justice and Delinquency Prevention Annual Report, 2008.* Raleigh, NC: North Carolina Department of Juvenile Justice and Delinquency Prevention.

Latessa, E., Lovins, B., and Ostrowski, K. (2009). *The Ohio Youth Assessment System: Final report.* Cincinnati OH : University of Cincinnati.

Lee, B., and Thompson, R. (2008). Comparing outcomes for youth in treatment foster care and family style group care, *Children and Youth Services Review*, 30, pp. 746–57.

Lee, S., Aos, S., Drake, E., Pennucci, A., Miller, M., and Anderson, L. (2012). *Return on investment: Evidence-based options to improve statewide outcomes*, April 2012 (Document No. 12–04–1201). Olympia, WA: Washington State Institute for Public Policy.

Legislative Budget Board. (2011). Statewide criminal justice recidivism and revocation rates. Austin, Texas: Legislative Budget Board.

Lerman, P., and Pottick, K. J. (1995). *The parents' perspective: Delinquency, aggression, and mental health.* Chur, Switzerland: Harwood.

Levene, K. S., Augimeri, L. K., Pepler, D. J., Walsh, M., Koegl, C. J., and Webster C. D. (2001). *Early assessment risk list for girls: EARL-21G, Version 1, Consultation Edition.* Toronto: Earlscourt Child and Family Centre.

Leiber, M. J., and Brubaker, S. J. (2010). Does the gender of the intake probation officer contextualize the treatment of Black youth? *Justice Research and Policy*, 12, 51–76.

Leiber, M., and Rodriguez, N. (2011). The implementation of the disproportionate minority confinement/contact (DMC) mandate: A failure or success? *Race and Justice*, 1, 103–124.

Liebman, J. S., Fagan, J., and West, V. (2000). *A broken system: Error rates in capital cases, 1973–1995.* New York: School of Law, Columbia University.

Lipsey, M. W. (1992). Juvenile delinquency treatment: A meta-analytic inquiry into the variability of effects. In T. D. Cook, H. Cooper, D. S. Cordray, H. Hartman, L.V. Hedges, R. J. Light, T. A. Louis, and F. Mosteller (eds.). *Meta-Analysis for Explanation* (pp. 83–127). New York, NY: Russell Sage Foundation.

———. (1995). What do we learn from 400 research studies on the effectiveness of treatment with juvenile delinquents? In J. McGuire (ed.). *What works? Reducing reoffending* (pp. 63–78). New York, NY: John Wiley.

———. (1998). Design sensitivity: Statistical Power for Experimental Research. In L. Bickman, and D. J. Rog (eds). *Handbook of applied social research methods* (pp. 39-68). Thousand Oaks, CA: Sage Publications.

———. (1999a). Can rehabilitative programs reduce the recidivism of juvenile offenders? An inquiry into the effectiveness of practical programs. *The Virginia Journal of Social Policy and the Law*, 6, 611–641.

———. (1999b). Can intervention rehabilitate serious delinquents? *Annals of the American Academy of Political and Social Science*, 564 (July), 142–166.

———. (2002). Meta-analysis and program outcome evaluation. *Socialvetenskaplig Tidskrift*, 9, 194-208.

———. (2006a). The effects of community-based group treatment for delinquency: A meta-analytic search for cross-study generalizations. In K. A. Dodge, T. J. Dishion, and J. E. Lansford (eds.), *Deviant peer influences in programs for youth: Problems and solutions*, (pp. 162–184). New York: Guilford Press.

———. (2006b). *The evidence base for effective juvenile programs as a source for best practice guidelines.*Nashville, TN: Vanderbilt University, Center for Evaluation Research and Methodology.

———. (2007). *The evidence base for effective juvenile programs as a source for best practice guidelines.* Nashville, TN: Vanderbilt University, Center for Evaluation Research and Methodology.

———. (2008). *The Arizona Standardized Program Evaluation Protocol (SPEP) for Assessing the Effectiveness of Programs for Juvenile Probationers: SPEP Ratings and Relative Recidivism Reduction for the Initial SPEP Sample. A Report to the Juvenile Justice Services Division, Administrative Office of the Courts, State of Arizona.* Center for Evaluation Research and Methodology, Vanderbilt Institute for Public Policy Studies. Retrieved from http://peabody.vanderbilt.edu/research/pri/publications.php.

———. (2009). The primary factors that characterize effective interventions with juvenile offenders: A meta-analytic overview. *Victims and Offenders*, 4, 124–147.

Lipsey, M. W., and Cullen, F. T. (2007). The effectiveness of correctional rehabilitation: A review of systematic reviews. *Annual Review of Law and Social Science*, 3, 297–320.

Lipsey, M. W., and Derzon, J. H. (1998). Predictors of violent or serious delinquency in adolescence and early adulthood: A synthesis of longitudinal research. In R. Loeber and D. P. Farrington (eds.), *Serious and violent juvenile offenders: Risk factors and successful interventions* (pp. 86–105). Thousand Oaks, CA: Sage.

Lipsey, M. W., and Howell, J. C. (2012). A broader view of evidence-based programs reveals more options for state juvenile justice systems. *Criminology and Public Policy*, 11, 515–523.

Lipsey, M. W., Howell, J. C., Kelly, M. R., Chapman, G. L., and Carver, D. (2010). *Improving the effectiveness of juvenile justice programs: A new perspective on evidence-based practice.* Washington, DC: Georgetown University, Center for Juvenile Justice Reform. Retrieved from http://peabody.vanderbilt.edu/research/pri/publications.php.

Lipsey, M. W., Howell, J. C., and Tidd, S. T. (2007). *A practical approach to evaluating and improving juvenile justice programs utilizing the Standardized Program Evaluation Protocol (SPEP): Final evaluation report.* Nashville, TN: Vanderbilt University, Center for Evaluation Research and Methodology. Retrieved from http://peabody.vanderbilt.edu/research/pri/publications.php.

Lipsey, M. W., and Landenberger, N. A. (2006). Cognitive–behavioral interventions. In B. C. Welsh and D. P. Farrington (eds.), *Preventing crime: What works for children, offenders, victims, and places* (pp. 57–71). Belmont, CA: Wadsworth.

Lipsey, M. W., and Wilson, D. B. (1993). The efficacy of psychological, educational, and behavioral treatment: Confirmation from meta-analysis. *American Psychologist*, 48, 1181–1209.

———. (1998). Effective intervention for serious juvenile offenders: A synthesis of research. In R. Loeber and D.P. Farrington (eds.), *Serious and violent juvenile offenders: Risk factors and successful interventions* (pp. 313–345). Thousand Oaks, CA: Sage.

———. (2001). *Practical meta-analysis*. Thousand Oaks, CA: Sage.

Lipsey, M. W., Wilson, D. B., and Cothern, L. (2000). Effective interventions for serious and violent juvenile offenders. *Juvenile Justice Bulletin*. Washington, DC: U.S. Department of Justice, Office of Juvenile Justice and Delinquency Prevention.

Lipton, D., Martinson, R., and Wilks, J. (1975). *The effectiveness of correctional treatment: A survey of treatment evaluation studies*. New York, NY: Praeger.

Lizotte, A. J., Krohn, M. D., Howell, J. C., Tobin, K., and Howard, G. J. (2000). Factors influencing gun carrying among young urban males over the adolescent-young adult life course. *Criminology*, 38, 811–834.

Loeber, R., and Ahonen, L. (2013). Invited address: Street killings: Prediction of homicide offenders and their victims. *Journal of Youth Adolescence*, 42, 1640-1650.

Loeber, R., and Farrington, D. P., eds. (1998). *Serious and violent juvenile offenders: Risk factors and successful interventions*. Thousand Oaks, CA: Sage.

———., eds. (2001). *Child delinquents: Development, intervention, and service needs*. Thousand Oaks, CA: Sage.

———. (2011). *Young homicide offenders and victims: Risk factors, prediction, and prevention from childhood*. New York: Springer.

———., eds. (2012). *From juvenile delinquency to adult crime*. New York: Oxford University Press.

Loeber, R., Farrington, D. P., Howell, J. C., and Hoeve, M. (2012). Overview, conclusions and key recommendations. In R. Loeber and D. P. Farrington (eds.), *From juvenile delinquency to adult crime* (pp. 315–383). New York: Oxford University Press.

Loeber, R., Farrington, D. P., Stouthamer-Loeber, and White, H. (2008). Conclusions and policy implications. In R. Loeber, D. P. Farrington, M. Stouthamer-Loeber, and H. White (eds.). *Violence and serious theft: Development and prediction from childhood to adulthood* (pp. 309–334). New York: Routledge.

Loeber, R., Farrington, D. P., Stouthamer-Loeber, M., White, H. R., and Wei, E. (2008), *Violence and serious theft: Development and prediction from childhood to adulthood*. New York: Routledge.

Loeber, R., Farrington, D. P., and Waschbush, D. A. (1998). Serious and violent juvenile offenders. In R. Loeber and D. P. Farrington (eds.), *Serious and violent juvenile offenders: Risk factors and successful interventions* (pp. 13–29). Thousand Oaks, CA: Sage.

Loeber, R., Hoeve, M., Farrington, D. P., Howell, J. C., Slott, N. W., and Van Der Laan, P. H. (2012). Overview, conclusions, and policy and research recommendations. In R. Loeber, M. Hoeve, N. W. Slott, and and P. H. Van Der Laan (eds.), *Persisters and desisters in crime from adolescence into adulthood* (pp. 335–412). Burlington, VT: Ashgate.

Loeber, R., Hoeve, M., Slott, N. W., and Van Der Laan, P. H. (eds.) (2012). *Persisters and desisters in crime from adolescence into adulthood*. Burlington, VT: Ashgate.

Loeber, R., Keenan, K., and Zhang, Q. (1997). Boys' experimentation and persistence in developmental pathways toward serious delinquency. *Journal of Child and Family Studies*, 6, 321–357.

Loeber, R., Slott, W., and Stouthamer-Loeber, M. (2008). A cumulative developmental model of risk and promotive factors. In R. Loeber, H. M. Koot, N. W. Slott, P. H. Van der Laan, and and M. Hoeve (eds.), *Tomorrow's criminals: The development of child delinquency and effective interventions* (pp. 3–17). Hampshire, England: Ashgate.

Loeber, R., Slott, N. W., Van Der Laan, P. H., and Hoeve, M. (2008). *Tomorrow's criminals: The development of child delinquency and effective interventions*. Burlington, VT: Ashgate.

Loeber, R., Wei, E., Stouthamer-Loeber, M., Huizinga, D., and Thornberry, T. P. (1999). Behavioral antecedents to serious and violent offending: Joint analyses from the Denver Youth Survey, Pittsburgh Youth Study, and the Rochester Youth Development Study. *Studies on Crime and Crime Prevention, 8*, 245–263.

Loeber, R., and Wikstrom, P. H. (1993). Individual pathways to crime in different types of neighborhood. In D. P. Farrington, R. J. Sampson, and P. H. Wikstrom (eds.), *Integrating individual and ecological aspects of crime* (pp. 169–204). Stockhom: SWE: National Council for Crime Prevention.

Loeber, R., Wung, P., Keenan, K., Giroux, B., Stouthamer-Loeber, M., Van Kammen, W. B., and Maughan, B. (1993). Developmental pathways in disruptive child behavior. *Development and Psychopathology*, 5, 103–133.

Lösel, F., and Bender, D. (2003). Protective factors and resilience. In D. P. Farrington, and J. W. Coid (eds.). Early Prevention of Adult Antisocial Behavior (pp. 130-204). Cambridge, UK: Cambridge University Press.

Lösel, F., and Farrington, D. P. (2012). Direct protective and buffering protective factors in the development of youth violence. *American Journal of Preventive Medicine*, 43, 8–23.

Loughran, T. A., Mulvey, E. P., Schubert, C. A., Fagan, J., Piquero, A. R., and Losoya, S. H. (2009). Estimating a dose-response relationship between length of stay and future recidivism in serious juvenile offenders. *Criminology*, 47, 699–740.

Loughran, T. A., Piquero, A. R., Fagan, J., and Mulvey, E. P. (2012). Differential deterrence: Studying heterogeneity and changes in perceptual deterrence among serious youthful offenders. *Crime and Delinquency*, 58, 3–27.

Lovins, B., and Latessa, E. (2013). Creation and validation of the Ohio Youth Assessment System (OYAS) and strategies for successful implementation. *Justice Research and Policy*, 15, 67–93.

Lowenkamp, C. T., and Latessa, E. J. (2004). Understanding the risk principle: How and why correctional interventions can harm low risk offenders. In *Topics in community corrections: Assessment issues for managers* (pp. 3–8). Washington, DC: U.S. Department of Justice, National Institute of Corrections.

Lowenkamp, C. T., Makarios, M. D., Latessa, E. J., Lemke, R., and Smith, P. (2010). Community corrections facilities for juvenile offenders in Ohio: An examination of treatment integrity and recidivism. *Criminal Justice and Behavior*, 37, 695–708.

Macleod, J. F., Groves, P. G., and Farrington, D. P. (2012). *Explaining criminal careers*. Oxford: Oxford University Press.

Maguin, E., and Loeber, R. (1996). Academic performance and delinquency. In M. Tonry (ed.), *Crime and Justice: A Review of Research*, Vol. 20. Chicago, IL: University of Chicago Press, pp. 145–264.

Males, M., and Macallair, D. (2010). California miracle: Drastically reduced youth incarceration, drastically reduced youth crime. San Francisco: Center on Juvenile and Criminal Justice.

Mallett, C. A., Stoddard-Dare, P., and Seck, M. M. (2011). Explicating correlates of juvenile offender detention length: The impact of race, mental health difficulties, maltreatment, offense type, and court dispositions, *Youth Justice*, 11, 134–149.

Martinson, R. (1974). What works? Questions and answers about prison reform. *Public Interest*, 35, 22–54.

Matsueda, R. L., Kreager, D. A., and Huizinga, D. (2006). Deterring delinquents: A rational choice model of theft and violence. *American Sociological Review*, 71, 95–122.

McCord, J. (1985). Deterrence and the light touch of the law. In D. P. Farrington and J. Gunn (eds.), *Reactions to crime: The public, the police, courts, and prisons* (pp. 73–85). New York: John Wiley.

McCord, J., Widom, C. S., and Crowell, N. A. (eds.). (2001). *Juvenile crime, juvenile justice*. Washington, DC: National Academy Press.

McGowan, A., Hahn, R., Liberman, A., Crosby, A., Fullilove, M., Johnson, R., Moscicki, E., et al. (2007). Effects on violence of laws and policies facilitating the transfer of juveniles from the juvenile justice system to the adult justice system: A systematic review. *American Journal of Preventive Medicine*, 32 (4, Suppl. #1), 7–28.

McReynolds, L. S., Schwalbe, C. S., and Wasserman, G. A. (2010). The contribution of psychiatric disorder to juvenile recidivism. *Criminal Justice and Behavior*, 37, 204–216.

McReynolds, L. S., Wasserman, G. A., DeComo, R. E., John, R., Keating, J. M., and Nolen, S. (2008). Psychiatric disorder in a juvenile assessment center. *Crime and Delinquency*, 54, 313–334.

Mears, D. P., Cochran, J. C., Greenman, S. J., Bhati, A. S., and Greenwald, M. A. (2011). Evidence on the effectiveness of juvenile court sanctions. *Journal of Criminal Justice*, 39, 509–520.

Medaris, M. L. (1998). *A guide to the Family Educational Rights and Privacy Act*. Washington, DC: U.S. Department of Justice, Office of Juvenile Justice and Delinquency Prevention.

Mendel, R. A. (2011). No place for kids: *The case for reducing juvenile incarceration*. Baltimore, MD: Annie E. Casey Foundation.

Medaris, M. L., Campbell, E., and James, B. (1997). *Sharing information: A guide to the Family Educational Rights and Privacy Act and participation in juvenile justice programs*. Washington, DC: U.S. Department of Justice, Office of Justice Programs, Office of Juvenile Justice and Delinquency Prevention.

Mihalic, S., Irwin, K., Elliott, D., Fagan, A., and Hansen, D. (2001). Blueprints for violence prevention. *Juvenile Justice Bulletin*. Washington, DC: Office of Juvenile Justice and Delinquency Prevention.

Miller, J., and Maloney, C. (2013). Practitioner compliance with risk/needs assessment tools: A theoretical and empirical assessment. *Criminal Justice and Behavior*, 40, 716–736.

Missouri Juvenile and Family Division. (2013). *Annual report: Calendar 2012.* Jefferson City, MO: Juvenile and Family Division, Office of State Courts Administrator.

Moffitt, T. E. (1993). Adolescence-limited and life-course–persistent antisocial behavior: A developmental taxonomy. *Psychological Review,* 100, 674–701.

Moffitt, T. E., Caspi, A., Rutter, M., and Silva, P. A. (2001). *Sex differences in antisocial behavior: Conduct disorder, delinquency, and violence in the Dunedin Longitudinal Study.* New York: Cambridge University Press.

Monahan, K. C., and Piquero, A. R. (2009). Investigating the longitudinal relation between offending frequency and offending variety. *Criminal Justice and Behavior,* 36, 653–673.

Moore, J. E., Bumbarger, B. K., and Cooper, B. R. (2013). Examining adaptations of evidence-based programs in natural contexts. *Journal of Primary Prevention,* 34, 147–161.

Mulvey, E. P. (2011). Highlights from pathways to desistance: A longitudinal study of serious adolescent offenders. *Juvenile Justice Bulletin.* Washington, DC: U.S. Department of Justice, Office of Juvenile Justice and Delinquency Prevention.

Mulvey, E. P., Schubert, C. A., and Chung, H. L. (2007). Service use after court involvement in a sample of serious adolescent offenders. *Child and Youth Services Review,* 29, 518–44.

Mulvey, E.P., Steinberg, L., Fagan J., Cauffman, E., Piquero, A., and Chassin, L. et al. (2004). Theory and research on desistance from antisocial activity among serious adolescent offenders. *Youth Violence and Juvenile Justice,* 2, 213–236.

Mulvey, E. P., Steinberg, L., Piquero, A. R., Besana, M., Fagan, J., Schubert, C., and Caufman, E. (2010). Trajectories of desistance and continuity in antisocial behavior following court adjudication among serious adolescent offenders. *Developmental Psychopathology,* 22, 453–475.

National Center on Addiction and Substance Abuse. (2010). *National survey of American attitudes on substance abuse XV: Teens and parents,* 2010. New York: National Center on Addiction and Substance Abuse, Columbia University.

National Gang Center. (2010). *Best practices to address community gang problems: OJJDP's Comprehensive Gang Model.* Washington, DC: Author.

National Juvenile Justice Evaluation Center. (2012). *Evaluation-related needs of state, local, and tribal juvenile justice grantees.* Washington, DC: Justice Research and Statistics Association.

National Research Council. (2013). *Reforming juvenile justice: A developmental approach.* Washington, DC: National Academy of Sciences, National Academies Press.

Nugent, W. R., Bruley, C., and Allen, P. (1999). The effects of Aggression Replacement Training on male and female antisocial behavior in a runaway shelter. *Research on Social Work Practice,* 9, 466–82.

Office of Juvenile Justice and Delinquency Prevention. (2010). Conditions of confinement. *Juvenile Justice Bulletin.* Washington, DC: U.S. Department of Justice, Office of Juvenile Justice and Delinquency Prevention.

Office of State Courts Administrator. (2002). *Missouri's juvenile offender risk and needs assessment and classification system: User manual.* Jefferson City, MO: Juvenile and Adult Court Programs Division, Office of State Courts Administrator.

———. (2004). *Report on standards for the administration of juvenile justice.* Jefferson City, MO: Juvenile and Adult Court Programs Division, Office of State Courts Administrator.

———. (2009). *Juvenile offender recidivism report: 2009 statewide juvenile court report.* Jefferson City, MO: Juvenile and Adult Court Programs Division, Office of State Courts Administrator.

Oldenettel, D., and Wordes, M. (2000). The community assessment center concept. *Juvenile Justice Bulletin.* Washington, DC: U.S. Department of Justice, Office of Juvenile Justice and Delinquency Prevention.

Olds, D.; Hill, P.; Mihalic, S.; and O'Brien, R. (1998). *Blueprints for Violence Prevention, Book Seven: Prenatal and Infancy Home Visitation by Nurses.* Boulder, CO: Center for the Study and Prevention of Violence.

Olson, D. (2007). Florida makes PACT with state's youthful offenders. *Juvenile and Family Justice Today,* Winter, 6–9.

Olver, M. E., Stockdale, K. C., and Wormith, J. S. (2009). Risk assessment with young offenders: A meta-analysis of three assessment measures. *Criminal Justice and Behavior, 36,* 329–353.

Pearl, N., Ashcraft, R. G. P., and Geis, K. A. (2009). Predicting juvenile recidivism using the San Diego Regional Resiliency Check-Up. *Federal Probation, 7,* 46–49.

Pennsylvania Commission on Crime and Delinquency. (2012a). *A family guide to Pennsylvania's juvenile justice system.* Harrisburg, PA: Pennsylvania Commission on Crime and Delinquency. Retrieved from: http://www.pachiefprobation officers.org/ library.php.

———. (2012b). *Pennsylvania's juvenile justice system enhancement strategy.* Harrisburg, PA: Pennsylvania Commission on Crime and Delinquency. Harrisburg, PA: Pennsylvania Commission on Crime and Delinquency. Retrieved from: http://pachiefprobationofficers.org/docs/JJSES_Monograph.pdp.

———. (2013). *The Pennsylvania Juvenile Justice Recidivism Report: Juveniles with a 2007 Case Closure.* Harrisburg, PA: Pennsylvania Commission on Crime and Delinquency.

Pepler, D., Walsh, M., Yuile, A., Levene, K. Jiang, D., Vaughan, A., and Webber, J. (2010). Bridging the gender gap: Interventions with aggressive girls and their parents. *Prevention Science, 11,* 229–238.

Petersen, R. and Howell, J.C. (2013). Girls Involvement in gangs: A review of research, programs, and policies, *Criminal Justice Review, 38,* 491–509.

Peterson, D. (2012). Girlfriends, gun-holders, and ghetto-rats? Moving beyond narrow views of girls in gangs. In S. Miller, L. D. Leve, and P. K. Kerig (eds.), *Delinquent girls: Contexts, relationships, and adaptation* (pp. 71–84). New York: Springer.

Pratt, G. W. (2004). *Report on mental health services in the North Carolina Department of Juvenile Justice and Delinquency Prevention.* Raleigh, NC: Department of Juvenile Justice and Delinquency Prevention.

Prior, D., Farrow, K., Hughes, N., Kelly, G., Manders, G., White, S., and Wilkinson, B. (2011). *Maturity, young adults, and criminal justice.* Birmingham: Institute of Applied Social Studies, School of Social Policy, University of Birmingham.

Puzzanchera, C., and Adams, B. (2011). Juvenile arrests, 2009. *Juvenile Justice Bulletin.* Washington, DC: U.S. Department of Justice, Office of Juvenile Justice and Delinquency Prevention.

Puzzanchera, C., Adams, B., and Hockenberry, S. (2012). *Juvenile court statistics, 2009.* Pittsburgh, PA: National Center for Juvenile Justice.

Pyrooz, D. C., Sweeten, G., and Piquero, A. R. (2013). Continuity and change in gang membership and gang embeddedness. *Journal of Research in Crime and Delinquency,* 50, 239–271.

Redpath, D. P., and Brandner, J. K. (2010). *The Arizona Standardized Program Evaluation Protocol (SPEP) for assessing the effectiveness of programs for juvenile probationers: SPEP rating and relative recidivism reduction: An update to the January 2008 report by Dr. Mark Lipsey.* Phoenix: Arizona Supreme Court, Administrative Office of the Courts, Juvenile Justice Service Division. Retrieved from http://peabody.vanderbilt.edu/peabody research institute/publications.xml.

Rhoades, B. L., Bumbarger, B. K., and Moore, J. E. (2012). The role of a state-level prevention support system in promoting high-quality implementation and sustainability of evidence-based programs. *American Journal of Community Psychology,* 50, 386–401.

Robers, S., Zhang, J., Truman, J., and Snyder, T. D. (2012). *Indicators of school crime and safety, 2011.* Washington, DC: U.S. Department of Justice, National Center for Education Statistics, Bureau of Justice Statistics.

Rodriguez, N. (2010). The cumulative effect of race and ethnicity in juvenile court outcomes and why preadjudication detention matters. *Journal of Research in Crime and Delinquency,* 47, 391–413.

Rosenfeld, R., White, H., and Esbensen, F. (2012). Special categories of serious and violent offenders: Drug dealers, gang members, homicide offenders, and sex offenders. In R. Loeber and D. P. Farrington (eds.), *From juvenile delinquency to adult crime* (pp. 118–149). New York: Oxford University Press.

Sametz, L., and Hamparian, D. (1990). *Innovative programs in Cuyahoga County juvenile court: Intensive probation supervision and probation classification.* Cleveland, OH: Federation for Community Planning.

Schneider, A. L. (1990). *Deterrence and juvenile crime: Results from a national policy experiment.* New York: Springer-Verlag.

Schneider, A. L., and Ervin, L. (1990). Specific deterrence, rational choice, and decision heuristics: Applications in juvenile justice. *Social Science Quarterly,* 71, 585–601.

Schubert, C. A., Mulvey, E. P., and Glasheen, C. (2011). The influence of mental health and substance use problems and criminogenic risk on outcomes in serious juvenile offenders. *The Journal of the American Academy of Child and Adolescent Psychiatry,* 50, 925–937.

Schumacher, M., and Kurz, G. (2000). *The 8% solution: Preventing serious, repeat juvenile crime.* Thousand Oaks, CA: Sage Publications.

Schwalbe, C. S. (2007). A meta analysis of juvenile justice risk assessment predictive validity. *Law and Human Behavior,* 31, 449–462.

———. (2008). A meta-analysis of juvenile justice RAI: Predictive validity by gender. *Criminal Justice and Behavior,* 35, 1367–1381.

Schwalbe, C. S., Fraser, M. W., Day, S. H., and Arnold, E. M. (2004). North Carolina Assessment of Risk (NCAR): Reliability and predictive validity with juvenile offenders. *Journal of Offender Rehabilitation,* 40, 1–22.

Schwalbe, C. S., Fraser, M. W., and Day, S. H. (2007). Predictive validity of the Joint Risk Matrix with juvenile offenders: A focus on gender and race/ethnicity. *Criminal Justice and Behavior, 34*, 348–361.

Schwalbe, C. S., Fraser, M. W., Day, S. H., and Cooley, V. (2006). Classifying juvenile offenders according to risk of recidivism: Predictive validity, race/ethnicity, and gender. *Criminal Justice and Behavior, 33*, 305–324.

Schwalbe, C. S., Gearing, R. E., MacKenzie, M. J., Brewer, K. B., and Ibrahim, R. (2012). A meta-analysis of experimental studies of diversion for juvenile offenders. *Clinical Psychology Review, 32*, 26–33.

Schwalbe, C. S., Macy, R. J., Day, S. H., and Fraser, M. W. (2008). Classifying offenders: An application of latent class analysis to needs assessment in juvenile justice. *Youth Violence and Juvenile Justice, 6*, 279–294.

Sedlak, A. J., and McPherson, K. S. (2010). Youth's needs and services: Findings from the survey of youth in residential placement. *Juvenile Justice Bulletin.* Washington, DC: Office of Juvenile Justice and Delinquency Prevention.

Shannon, L.W. (1991). *Changing patterns of delinquency and crime: A longitudinal study in Racine.* Boulder, CO: Westview.

Shlonsky, A., and Wagner, D. (2005). The next step: Integrating actuarial risk assessment and clinical judgment into an evidence-based practice framework in CPS case management. *Children and Youth Services Review, 27*, 409–427.

Shook, J. J and Sarri, R. C. (2007). Structured decision making in juvenile justice: Judges' and probation officers' perceptions and use. *Children and Youth Services Review, 29*, 1335-1351.

Shufelt, J. S., and Cocozza, J. C. (2006). *Youth with mental health disorders in the juvenile justice system.* Delmar, NY: National Center for Mental Health and Juvenile Justice.

Simon, T. R., Ritter, N. M., and Mahendra, R. R., eds. (2013). *Changing course: Preventing gang membership.* Washington, DC: U.S. Department of Justice, U.S. Department of Health and Human Services.

Singh, J. P., Desmarais, S. L., Sellers, B. G., Hylton, T., Tirotti, M., and Van Dorn, R. A. (2013). From risk assessment to risk management: Matching interventions to adolescent offenders' strengths and vulnerabilities. *Children and Youth Services Review.*

Skowyra, K., and Cocozza, J. J. (2006). *A blueprint for change: A comprehensive model for the identification and treatment of youth with mental health needs in contact with the juvenile justice system.* Delmar, NY: National Center for Mental Health and Juvenile Justice.

Slobogin, C. (2013). Risk assessment and risk management in juvenile justice. ABA *Criminal Justice Magazine, 27* (Winter), 16–25.

Slobogin, C., and Fondacaro, M. R. (2011). *Juveniles at risk: A plea for preventive justice.* New York: Oxford University Press.

Smith, C., Lizotte, A. J., Thornberry, T. P., and Krohn, M. D. (1995). Resilient youth: Identifying factors that prevent high-risk youth from engaging in delinquency and drug use. In Z. S. Blau and J. Hagan (eds.), *Current perspectives on aging and the life cycle* (pp. 217–247). Greenwich, CT: JAI.

Snyder, H. N. (1998). Serious, violent and chronic juvenile offenders: An assessment of the extent of and trends in officially recognized serious criminal behavior in a delinquent population. In R. Loeber and D.P. Farrington (eds.), *Serious and violent juvenile offenders: Risk factors and successful interventions* (pp. 428–444). Thousand Oaks, CA: Sage.

———. (2001). Epidemiology of official offending. In R. Loeber and D.P. Farrington (eds.), *Child delinquents: Development, interventions, and service needs* (pp. 25–46). Thousand Oaks, CA: Sage.

Snyder, H. N., and Sickmund, M. (2006). *Juvenile offenders and victims: 2006 national report.* Washington, DC: U.S. Department of Justice, Office of Juvenile Justice and Delinquency Prevention.

Soler, M., Shoenberg, D., and Schindler, M. (2009) Juvenile justice: Lessons for a new era. *Georgetown Journal on Poverty Law and Policy,* Volume XVI, Symposium Issue.

Spanjaard, H. J. M., Van der Knaap, L. M., Van der Put, C. E., and Stams, G. J. (2012). Risk assessment and the impact of risk and protective factors. In R. Loeber, M. Hoeve, N.W. Slott, and P.H. Van Der Laan (eds.), *Persisters and desisters in crime from adolescence into adulthood* (Vol. 127–157). Burlington, VT: Ashgate.

Spergel, I. A., Wa, K. M., and Sosa, R. V. (2006). The comprehensive, community-wide, gang program model: Success and failure. In J. F. Short and L. A. Hughes (eds.), *Studying youth gangs* (pp. 203–224). Lanham, MD: AltaMira Press.

Steffensmeier, D., Zhong, H., Ackerman, J., Schwartz, J., and Agha, S. (2006). Gender gap trends for violent crimes, 1980 to 2003: A UCR-NCVS comparison. *Feminist Criminology,* 1, 72–98.

Stevens, T., Morash, M., and Park, S. (2011). Late-adolescent delinquency: Risks and resilience for girls differing in risk at the start of adolescence. *Youth and Society,* 43, 1433–1458.

Stouthamer-Loeber, M., and Loeber, R. (2002). Lost opportunities for intervention: Undetected markers for the development of serious juvenile delinquency. *Criminal Behavior and Mental Health,* 12, 69–82.

Stouthamer-Loeber, M., Loeber, R., Stallings, R., and Lacourse, E. (2008). Desistance from and persistence in offending. In R. Loeber, D. P. Farrington, M. Stouthamer-Loeber, and H. R. White (eds.), *Violence and serious theft: Development and prediction from childhood to adulthood* (pp. 269–306). New York: Routledge.

Strom, K. J., Colwell, A., Dawes, D., and Hawkins, S. (2010). *Evaluation of the Methodist Home for Children's value-based therapeutic environment model.* Research Triangle Park, NC: Research Triangle Institute.

Suter, J. C., and Bruns, E. J. (2009). Effectiveness of the wraparound process for children with emotional and behavioral disorders: A meta-analysis. *Clinical Child and Family Psychology Review,* 12, 336–351.

Sweeten, G. (2006). Who will graduate? Disruption of high school education by arrest and court involvement. *Justice Quarterly,* 23, 462–480.

Sweeten, G., Pyrooz, D. C., and Piquero, A. R. (2013). Disengaging from gangs and desistance from crime. *Justice Quarterly,* 30, 469–500.

Tanner-Smith, E. (2012). Pubertal development and adolescent girls' substance use: Race, ethnicity, and neighborhood contexts of vulnerability, *The Journal of Early Adolescence,* 32, 621–649.

Tanner-Smith, E. E., Wilson, S. J., and Lipsey, M. L. (2013a). Risk factors and crime. In F.T. Cullen and P. Wilcox (eds.), *The Oxford handbook of criminological theory* (pp. 89–111). New York: Oxford University Press.

———. (2013b). The comparative effectiveness of outpatient treatment for adolescent substance abuse: A meta-analysis. *Journal of Substance Abuse Treatment*, 44, 145–158.

Task Force on Community Preventive Services. (2007). Recommendation against policies facilitating the transfer of juveniles from juvenile to adult justice systems for the purpose of reducing violence. *American Journal of Preventive Medicine*, 32(4 Suppl. #1), 5–6.

Taxman, F. S. (2013a). The technical background of the Risk, Need, Responsivity (RNR) Simulation Tool. Fairfax, VA: Center for Advancing Correctional Excellence, George Mason University.

———. (2013b). Keys to "Make EBPs Stick": Lessons from the field. *Federal Probation*, September, 76–86.

Teplin, L. A., Abram, K. M., McClelland, G. M., Dulcan, M. K., and Washburn, J. J. (2006). Psychiatric disorders of youth in detention. *Juvenile Justice Bulletin*. Washington, DC: Office of Juvenile Justice and Delinquency Prevention.

Teske, S. C., and Huff, J. B. (2011). When did making adults mad become a crime? The court's role in dismantling the school-to-prison pipeline. *Juvenile and Family Justice Today*, Winter, 14–17.

Thornberry, T. P. (1998). Membership in youth gangs and involvement in serious and violent offending. In R. Loeber and D.P. Farrington (eds.), *Serious and violent juvenile offenders: Risk factors and successful interventions* (pp. 147–166). Thousand Oaks, CA: Sage.

———. (2005). Explaining multiple patterns of offending across the life course and across generations. *The Annals of the American Academy of Political and Social Science*, 602, 156–195.

Thornberry, T.P., Giordano, P. C., Uggen, C., and Matsuda, M. (2012). Explanations for offending. In R. Loeber and D. P. Farrington (eds.), *From juvenile delinquency to adult crime* (pp. 47–85). New York: Oxford University Press.

Thornberry, T. P., Huizinga, D., and Loeber, R. (1998). The prevention of serious delinquency and violence: Implications from the program of research on the causes and correlates of delinquency. In J. C. Howell, B. Krisberg, J. D. Hawkins, and J. J. Wilson (eds.). *Sourcebook on serious, violent, and chronic juvenile offenders* (pp. 213–237). Thousand Oaks, CA: Sage Publications, Inc.

Thornberry, T. P., and Krohn, M. D. (2001). The development of delinquency: An interactional perspective. In S. O. White (ed.), *Handbook of youth and justice* (pp. 289–305). New York: Plenum.

Thornberry, T. P., Krohn, M. D., Lizotte, A. J., Smith, C. A., and Tobin, K. (2003). *Gangs and delinquency in developmental perspective*. New York: Cambridge University Press.

Thornberry, T. P., Smith, C. A., Rivera, C., Huizinga, D., and Stouthamer-Loeber, M. (1999). Family disruption and delinquency. *Juvenile Justice Bulletin*. Washington, DC: U.S. Department of Justice, Office of Juvenile Justice and Delinquency Prevention.

Tolan, P. H., Gorman-Smith, D., and Loeber, R. (2000). Developmental timing of onsets of disruptive behaviors and later delinquency of inner-city youth. *Journal of Child and Family Studies, 9,* 203–330.

Tonry, M. (2007). Treating juveniles as adult criminals: An iatrogenic violence prevention strategy if ever there was one. *American Journal of Preventive Medicine, 32,* 3–4.

———. (2009). Explanations of American punishment policies: A national history. *Punishment and Society,* 11, 377–394.

Towberman, D. B. (1992). A national survey of juvenile risk assessment. *Family and Juvenile Court Journal,* 43, 61–67.

U.S. Department of Justice. (2007). *Department of Justice activities under the Civil Rights of Institutionalized Persons Act: Fiscal year 2006.* Washington, DC: Office of the Attorney General, U.S. Department of Justice.

———. (2012). *Department of Justice activities under the Civil Rights of Institutionalized Persons Act: Fiscal year 2011.* Washington, DC: Office of the Attorney General, U.S. Department of Justice.

Van der Geest, V., Blokland, A., and Bijleveld, C. (2009). Delinquent development in a sample of high-risk youth: Shape, content, and predictors of delinquent trajectories from age 12 to 32. *Journal of Research in Crime and Delinquency,* 46, 111–143.

Van Der Put, C. E., Dekovic, M., Geert, J. J., Stams, G. J., Van Der Laan, P. H., Hoeve, M., and Van Amelsfort, L. V. (2011). Changes in risk factors during adolescence: Implications for risk assessment. *Criminal Justice and Behavior, 38,* 248–262.

Van Der Put, C. E., Dekovic, M., Stams, G. J., Hoeve, M., Dekovic, M., Spanjaard, H. J. M., Van Der Laan, P. H., and Barnoski, R. P. (2012). Changes in the relative importance of dynamic risk factors on recidivsm during adolescence. *International Journal of Offender Therapy and Comparative Criminology,* 56, 296–316.

Van Der Put, C. E., Van Vugt, E. S., Stams, G. J., Dekovic, M., and Van Der Laan, P. H. (2013). Differences in the prevalence and impact of risk factors for general recidivism between different types of juveniles who have committed sexual offenses (JSOs) and juveniles who have committed nonsexual offenses (NSOs). *Sexual Abuse: A Journal of Research and Treatment,* 25, 41–68.

Van Domburgh, L., Vermeiren, R., and Doreleijers, T. (2008). Screening and assessments. In R. Loeber, H. M. Koot, N. W. Slott, P. H. Van der Laan, and and M. Hoeve (eds.), *Tomorrow's criminals: The development of child delinquency and effective interventions* (pp. 165–178). Hampshire, England: Ashgate.

Vieira, T. A., Skilling, T. A., and Peterson-Badali, M. (2009). Matching court-ordered services with treatment needs: Predicting treatment success with young offenders. *Criminal Justice and Behavior,* 36, 385–401.

Villarruel, F. A., and Walker, N. E. (2002). *Donde esta la justicia? A call to action on behalf of Latino and Latina youth in the U.S. justice system.* Washington, DC: Building Blocks for Youth.

Vincent, G. M., Guy, L. S., and Grisso, T. (2012). *Risk assessment in juvenile justice: A guidebook for implementation.* Chicago, IL: John D. and Catherine T. MacArthur Foundation.

Virginia Department of Juvenile Justice. (2005). Juvenile recidivism in Virginia. *DJJ Research Quarterly*, III, 1–12.

Wagner, D. (2009). Recommendations for developing a quality assurance program: Alaska Division of Juvenile Justice. Madison, WI: National Council on Crime and Delinquency.

Waint, G. (2002). *Standards for the administration of juvenile justice: The need to evaluate performance, identify barriers and incentives for their use.* Williamsburg, VA: National Center for State Courts, Institute for Court Management.

Warren, R. (2007). Evidence-based practice to reduce recidivism: Implications for state judiciaries. Williamsburg, VA: National Center for State Courts, National Institute of Corrections.

Wasserman, G. A., and Ko, S. J. (2003). Columbia Guidelines for Child and Adolescent Mental Health Referral. New York: Columbia University Department of Child and Adolescent Psychiatry, Center for the Promotion of Mental Health in Juvenile Justice (www.promotementalhealth.org).

Wasserman, G. A., Ko, S. J., and McReynolds, L. S. (2004). Assessing the mental health status of youth in juvenile justice settings. *Juvenile Justice Bulletin.* Washington, DC: U.S. Department of Justice, Office of Juvenile Justice and Delinquency Prevention.

Wasserman, G.A., and McReynolds, L.S. (2011). Contributors to traumatic exposure and posttraumatic stress disorder in juvenile justice youths. *Journal of Traumatic Stress*, Vol. 24(4): 422–429.

Wasserman, G. A., McReynolds, L. S., Ko, S. J., Katz, L. M., and Carpenter, J. (2005). Gender differences in psychiatric disorders at juvenile probation intake. *American Journal of Public Health*, 95, 131–137.

Wasserman, G. A., McReynolds, L. S., Lucas, C., Fisher, P., and Santos, L. (2002). The Voice DISC-IV with incarcerated male youth: Prevalence of disorder. *Journal of the American Academy of Child and Adolescent Psychiatry*, 41, 314-321.

Wasserman, G. A., McReynolds, L. S., Musabegovic, H., Whited, A. L., Keating, J. M., and Huo, Y. (2009). Evaluating Project Connect: Improving juvenile probationers' mental health and substance use service access. *Administration and Policy in Mental Health and Mental Health Services Research*, 36, 393–405.

Wasserman, G. A., McReynolds, L. S., Schwalbe, C. S., Keating, J. M., and Jones, S. A. (2010). Psychiatric disorder, comorbidity, and suicidal behavior in juvenile justice youth. *Criminal Justice and Behavior*, 37, 1361–1376.

Watson, L., and Edelman, P. (2012). *Improving the juvenile justice system for girls: Lessons from the states.* Washington, DC: Georgetown Center on Poverty, Inequality, and Public Policy.

Welsh, B. C., and Farrington, D. P. (2006). Evidence-based crime prevention. In B. C. Welsh and D. P. Farrington (eds.), *Preventing crime: What works for children, offenders, victims, and places* (pp. 1–17). Dordrecht, The Netherlands: Springer.

Welsh, B. C., Loeber, R., Stevens, B. R., Stouthamer-Loeber, M., Coehn, M. A., and Farrington, D. P. (2008). Costs of juvenile crime in urban areas. *Youth Violence and Juvenile Justice*, 6, 3–27.

Welsh, B. C., Sullivan, C. J., and Olds, D. L. (2010). When early crime prevention goes to scale: A new look at the evidence. *Prevention Science*, 11, 115–125.

Welsh, B. C., and Farrington, D. P. (2007). Save children from a life of crime. *Criminology and Public Policy*, 6, 871–880.

West, C. (1993). *Race matters*. Boston: Bacon.

Wiebush, R. G., ed. (2002).*Graduated sanctions for juvenile offenders: A program model and planning guide*. Oakland, CA: National Council on Crime and Delinquency and National Council of Juvenile and Family Court Judges.

Wiebush, R. G., Baird, C., Krisberg, B., and Onek, D. (1995). Risk assessment and classification for serious, violent, and chronic juvenile offenders. In J.C.Howell, B.Krisberg, J.D.Hawkins, and J.J.Wilson (eds.). *Sourcebook on serious, violent and chronic juvenile offenders* (pp. 171-212). Thousand Oaks, CA: Sage Publications, Inc.

Wiebush, R. G., and Hamparian, D. M. (1991). Variations in "doing" intensive supervision: Programmatic issues in four Ohio jurisdictions. In T.L. Armstrong (ed.), *Intensive interventions with high-risk youths: Promising approaches in juvenile probation and parole* (pp. 153–188). Monsey, NY: Criminal Justice Press.

Wilson, H. A., and Hoge, R. D. (2013). The Effect of Youth Diversion Programs on Recidivism : A Meta-Analytic Review. *Criminal Justice and Behavior*, 40, 497–518.

Wilson, J. J., and Howell, J. C. (1993). *A comprehensive strategy for serious, violent and chronic juvenile offenders*. Washington, DC: Office of Juvenile Justice and Delinquency Prevention.

——. (1994). OJJDP's comprehensive strategy for serious, violent, and chronic juvenile offenders. *The Juvenile and Family Court Journal*, 45, 3–12.

——. (1995). Comprehensive strategy for serious, violent and chronic juvenile offenders. In J.C. Howell, B. Krisberg, J.D. Hawkins, and J.J. Wilson (eds.), A *Sourcebook: Serious, violent, and chronic juvenile offenders* (pp. 36–46). Thousand Oaks, CA: Sage.

Wilson, J. J., Kelly, M. R., and Howell, J. C. (2012). *Delaware Report: The Little Engine that Could*. Richmond, VA: The Comprehensive Strategy Group.

Wilson, J. Q. (1995). Crime and public policy. In J. Q. Wilson and J. Petersilia (eds.), *Crime* (pp. 489–507). San Francisco: ICS Press.

Wilson, S. J., Lipsey, M. W., and Derzon, J. H. (2003). The effects of school-based intervention programs on aggressive behavior: A meta-analysis. *Journal of Consulting and Clinical Psychology*, 71, 136–149.

Winokur-Early, K., Hand, G. A., and Blankenship, J. L. (2012). Validity and Reliability of the Florida Positive Achievement Change Tool (PACT) Risk and Needs Assessment Instrument: A Three-Phase Evaluation (Validation Study, Factor Analysis, Inter-Rater Reliability). Tallahassee, FL: Justice Research Center.

Wolfgang, M. E., Figlio, R. M., and Sellin, T. (1972). *Delinquency in a birth cohort*. Chicago: University of Chicago Press.

Wong, T. M. L., Slottboom, A.-M, and Bijleveld, C. C. J. H. (2010). Risk factors for delinquency in adolescent and young adult females: A European review. *European Journal of Criminology*, 7, 266–284.

Wooldredge, J. D. (1988). Differentiating the effects of juvenile court sentences on eliminating recidivism. *Journal of Research in Crime and Delinquency*, 25, 264–300.

Wright, B. R. E., Caspi, A., Moffitt, T. E., and Paternoster, R. (2004). Does the perceived risk of punishment deter criminally prone individuals? Rational choice, self-control, and crime. *Journal of Research in Crime and Delinquency, 41,* 180–213.

Yan, J. (2009). A multidisciplinary study on juvenile recidivism and multilevel impacts: Risk factors, neighborhood features, and juvenile justice intervention. Unpublished doctoral dissertation, University of Missouri, Columbia, Missouri.

Young, D., Moline, K., Farrell, J., and Bierie, D. (2006). Best implementation practices: Disseminating new assessment technologies in a juvenile justice agency. *Crime and Delinquency, 52,* 135–158.

Zahn, M. A., Agnew, R., Fishbein, D., and Miller, S. (2010). Causes and correlates of girls' delinquency. *Juvenile Justice Bulletin.* Washington, DC: U.S. Department of Justice, Office of Juvenile Justice and Delinquency Prevention.

Zahn, M. A., Day, J. C., Mihalic, S. F., and Tichavsky, L. (2009). Determining what works for girls in the juvenile justice system: A summary of evaluation evidence. *Crime and Delinquency, 55,* 266–293.

Zara, T., and Farrington, D. P. (2013). Assessment of risk for juvenile compared with adult criminal onset: Implications for policy, prevention, and intervention. *Psychology, Public Policy, and Law, 19,* 235–249.

Zavlek, S. (2005). Planning community-based facilities for violent juvenile offenders as part of a system of graduated sanctions. *Juvenile Justice Bulletin.* Washington, DC: U.S. Department of Justice, Office of Juvenile Justice and Delinquency Prevention.

Zimring, F. E. (1998). *American youth violence.* New York: Oxford University Press.

Index

About the Authors

James C. (Buddy) Howell is a partner in Comprehensive Strategies for Juvenile Justice. He worked at the federal Office of Juvenile Justice and Delinquency Prevention (OJJDP) in the U.S. Department of Justice for twenty-one years, mostly as Director of Research and Program Development. He also served as Deputy Administrator of OJJDP. He currently is Senior Research Associate with the National Gang Center in Tallahassee, Florida, where he has researched youth gangs for the past eighteen years. He has published many works on juvenile justice, youth violence, and gangs, including four books. Some of his published works have appeared in *Crime and Delinquency, Criminology and Public Policy, Journal of Research in Crime and Delinquency,* and *Youth Violence and Juvenile Justice.* Dr. Howell is very active in helping states and localities reform their juvenile justice systems and employ evidence-based programs, and in working with these entities in addressing youth violence and gang problems in a research-based, data-driven, and balanced approach. He has received several awards for contributions to the field of juvenile justice from organizations including the National Council of Juvenile and Family Court Judges, the National Council on Crime and Delinquency, and the National Juvenile Court Services Association.

Mark W. Lipsey is director of the Peabody Research Institute and a research professor at Vanderbilt University. He specializes in program evaluation with a focus on programs for at-risk children and youth. His research activities include the study of risk factors and effective interventions for antisocial behavior and delinquency. His meta-analysis

191

research on interventions for juvenile offenders has identified many effective programs and led to recent initiatives to better translate this research into practice in collaboration with the Center for Juvenile Justice Reform at Georgetown University and the Office of Juvenile Justice and Delinquency Prevention. This research has been funded by major federal agencies and private foundations and recognized with awards from such organizations as the American Probation and Parole Association, the Association for the Advancement of Evidence-Based Practice, the Society for Prevention Research, and the American Society of Criminology. Prof. Lipsey is a member of the Science Advisory Board for the federal Office of Justice Programs (chairing the OJJDP Subcommittee), and the Advisory Committee for the National Science Foundation Directorate for Education and Human Resources. He has served on the National Research Council Committee on Law and Justice, the Crime and Justice Coordinating Group of the Campbell Collaboration, and is a recent co-editor-in-chief of *Research Synthesis Methods* and *Campbell Systematic Reviews*.

John J. Wilson is a partner in Comprehensive Strategies for Juvenile Justice. From 1974–2005 he held a variety of legal and programmatic positions in the U.S. Department of Justice, Office of Justice Programs. In 1991, he joined the federal Office of Juvenile Justice and Delinquency Prevention (OJJDP), where he served as Acting Administrator, Deputy Administrator, and Counsel to the Administrator. While at OJJDP, he coauthored and led national testing and implementation of OJJDP's *Comprehensive Strategy for Serious, Violent, and Chronic Juvenile Offenders* (1993) and was an editor of *A Sourcebook: Serious, Violent, and Chronic Juvenile Offenders* (1995). He has lectured and taught courses in the legal rights of children, juvenile justice, and family law, and has been published in *Children's Legal Rights Journal*, the *Juvenile and Family Court Journal*, and *Corrections Today*. He also served as a member of the U.S. Advisory Board on Child Abuse and Neglect. Since 2005, Mr. Wilson has worked as a consultant on juvenile justice issues, participated on the Editorial Review Panel of the National Council of Juvenile and Family Court Judges' *Juvenile and Family Court Journal*, and served on the Board of Directors of the National Juvenile Defender Center.

CPSIA information can be obtained at www.ICGtesting.com
Printed in the USA
BVOW05*1329100614

355926BV00004B/4/P

0 1341 1571951 7